WAR AND SOCIETY IN EUROPE 1870–1970

BRIAN BOND

McGill-Queen's University Press
Montreal & Kingston · London · Ithaca

ISBN 0-7735-1763-4

Legal deposit first quarter 1998
Bibliothèque nationale du Québec
Reprinted 2003, 2005

First published in 1984 by Fontana Paperbacks.
This edition published simultaneously in the European Union by
Sutton Publishing Limited.

McGill-Queen's University Press acknowledges the support of the Canada
Council for the Arts for our publishing program. We also acknowledge the
financial support of the Government of Canada through the Book Publishing
Industry Development Program (BPIDP) for our publishing activities.

Canadian Cataloguing in Publication Data

Bond, Brian, 1936–
War and society in Europe, 1870–1970
(Fontana history of war and European society series)
Rev. ed.
Includes bibliographical references and index.
ISBN 0-7735-1763-4
1. Europe – History, Military – 19th century.
2. Europe – History, Military – 20th century.   3. Europe – Social
conditions – 1789–1900.   4. Europe – Social conditions – 20th century.
I. Title.   II. Series.
D396.B63 1998   940.'8   C97-901200-7

Cover illustration: *Day of Liberation, March 1945* by Stankovitch.
Galley of Yugoslav People's Army Club,
Belgrade/Bridgeman Art Library, London

Contents

EDITOR'S PREFACE

The re-issue of a series of books after fifteen years' exploitation of its field invites justification and prompts reflection. The justification – other than what lies in the qualities of the books themselves – is simply that no comparable series has appeared to replace it. Our purpose was to sum up what had so far been achieved in the rather new study of 'war and society' and to make it available as an attractive accompaniment to the Fontana and other general series on the history of Europe and its empires. That we were right to sense a need for such enlargement of view on the military side, has been amply confirmed by the army of historians and history-minded social scientists who have continued active in the field, and whose relevant contributions will be duly noted in our revised reading lists. Some of them, especially in the United States, march under the banner of 'the new military history'; which however boils down to much the same thing as was meant by the 'war and society' pioneers, a generation ago. The more recent writers evidently having shared with the earlier ones the aim of distinguishing their historical operations from those of the 'old' military history, it seems worth while to reconsider what I wrote about the series' purposes and principles, fifteen years or so ago.

The 'war and society' movement took shape in the 1960s, to make good what had come to be felt as something missing in the traditional style of histories of wars and warfare. Although the latter had paid much attention to what armed forces did to one another in war, they normally showed little interest in how those armed forces related to the societies from which they were drawn and in what war itself – the experience of it while it was going on, the perhaps huge net effect of it once it was over – did to the societies which engaged in it. The years 1935–1945 were crucial to the new perception. Each of the Second World War's major participants experienced social mobilization on a scale of totality historically unprecedented. Even before it was over, official histories of it were being planned to do justice to everything that happened away from the firing lines as well as on them; and those who survived it tended to feel sure that it must have caused great social changes. Particular inquiries into

v

this latter possibility were what brought to the forefront of the movement the historian who more than anyone else launched 'war and society' as a viable and (to the limited extent that any area of historical studies can be so) self-sufficient branch of historical studies. Arthur Marwick effected this notable step forward when his history department at the Open University produced in 1973 its famous third-year course 'War and Society', in which pretty well every apposite part of the field came into view. About five thousand students took this course during its six years' lifetime, the teaching units expressly produced for it acquired a wide circulation, and some of them remain among the best things so far written. (Nor is that the end of the story; over six thousand students have, by the time of writing, taken its successor 'War, Peace and Social Change'.)

This new approach to war history's popularity was no doubt partly because it offered to those who disliked war (numerous indeed after the Second World War, and subsequently under the shadow of nuclear weapons) a way of studying war without what seemed to them its rebarbative and retrogressive aspects. From certain morally committed standpoints the new approach might appear to be positively progressive. After all, it was happening during the same years as the movement within the social sciences to learn more about the causes of war – and thus a hoped-for preventability of war – than had been made apparent in the well-established genres of political and diplomatic history. From the traditional point of view, these were the very novelties and connections which invited criticism. Practitioners of military history proper, continuing to work within the parameters of the tradition, pointed out that the new fashion, too enthusiastically followed, failed to do justice to certain inescapable historical facts: for instance, that war was about the use of force, that force normally made itself felt as armed violence, and that books about war without the battles which usually brought it to a close were not to be taken seriously. That such books, ignoring what they did not like to recognize, did surface on the further edges of the field, cannot be denied. Our series, however, seeks to avoid such imbalance. Far from rejecting, we gladly acknowledge the parallel labours of those (one of the most distinguished of them, a contributor to this series) who prefer still to be known by the honourable title of military historian. Their campaigns and commanders, their armies and battles and the ways in which they were fought are all to be found here, in proportionate relation to the societies which supported them and which would in the natural course of events be affected by them. All that is missing is, inevitably, space to dwell as much on any of the many relevant aspects as keen inquirers may wish; and for them, our up-dated reading lists will show the way forward.

There are some passions for military history and war studies which the 'war and society' approach will never satisfy. Believing that the place of war in the world is best studied with as much detachment and objectivity as can be managed, it avoids the nationalistic and hyper-patriotic attitudes which were the norm in military history writing (one might just as well say, in national history writing) before the early twentieth century, and which continue to colour many of its popular productions. Nor can 'war and society' history appeal to men who find excitement and stimulus in tales of violence and in the contemplation of instruments of violence: all those guns and knives, etc. which fill a certain class of magazines and picture books, and which (along perhaps with innocent interests in military uniforms and model soldiers) are evidently what many 'militaria' fans alone are interested in. In the face of those interests, and in obvious contrast with them, our war and society approach is no doubt better suited to the interests of the peace-minded than the military enthusiast. There is no reason why it should not prove interesting to military persons – indeed, one volume in the series has seemed interesting enough to the Spanish Ministry of Defence to have been translated into their language – but it will not long hold the attention of the militaristic.

The attractiveness of the kind of war studies which this series has helped to popularize is no doubt partly because it matches the very common civilian feeling that war and soldiering – ancient, admirable and 'normal' though they may seem to be – are worth more critical inquiry than military men and their numerous admirers used to seem to like, and the not uncommon realization by thoughtful people that war and peace, after all, are two sides of the same medal. Ideal as a title would be 'peace, war and society'. That alone comprehends the two poles of moral and historical interest between which 'war and society' studies oscillate. Why do wars happen at all?, is a question much more likely to be in the mind of a historian now than it was before the Second World War. Like the post-war boom in 'conflict analysis and peace research', it is related to the preoccupations of the generation born under that shadow of the mushroom-shaped cloud.

But it is nothing new, that the more reflective of our humankind should ponder upon the idea of war itself. War and the imagination of it are the ultimate link between armed forces and society. Human society, politically organized, becomes a State; and States have traditionally distinguished themselves from other States, to put it bluntly, by their abilities to defend their borders and, should they be of the expanding sort, to extend them. Whether there is something congenital in the natures of men (I say 'men' deliberately, because women may be different) and States which impels them towards competitiveness and conflict, is an enormous field of inquiry which has for long engaged the attention of some of the most thoughtful and caring of our kind. The idea of war may, to many living now, have become repulsive, unnatural and essentially destructive. The historian has to note that this marks a big change from the past. War appeared in quite a different light through the greater part of history. It was the normal accompaniment of State-making and almost inevitably the means by which States gathered empires around them. Societies which benefited from these processes thought nothing wrong in them; societies which lost out, bemoaned only the failure of their fights to defend themselves. Win or lose, the literatures and traditional ethics and (if they had them) written histories of societies throughout all history before the twentieth century accepted war as a fact of international life and admired the heroes who were good at it. War may not wholly begin in the minds of men (a lot of it begins simply in material need or greed, and in the gross appetites attached thereto) but a good case can be made for saying that it begins there more than anywhere else. The idea of war therefore, the place of war in what the French and many of the rest of us call *mentalité*, is of itself a matter of giant historical importance: how at particular epochs and in particular societies the idea of war is diffused, articulated, coloured and connected. Only by way of that matrix of ideas about God and man, nature and society, can come full understanding of the causes of wars that have happened, and of the armed forces which have for the most part conducted them.

Ideas, then, we consider to matter at least as much as the social and economic history of war and of readiness for war; they form the, so to speak, cultural and material envelope within which exist the armed forces whose existence and activities lie at the centre of our common interest, and about which something more must be said. Armed forces are a very special sort of social organization. They can be more nearly 'complete societies' than any other of the 'secular' associations and interest groups which structure society within States so far as governments permit. Their internal life is by nature peculiarly structured, tough and ritualistic; their business – discipline, force, violence, war – makes them exceptionally formidable; by definition they subscribe to codes of behaviour – honour, loyalty, obedience, etc. – which emphasize their solidarity and reinforce their apparent differences from the societies beside and around them. It is not difficult to understand why so much that has been written about them (not least, by 'old' military historians) has treated them as if they were absolutely different and apart.

But of course they are by no means wholly so. Except in cases where an armed force or a coalition of armed forces succeeds in totally militarizing society, or where a 'war-minded' ideology possesses a whole society to the extent that every citizen is as much a soldier as any other, there are bound to remain differences and distinctions between armed forces on the one hand, and the societies from which they spring on the other. And yet, while there are differences and distinctions, there must also be relationships and interactions. So they can and to some extent must be studied 'on their own', because in their own right they tend to be so remarkable and influential; but in other respects their history, nature, and influence demands that they be studied in their relationship with the world they belong to. We try, within the limits of our enterprise, to acknowledge both demands.

War, to sum up, is a unique human interest and activity, with its own character, its own self-images, its own mystiques, its own forms or organization and, to crown all, a prime place in determining the standards of national societies and their political viability as States. Such is our case for picking out of the whole seamless web of history the scarlet warps of war, for putting the more social and cultural of them under a magnifying microscope, and for writing about them in a way which the general historical reader, who is not normally a 'military buff', will appreciate. This was brilliantly done in miniature by Michael Howard in his *War in European History* (1976), a few years before this series began to appear. At that time, there was not much of similarly relevant character that had to be pointed out besides his book, the pioneer classics by Alfred Vagts (*A History of Militarism, Civilian and Military*, 1937) and Preston and Wise (*Men in Arms: A History of Warfare and its Interrelationships with Western Society*, 1956), and such specialized periodicals as the American periodical *Armed Forces and Society* and the *War and Society Newsletter*, since 1975 an English-language annual supplement to the celebrated German periodical *Militärgeschichtliche Mitteilungen*, and an ideal way to scan everything that is published year by year. A good deal has come out since then (besides the Open University material already mentioned) and this general preface may appropriately close by highlighting some of the most useful items.

Conspicuous among the war-and-warfare publications of the past twenty years are some of encyclopaedic type, worth mentioning because they should be available in most libraries and because within their broad spans of coverage, particular war-and-society interests may find satisfaction. The most impressive is the improved English-language version of what was begun by the most eminent French historian in the field; it now appears as the *Dictionary of Military History and the Art of War*, edited by André Corvisier, revised and expanded by John Childs, translated by Christopher Turner (1994). Still international, but slighter and more conventional is Charles Townshend (ed.), *The Oxford Illustrated History of Warfare: the triumph of the west* (1995); of national interest merely are David Chandler (ed.), *The Oxford Illustrated History of the British Army* (1994) and John Pimlott (ed.), *The Guinness History of the British Army* (1993). Another feature of the past twenty years or so is the appearance of several periodicals dedicated to the history of war in its broader sense: probably most appropriate are the Australian *War and Society* and the British *War in History* and the *Imperial War Museum Review*.

Of the writing of long-span histories of war and/or warfare, especially by retired generals, there is no end; the only ones known to me as doing justice to the war-and-society aspects of the subject are, in their different ways, William H. McNeill, *The Pursuit of Power. Technology, Armed Forces and Society since AD 1000* (1983) and John Keegan, *A History of Warfare* (1993). Readers with an understandable curiosity as to how the outbreaks and conclusions of wars have been conditioned by the practices, customs and laws of the society of States, a.k.a. international society, within which they were all contained, will find instruction in F.H. Hinsley, *Power and the Pursuit of Peace* (1963), Kalevi J. Holsti, *Peace and War: Armed Conflicts and International Order, 1648–1989* (1991), and (though the title hardly suggests it) Martin Wight, *International Theory: The Three Traditions* (1991, ed. G. Wight and B. Porter). Two ambitious works of sociological inspiration with pockets of the suggestively relevant in them are: Michael Mann, *The Sources of Social Power* (2 v., 1986 and 1993), and David Evan Luard, *War in International Society* (1987). And it is good, at the last moment before going to press, to be able to mention Peter Paret's very instructive and finely illustrated book *Imagined Battles. Reflections of War in European Art* (1997), which begins in the Renaissance and comes right up to the present.

Geoffrey Best
Oxford, 1997

AUTHOR'S PREFACE

The world of unrelenting great power rivalries, nuclear deterrence and the dread of large-scale conventional war in an ideologically divided Europe has changed almost beyond recognition since this book was written in the early 1980s. The Soviet Union has disintegrated, the former Warsaw Pact countries have largely abandoned Communism and all without major conflicts in Europe. Contrary to the predictions of many experts right up until it happened, the Berlin Wall was demolished and the two Germanies were united without Soviet intervention or civil war.

Consequently the pressure to maintain nuclear deterrence and the war-readiness of large conscript-based armies has greatly relaxed and certainly receives less public attention. Rather the principal role of smaller and highly trained professional forces is perceived to lie in alliance actions in a variety of 'peace-keeping' tasks in the Balkans and other anarchic areas.

While the forces of East–West confrontation and the possibility of nuclear war have almost disappeared, terrorism and various forms of low intensity conflict continue to trouble several European states, creating an impression that, for example, Britain and Spain are not truly at peace due to the activities of the IRA and ETA respectively. Democracies, faced with the classic dilemma of how to combat anti-democratic movements without resorting to methods which will alienate their electorates, seem to veer uncertainly between military suppression and appeasement.

As the twentieth century draws to a close an ever-diminishing percentage of Europeans will have experienced any form of military service. National Service ended in Britain in the early 1960s and it is inconceivable that it will be re-introduced. Several European states including, rather surprisingly, France are also in the process of converting to smaller, all-volunteer forces. Henceforth, therefore, historians of war and society in Europe will be writing in a very different political atmosphere from the generation which grew up during the Second World War and the early post-war decades. Few of their readers will have experienced the drill, discipline and tedious routines of military life, let alone the challenges of combat. Whether these new circumstances will reduce the general public's appetite for studying military history is uncertain; but it is possible that vicarious interest will increase as the prospects of direct experience diminish. These reflections apply essentially to Western and Central Europe. Recent or on-going conflicts in the Balkans, Central Africa and Afghanistan must check any optimistic predictions about the propsects of a world free from conventional wars and 'low intensity conflicts' which are intense enough for the civilians who suffer them.

When we turn from the broad European scene to focus on research, publications and study in the field of war and society the impression is one of encouraging developments since the appearance of Sir Michael Howard's *War in European History* in 1976 and Fontana's *War and Society* series in the 1980s. In the English-speaking world, at least, interest in the study of warfare is booming, and, coinciding with scholarly trends, has resulted in the launching of new journals, the holding of numerous conferences and a surge of publications which can only be hinted at in this volume's up-dated bibliography. It should be noted, however, that while some topics receive saturation coverage, others of equal importance are neglected. There are, for example, sufficient publications on aspects of war and society in the Nazi era to fill virtually the whole bibliography.

Let us first briefly discuss some of the outstanding recent publications on the British experience. As long ago as 1971 Martin Middlebrook's *The First Day on the Somme* indicated what has since become a very popular genre by relying heavily on recorded interviews with veterans. His concentration on the single most tragic day of the war on the Western Front – 1 July 1916 – has been followed, too obsessively and narrowly in some cases, by books devoted to individual 'Pals' battalions, many of which suffered heavy losses on that day. Middlebrook's more significant achievement, beyond his method of using oral evidence to enhance the documentary sources, was to give more prominence to the hitherto largely neglected experience of the other ranks. Middlebrook's approach was developed by other writers on the war including Denis Winter (*Death's Men*, 1978) and Tony Ashworth (*Trench Warfare 1914–1918: The Live and Let Live System*, 1980). Ashworth avowedly sought to demonstrate that even in the midst of total war front line fighters can exercise some degree of influence over their environment, sometimes in collusion with the enemy in defiance of their own high command. A common feature of these books which focus on the experience of ordinary soldiers is to play down the constrast between 'us' and 'them': Middlebrook's study is charcteristically dedicated to 'the front-line soldiers of all nations, 1914–1918'. Two recent publications of conference proceedings demonstrate that this approach to war has become truly international; namely H. Cecil and P. Liddle (eds) *Facing Armageddon: The First World War Experienced* (1996), and P. Addison and A. Calder (eds) *Time to Kill: The Soldier's Experience of War in the West, 1939–1945* (1977). Another excellent critical survey is Peter Simkins' 'Everyman at War: Recent Interpretations of the Front Line Experience' in Brian Bond (ed.) *The First World War and British Military History* (1991).

As regards new journals, *War and Society* (published in Australia since 1983) is the clearest example of the tendency to place more emphasis on the social underpinning and repercussions of war (economic and manpower mobilisation, the role of women, the press and public opinion, the demographic consequences) at the expense of command, tactics and battle, which are still adequately covered elsewhere. A similar 'modern' approach has been adopted by the editors of *War in History* (a joint Anglo-American venture since 1994). Also worthy of mention is the Imperial War Museum's annual *Review* (since 1986) whose contributions evince a strong and original interest in war paintings, film, photography and personal experience.

The institution which perhaps most fully exemplifies the new approach to war and society, in its name, prospectus and publications is the Historial de la grande guerre, established and opened with an international conference at Péronne on the Somme in 1992. The Historial's governing body downplays strategic and command issues and also the painful matter of winning and losing: rather it seeks to encourage European cooperation as the principal lesson to be learned from the suffering and destruction resulting from the two world wars. Its research programme and publications (in association with Berg) strikingly illustrate some of the new avenues under exploration; for example Antoine Prost *In the Wake of War: 'Les Anciens Combattants' and French Society 1914–1939*; Patrick Fridenson *The French Home Front 1914–1918* and Gerald Feldman *Army, Industry and Labour in Germany 1914–1918*.

Lastly, it should also be noted that the developing interest in the social ramifications of warfare is not confined to Europe, either as regards participants or the area for study. This is demonstrated by a recent international conference (July 1997) at Wolfson College, Cambridge on 'The New Military History of South Asia' in which the main themes included the relations between armies and states; the effects of enlistment on society; the loyalty of native soldiers to European regimes; and the economic consequences of military expenditure.

Thus future historians of the hundred year period covered by this volume will have the advantage not only of a vastly expanded historiography and documentary sources, but also of interaction with an international community of scholars with similar interests. But an even greater challenge will confront the historian of the later twentieth century in Europe, mercifully deprived of the landmarks provided by great wars, but obliged to cover seemingly endless and insoluble low intensity conflicts and international terrorism. The two components of this series, 'War and Society', whose meanings and connotations have undergone subtle changes since the starting point of Sir John Hale's opening volume in 1450, are likely to experience a further transformation in which 'Society' will loom larger and the fierce clarity of 'War' will be replaced by the all-embracing and more euphemistic term 'Security'.

Brian Bond
Medmenham, Buckinghamshire
October 1997

1

THE WARS OF THE 1860s AND THEIR AFTERMATH

The wars of the 1860s shattered the hopes of those optimists who believed that Europe was entering an era of enduring peace founded upon expanding industrialization, free trade and international cooperation. The creation of a German empire, forged by Prussian military might, drastically altered the power structure of the European states, and also provided the first dreadful foretaste of the nature of modern 'total' warfare between industrializing nations capable of raising huge conscript armies and maintaining them in the field. The unification of Italy, again largely by military means, dealt a blow to the prestige of the Hapsburg empire and gave encouragement to the latter's subject peoples; while Germany's annexation of Alsace and Lorraine ensured the undying enmity of France. Curiously enough, the forty years of peace following the Congress of Vienna in 1815 were to be matched by a similar period after the Treaty of Frankfurt in 1871. But if the major European powers contrived to avoid open conflict, the period 1871–1914 was far from tranquil; it was characterized rather by the formation of ominous alliances, desperate arms races and increasing expectation of an eventual Armageddon.

The aim of this chapter is to establish some of the main themes and problems which will be explored more fully later. What, for example, were the main features of the new style of warfare which fascinated or perplexed contemporary observers and gave rise to a great outpouring of professional literature? In what ways did military conduct depart from accepted civilized standards, and how successful were the counterefforts to introduce limitations, restraints and humanity into the most terrible trade of war? What were the causes of a new brand of 'militarism' which was already evident in the 1870s but became more pronounced by the end of the century? Finally, what were the consequences, not simply in military organization but also in terms of political and social tensions, for all the European states which strove to emulate Germany's standards of military efficiency and preparedness for war?

With the wisdom of hindsight it is easy to exaggerate Prussia's military prowess in 1866 and to underrate Austria's. But contemporary military pundits, including Friedrich Engels, who wrote with considerable insight for the *Manchester Guardian*, could be excused for anticipating an Austrian victory. The latter had a long-service professional army, more breech-loading cannon with better gunners, and a superior cavalry. But her staff work and tactics were obsolete, her command system chaotic. Her best army was relegated to the secondary theatre (Italy) and Benedek, the commander in chief in Bohemia, was a pessimist. In sum, the Austrians were good by Napoleonic standards, but were defeated by more modern organization and tactics. The Austrians mobilized first but too slowly and lethargically to attack either of the two main Prussian armies in isolation. Instead, they fell back on to the defensive in Bohemia, thus allowing the dangerously dispersed Prussian armies to converge and envelop them. Moltke made good use of railways for the rapid movement of his armies to the enemy frontier, and of the electric telegraph to control them from his Berlin office.

In retrospect, Moltke's decisive victory at Königgrätz or Sadowa appeared to be more the product of calculated strategy and superior tactics than was actually the case. In reality neither command knew much about the other due to their lamentable neglect of cavalry reconnaissance, and the decisive engagement resulted from one Prussian army blundering into Benedek's larger force. It was saved by the timely arrival of the other Prussian army which marched to the sound of gunfire and joined the battle piecemeal without waiting for orders. A quarter of the Prussians never reached the field but those that did inflicted three times as many casualties as they suffered. The Prussian infantry neglected to take full advantage of their superior 'needle gun' by firing it standing up, but they had a perfect target in the tightly bunched Austrian ranks whose superior artillery was held too far back. Sadowa was a transitional battle still reminiscent of the Napoleonic era. About a quarter of a million troops took part – the most combatants since the 'battle of the nations' at Leipzig in 1813 – and the west front at Sadowa was about nine miles long. Observers noted that the higher commanders exerted hardly any control once the battle had started: it was decided largely by luck and hard fighting.

In northern Italy the situation was reversed and the Italians were humiliatingly defeated by inferior numbers at Custozza and also got the worse of a naval battle at Lissa. These Austrian victories and the successful withdrawal of the bulk of Benedek's army after Sadowa, did not persuade the Austrian emperor to continue the war because of the risk to the internal stability of the empire. On the Prussian side, Bismarck managed to restrain Moltke and the field commanders from annihilating the Austrian forces and occupying Vienna. In the peace treaty concluded after only seven weeks of war, Austria suffered the humiliation neither of an indemnity nor occupation; she merely ceded Venetia to Italy and withdrew completely from the North German Confederation.

The Franco-Prussian conflict of 1870–1 marked a further step on the downwards course towards 'total war', for in none of the preceding mid-century wars in Europe had the state and people of one society been locked in a fight to the death with the state and people of another. Two of the most highly organized and nationalistic peoples of Europe 'tore at each other's throats'.[1] The completeness of Prussia's victory was in some ways even more surprising than in 1866, because although France had rested too long on Napoleon I's laurels, she possessed certain tangible advantages such as her superior rifle, the *chassepot*, and her more extensive railway network. These assets could not, however, offset the disastrous higher direction of the war by Napoleon III, compounded by the machinations of his empress and the irresolution of his principal army commanders, Bazaine and MacMahon. In the opening frontier battles at Spicheren and Worth the Germans lost more killed and wounded than the French but they kept on attacking. French valour was undermined by continuous retreat. A series of orders and counterorders allowed the Germans to get between the two French armies and Paris. Bazaine dithered and finally withdrew his army into the fortress of Metz whither MacMahon eventually set out to relieve him. MacMahon's army with the desperately sick emperor were surrounded at Sedan and pounded into surrender by longer-range artillery which the French could not even engage. On 1 September Napoleon surrendered and went into exile while more than 100,000 French soldiers became prisoners. This disaster caused a revolution in Paris; a Government of National Defence was set up and the Third Republic proclaimed.

By 19 September the Germans were employing nearly 150,000

troops to besiege Paris while the remainder of their armies besieged Metz and other fortresses in a desperate effort to open up and safeguard their highly vulnerable lines of communication. France's last real hope of staving off defeat ended when Bazaine surrendered Metz at the end of October. The French Government of National Defence excelled in raising amateur armies numbering about half a million men in all, notably in the Loire valley and in Paris, but these ill-trained and often poorly led levies were no match for the Prussians in open country in midwinter. None of these forces could break the German stranglehold on Paris and the large garrison of some 300,000 National Guardsmen, *Gardes Mobiles*, regulars and sailors made no concerted effort to break out. After a brief and controversial bombardment, demanded by Bismarck and opposed by Moltke, Paris surrendered on 28 January 1871 and an armistice was signed.

During the brief conflict France mobilized nearly two million troops in all and the German states nearly one and a half million. French losses in troops killed, wounded or who died of disease probably approached 300,000, whereas the Germans lost about 140,000. Ironically, however, the worst barbarities were perpetrated by Frenchmen on Frenchmen in the systematic massacres by which the regular forces of the new Republic crushed the revolutionary workers of Paris – the *Commune*.[2]

On 10 May 1871 the French Republic accepted without negotiation the harsh terms of the Treaty of Frankfurt. France ceded the fortresses of Metz and Strasbourg, the entire province of Alsace (except Belfort) and about a third of Lorraine with its valuable coal and iron-ore resources. She undertook in addition to pay an indemnity of five billion francs within three years, in the meantime supporting a German occupation. This may be seen as a ruthless reversal of roles in revenge for the French occupation of Prussia after 1806, but by 1871 more concern might have been expected for the democratic rights of the people of the annexed territory. Quite the contrary, however; as Professor Carlton Hayes put it, 'The provinces and their inhabitants were appropriated by Germany in a military way and primarily for military purposes.'[3] This was a harbinger of German material might during the ensuing years.

The value of Prussia's short-service conscripts drawn from a complete cross section of her young men had not in 1866 completely convinced conservative defenders of long-service professionals, but after 1870 there was no room for argument. True, Prussia's vital initial advantage derived from her superior mobilization arrangements which enabled Moltke to cross the frontier in the first week of August with about 370,000 troops as against France's 240,000. But the deeper cause lay in Prussia's retention after 1815 of universal liability to three years' military service followed by four years in the *landwehr*. Contrary to orthodox military dogma, the mass Prussian armies of the 1860s proved to be a match for their opponents in marching and fighting and superior to them in education and motivation. The French belief in quality against quantity, though eloquently articulated by their admirable theorist Colonel Ardant du Picq, who was himself killed in action in 1870, was proved to be mistaken. So too was subsequent faith in the untrained ardour of the people in arms. Henceforth the vital importance of short-service conscription, trained reserves and the ability to mobilize the largest possible force in the shortest time was scarcely challenged as an ideal among the continental powers.

Combat in the 1860s also raised perplexing tactical problems. Firepower, in the form of breech-loading rifles and cannon and primitive types of machine guns, was effective at ever-increasing range and was becoming more intense and accurate. Indeed a 'fire zone' several hundred yards deep now tended to occur in which it was difficult for horses and upright soldiers to survive. Cavalry charges and close-order infantry tactics proved suicidal in 1866, 1870 and above all in the fanatically contested American Civil War whose implications were unfortunately not much appreciated in Europe. Enhanced firepower when skilfully combined with entrenchments and palisades now conferred a marked superiority on the defensive, but this fact was only reluctantly accepted by officers indoctrinated in the Napoleonic virtue of attack. Neither side displayed sophisticated tactics in 1870, but of necessity dense attacking columns fragmented into skirmishing lines; shoulder-to-shoulder cavalry charges achieved some limited successes but also resulted in massacres at Morsbronn, Vionville and Floing; and at Sedan the excellent French *chassepot* was completely nullified by the superior range of the Prussian guns.

According to Alfred Vagts's classic *History of Militarism*, most militarists, 'being conservative in politics, are antimaterialist'.[4] While his book provides some evidence to support this bold generalization, the period under review shows that soldiers accepted very rapid changes in basic armaments even if they sometimes badly misused them tactically. The following summary provides some idea of the rapidity of change. By 1859 the French possessed an effective breech-loading field gun which performed well against the Austrians in north Italy. Seven years later the Austrian artillery excelled the Prussian, possessing over 700 rifled but still muzzle-loading cannon, whereas the latter had less than 300. By 1870, however, Prussia had converted to Krupp steel breech-loaders which, despite a tendency to explode in the faces of their gunners, completely outdistanced the French artillery. In compensation, the French had a far superior infantry rifle, the *chassepot*, as well as a primitive machine gun, the *mitrailleuse*, which was multi-barrelled, weighed a ton and could fire about 370 rounds per minute. The *mitrailleuse* provides a spectacular example of military mismanagement because the French had kept this 'wonder-weapon' so secret that their own troops were insufficiently trained in its use. Worse still, it was employed as an artillery piece rather than an infantry support weapon where it was fatally outranged. Thus, while it is certainly true that the tactical lessons of 1870 were not fully assimilated, it is possible to have some sympathy with the substantial number of military men who grappled with these problems in the professional journals. Perhaps it is not surprising that it took an outsider – Friedrich Engels – fully to grasp that superior armaments could be decisive in future wars and that this had important implications, not only for the industrial base, but also for the social relationship between workers, soldiers and governments.

A third feature of these wars which deeply impressed contemporaries, and which historians have tirelessly repeated, is the first significant use of railways. Prussia certainly gained an important initial advantage both in 1866 and 1870 from the speedier mobilization of her first-line troops and their movement by rail to her own frontiers. Thereafter, as recent research has demonstrated, the story of railways in the *supply* of advancing armies is largely one of congestion, confusion, chaos and breakdown. In 1866 Moltke was obliged by the belated order to mobilize to use all five lines available to distribute nearly 200,000 troops on a 200-mile-long arc along the Bohemian frontier. So far so good, but no arrangements had been made for supply trains with the result that supplies were rushed forward to the railheads until these were completely blocked. By the end of June some 18,000 tons of supplies were trapped and hundreds of railway wagons were serving as temporary magazines and could not have been used even had the lines been freed. As bread went stale, fodder rotted and cattle died, all connection between the troops and the railways was lost. From the first crossing of the Austrian frontier until after the battle of Sadowa, railways had not the slightest influence on the course of the campaign.[5]

Moltke and the Prussian general staff did attempt to profit from this experience. Contrary to popular belief, they correctly appreciated that France had a superior railway network, but incorrectly expected railways to favour the defender operating on interior lines. France did indeed attempt to seize the initiative by mobilizing more rapidly and by striking into Germany, but this plan was ruined by defective military organization. The French army, unlike the Prussian, was not localized in corps areas; troops were required to report to their depots whence they were directed to their concentration area. This involved some soldiers in ludicrous journeys to Africa before returning to their starting point; and the similarity with a disturbed ant heap was increased by many senior officers' adamant refusal to assist the harassed railway officials. Tragicomic messages flew to and fro, like the general who telegraphed to Paris on 21 July: 'Have arrived at Belfort. Not found my brigade. Not found general division. What should I do? Don't know where my regiments are.'[6]

The Prussians did rather better than this in moving their troops to railheads in the Rhineland but supplies were breaking down even before they crossed the French frontier. Thereafter they encountered the insuperable problem of Toul and other fortresses which prevented the pushing forward of railheads. As the Germans pressed on to Paris and the Loire valley, a huge backlog of blocked trains accumulated, stretching as far back as Frankfurt and Cologne. The Germans eventually operated three lines in France sufficiently freely to make the siege of Paris, with its huge consumption of ammunition, possible, but although more than 2000 miles of French track was being operated by the Germans when the war ended, conditions remained chaotic and – due to the attacks of *francs-tireurs* – dangerous. The German armies had to subsist by requisitioning and by living off the land which did not prove difficult in a rich agricultural country provided the troops kept moving. It is thus completely untrue that Moltke and his railway officials had solved the problem of supply in 1870. Once his armies advanced beyond the railheads they subsisted by traditional methods that differed little from Napoleonic times.[7] Railways had been exploited much more fully and successfully, for both supply and rapid movement of troops, by the North in the American Civil War but this achievement was not recognized in Europe. What can be said is that despite the contemporary exaggeration of Moltke's mastery of railways in 1870, the revolutionary *potential* of rail communication was becoming clear.

The last of Prussia's assets which so deeply impressed contemporaries was her superior military organization. Part of her secret lay in the existence of permanent army corps, each about 30,000 fighting men strong; the optimum organization of an army in miniature, self-sufficient in all arms and ancillary services. The Prussian army corps were localized in particular areas whence they drew all their recruits and reservists. The corps commander enjoyed considerable responsibility for peacetime training and administration as well as for carrying out mobilization at the outbreak of war.

The corps system was complemented by the general staff, which had passed through a lean spell after 1815 but grew steadily in prestige under Moltke from 1857. Moltke accomplished the rare feat of making service on the general staff a mark of distinction for ambitious officers rather than a despised refuge for idlers, scribblers and academic theorists. His other distinctive contribution was to insist that staff service alternate with tours of command, allowing only outstanding all-round officers to reach the higher staff appointments. Benedek belatedly recognized the importance of staff work after the Austrian defeat in 1866 when he remarked plaintively: 'How could we prevail against the Prussians? We have learned so little and they are such a studious people.'[8] Colonel Henderson later made the same point when he wrote that the staff officers of Austria and France, though they had more warlike experience, were inferior in every respect save physical courage: 'In small enterprise as in great . . . the lore of camp and barrack proved utterly incapable of dealing with the judgement and science of the *Kriegsakademie*.'[9] The development of a superior 'brain' and sinews of the army in the form of the general staff, with its chief at Imperial Headquarters and its officers attached to subordinate units, did not of course prevent the Prussian command from committing appalling blunders, particularly in the opening manoeuvres in 1870 preceding Sedan and Metz. But it *did* ensure that the spirit of cooperation prevailed over the unavoidable inertia and friction characteristic of all military operations. Whereas the Austrian and French commanders allowed themselves to be paralysed by want of orders or contradictory ones, the German generals marched to the sound of the guns, an elementary military principle which proved decisive.

Before examining the international repercussions of Prussia/ Germany's victories in the 1870s it is important to show briefly the interaction of military events and domestic politics in the 1860s. There is no need to rehearse here in full detail the prolonged struggle in Prussia in the 1860s between the progressive liberals in the Landtag who sought to develop their constitutional powers at the expense of the *Junker*-dominated army and the king of Prussia. Military reform significantly provided the issue on which the Landtag forced a crisis by cancelling all provisional grants. The ultra-conservative Bismarck, appointed chancellor to resolve the deadlock, was prepared to concede two-year service (instead of three-) but in return he asked that the size of the army be fixed at the constant proportion of 1.2 per cent of the population and that the funds to support it also be perpetuated at a given sum per head. William I, egged on by the reactionary General Manteuffel, refused to accept anything less than three-year service. When parliament was dissolved in 1863, Bismarck implemented the bold solution that the crown must in such circumstances collect its own taxes. Prussia's military triumphs of 1864 and 1866 showed that the opposition to the king and Bismarck was extremely susceptible to the appeal of national unity achieved by force of arms. The chancellor's unconstitutional measures were retrospectively condoned.

In 1866 all the states composing the new North German Confederation accepted Prussian terms of military service: every German male was liable to three years' colour service followed by four years in the reserve and five in the *landwehr*, which was now firmly associated with the regular army and lost the last vestiges of a distinct liberal institution. More significant still, politically, was that Bismarck largely prevailed in his determined effort to remove the army from parliamentary control. Henceforth the army would consist of 1 per cent of the population with its budgetary allocation settled for the period 1866–73. This measure served to institutionalize the social and political gulf between the royal army and the bourgeoisie and lower classes. The measure also ensured that there would be bitter conflict between parliament and the military interest on the rare occasions when the budget came up for reallocation. In 1874 the army leaders, with Bismarck, secured the exemption of the military budget from parliamentary debate for a further seven years (the so-called *Septennat*) which was widely denounced as an act of militarism. As Germany became increasingly industrialized and social democratic representation in the Reichstag grew this issue came to symbolize the constitutional struggle against the crown and its conservative supporters, the *Junkers* and Rhineland industrialists.

To sum up, Bismarck skilfully employed the prestige and power deriving from spectacular military victories to deflate liberal opposition and even to secure its assent to the perpetuation of the army as an antidemocratic royal institution largely removed from constitutional control. The ominous implications of this trend towards 'militarism' were muffled in the short run by Bismarck's success over Moltke in 1866 and again in 1870 when the chief of the general staff vainly strove to assert his supremacy in ruthlessly pressing home military advantages. Even so Bismarck got his way at a high price in 1871 by imposing draconian terms on France which were in accord with the generals' and the people's demands.[10]

Apart from the loss of Venetia to Italy, the Hapsburg empire did not suffer severely in territorial terms from the defeat in 1866. But her loss of all influence in the North German Confederation clearly signalled her inferiority to Prussia/Germany, and a further blow fell in 1867 when Franz Joseph was obliged to accept the split of his empire into two constituent parts of Austria and Hungary. The regular armies, which remained united under the war ministry in Vienna, were reorganized along Prussian lines by an energetic war minister, Field Marshal Kuhn (1868–75). So far as possible, regional privileges were reduced and an attempt was made to associate regiments with the districts from which they would draw their reserves. Shortage of money and fear of fostering nationalist opposition together ensured that Austria would not implement the full Prussian system of universal short-service conscription. Instead the annual contingent was split into two portions; the first served for three years in the colours, seven in the reserve and two in the *landwehr*, while the second portion merely served twelve years in the *landwehr*. In contrast to Prussia the *landwehr* was not fused with the regular armies and, a further complication, the Austrian and Hungarian *landwehr* were controlled by their respective ministries of national defence. This gave the Hungarian *landwehr* or *honved* enhanced significance as the nucleus of a future national army. On the whole this separation of the *landwehr* produced a healthy rivalry but flaws were revealed in the army organization shaped by Kuhn when it was first tested in the struggle over Bosnia-Herzegovina in 1876–8.[11]

France provides an interesting example of a once-great military nation which recognized its danger in good time but was unable to reform its military system before disaster struck. Napoleon III in particular realized in 1866 that too much faith was being placed in quality as against quantity of troops. He and his favoured war minister, Marshal Niel, attempted to push through radical changes in the terms of service so as to secure larger numbers with the colours supported by well-trained and numerous reserves. French public opinion as a whole, however, showed itself to be fiercely opposed to the concept of the 'nation in arms' and to 'the blood tax', as conscription was called. French society was vehemently opposed to the abolition of 'lucky numbers' or to ending the concession whereby those who drew an 'unlucky number' might purchase a substitute. Indeed there were even insurance companies which issued policies against the calamity of military service. Niel's new terms of service became law in January 1868 but they had suffered serious dilution in the legislature. The annual contingent was still divided into two parts, the first to serve five years with the colours but the second a mere five months. The *Garde Mobile* would provide another half a million men bringing the total of supposedly 'trained troops' available to over a million. French professional opposition to a mass army was vividly exemplified in provisions for training the *Garde Mobile*. Only two weeks were allowed for training which had to take place a day at a time and under conditions that enabled all the young recruits to return home in the evening. Not for a single night were they to be exposed to the corrupting influence of the barracks. So far from being 'ready down to the last gaiter button', as one complacent general remarked, very little improvement had been made by 1870: the French army went to war virtually unchanged from 1866. This did not of course inhibit the ignorant Parisiens from shouting 'On to Berlin'.

After the defeat of the regular French armies and the deposition of Napoleon III the Republican Government of National Defence, led by Freycinet and Gambetta, showed itself to be remarkably forward-looking in its approach to raising a nation in arms. Freycinet, in particular, carried the conscription of skilled civilians, such as doctors, engineers, architects and businessmen, to an extent that was not to be equalled by any belligerent until the later stages of the First

World War. The failure of these improvised amateur armies to turn the tide ought not to have obscured the lessons which their mobilization suggested for the waging of total war in the twentieth century. Ironically, the failure of amateurs in the second part of the war served to muffle the failure of the professionals in the first part. Indeed the remnants of the regular (and essentially imperial) armies regained some of their prestige by their ruthless suppression of the Paris *Commune*. In doing so they finally ended the stormy history of the National Guard and dealt a severe blow at the extreme (*Communard*) conception of the people in arms, disproving the boast that 'The people know nothing of scientific manoeuvres, but when it has a musket in its hand, and paving stones under its feet, it fears not all the strategists of the monarchist school'.[12]

The main military lesson of the Franco-Prussian war seemed to be that the era of small, long-service professional armies was over. The Austrian and French armies had really been quite good by Napoleonic standards but they had been no match for the German nation in arms. The challenge of emulating Germany's achievement posed problems far transcending the military sphere: problems of industrial, social and political organization. In the short term, however, it was the narrowly military issues of manpower and mobilization which caught the attention for reasons that are readily apparent. Germany's success in 1870 did not stem primarily from brilliance in generalship or manoeuvre, but it had been achieved quite quickly in the classical manner of great battles and sieges. In short, there had been no need for tremendous industrial and logistical efforts. The American Civil War had already provided an instructive example of the kind of total effort that would be required when neither side would accept the verdict of battle, but it took a generation or more for this to be fully appreciated in Europe.

The wars of the 1860s dashed the hopes of international cooperation in Europe in a non-militant federative spirit. That spirit lingered on in the Scandinavian kingdoms, Switzerland and the Netherlands, but elsewhere standards of political conduct came to be patterned on the military exploits of Piedmont and Prussia. The series of national wars and revolutions between 1848 and 1871 not only saw the emergence of new national states for Germans, Italians and Hungarians, but the dawn of a new era in which the states' material strength and competitiveness were emphasized. All became resigned, as one jingle put it, 'to the simple plan. They should take who have the power. And they should keep who can.'[13]

By the 1860s the leading European states were already following Britain's example in industrialization, even before Prussia's victory over France provided proof and justification for the competitive spirit. France had begun to industrialize before Germany but by 1870 the latter was forging ahead, producing for example 2 million tons of pig iron to France's 1½ million. The broader lesson of Prussia/Germany's victory seemed to be that a healthy competition prevailed between nations as between individuals, and that the materially strong must necessarily excel the materially weak.

Though the conflicts between 1854 and 1871 did not destroy the European system of sovereign powers they revealed – or caused – drastic changes in the relative status of the main actors. The Austrian empire was declining in status: expelled from Italy and Germany by 1866, it still dominated the mixed nationalities of the central Danubian basin but signalled its decline by sharing the government of the empire with Hungary. The Ottoman empire was declining and contracting even more rapidly but survived as a great power mainly due to Russia's temporary setbacks and to the rivalry of other powers, notably Britain and France. Russia, with the largest contiguous land empire in the world, could not be kept down for long by her defeat in the Crimean War. Her denunciation of the restrictive ('Black Sea') clauses of the Treaty of Paris during the Franco-Prussian war signalled her intention to resume the advance through the Balkans towards Constantinople. Italy, though lacking the raw materials to become a major industrial force and with only a recently achieved and brittle national sense of identity, was nevertheless grudgingly admitted to the club of great powers. Finally it was France that had suffered the most rapid and humiliating slump in prestige. But despite her overshadowing by a united Germany and the transformation from empire into republic, she remained an intensely patriotic, formidable power.

The cession of Alsace-Lorraine provided the most disturbing tangible legacy of the mid-century wars. A century earlier such a transfer of provinces would have been commonplace, while a century later it would have been brutally enforced by physical occupation and the expulsion of the population. But, as Michael Howard wrote,

To the nineteenth century, with its growing belief in national-determination and plebiscitary voting, the process, carried out in defiance of the wishes of the population, seemed an open flouting of that public law on whose development Europe was beginning to pride itself.[14]

The complex and even paradoxical manifestations of the warring spirit or 'militarism', vividly described in the epilogue of the preceding volume in this series, became more pronounced after 1870. As Vagts noted, the bourgeoisie, despite their plans for peace, were not really at bottom averse to war but might at times express war emotions more violently than actual soldiers. The civilian middle classes were sometimes willing to pay for war but not to risk their own lives. They might, like Charles Kingsley, offer 'Brave Words to Brave Soldiers' but not their own sons, preferring that the poorest of the working classes should offer theirs. In some instances, one suspects, even the identity of the enemy was not of vital importance to the 'civilian militarists'. In short, long before the era of Hitler, Stalin, Mussolini and their pusillanimous general staffs, there were times when 'the non-military were warlike and the military were not'.[15]

This is not to deny, however, that a new and exceedingly nasty note of pro-war sentiment was evident in some of the leading soldiers and military theorists after 1870. For example, Friedrich von Bernhardi held that war was one of the Christian virtues, while Colmar von der Goltz asserted that modern wars had become the nations' way of doing business. That a vocal section of the military was becoming markedly less humane and tolerant can hardly be denied, but the cultural – as distinct from the institutional – roots of this phenomenon after 1870 would repay further investigation. Geoffrey Best has recently emphasized the contributions of the cheap jingoistic press and the popularization of the distorted concepts of Darwin, as well as intoxicating ideas lifted from writers who encouraged the cult of antirationalism such as Nietzsche. But as he acutely perceives, some militaristic outbursts may be viewed as a defensive reaction to the growing influence of the 'peace party'. He instances the cultivated and sensitive Moltke's reaction to Bluntschli's model code of war law. The general favoured the alleviation of the evils of war but declared:

Perpetual peace is a dream, and not even a beautiful dream. War is an element of the divine order of the world. In it are developed the noblest virtues of man: courage and self-denial, fidelity to duty and the spirit of sacrifice; soldiers give their lives. Without war, the world would stagnate and lose itself in materialism.[16]

Lest it be thought that these are the ravings of a typical Prussian, it should be recalled that John Ruskin had voiced similar sentiments in his lectures on 'War' delivered at the Royal Military Academy, Woolwich in 1865 and published in *The Crown of Wild Olive*. What also needs to be stressed are the undertones of insecurity, anxiety and self-reassurance that pervade such warlike statements particularly in the approach to the great conflagration of 1914. Bismarck brilliantly described this insecurity to a Russian diplomat in 1879:

> The great powers of our time are like travellers, unknown to one another, whom chance has brought together in a carriage. They watch each other, and when one of them puts his hand into his pocket, his neighbour gets ready his own revolver in order to be able to fire the first shot.[17]

It is possible to detect similar apprehension and uncertainty in one of the dominant themes in the great outpouring of professional military literature after 1870; namely that Moltke had rediscovered the Napoleonic recipe for short and decisive campaigns leading to clear-cut, beneficial peace settlements. Austria's prompt acceptance of the verdict of Sadowa provided a perfect but misleading example. By contrast the American Civil War, though studied by specialists for technical and tactical information, was not viewed as a protracted 'total' war of human and material attrition. Rather it was complacently assumed that the length of the struggle was due to initial unpreparedness and the persisting military incompetence of amateurs at all levels. Even in Europe, however, there was the ominous example of France which had not surrendered after the apparently 'decisive' defeats of Sedan and Metz, but had on the contrary instituted a revolutionary republican government and attempted to carry on a people's war. Yet France had no hope of defeating Germany and very little of even securing a more favourable peace by demanding further sacrifices from the nation. Ironically a *guerre à outrance* could be seen as the proof of republican patriotism. As Gambetta wrote to Jules Favre early in 1871:

> We shall prolong the struggle to extermination, we shall ensure that there cannot be found in France a man or an Assembly to

adhere to the victory of force, and we shall thus strike with impotence conquest and occupation.[18]

The Franco-Prussian war witnessed a decline in the standard of military conduct which proved a bitter disappointment to the international peace movements that had flourished since 1815. Some acts of indiscriminate brutality were patently unjustifiable, but in others the flood of accusation and counteraccusation obscured the fact that certain problems of morality versus 'military necessity' were inseparable from the nature of modern warfare.

The Prussian bombardment of the civilian districts of Strasbourg and Paris provoked particularly violent controversy. There was no military reason for indiscriminate attack on civilians, but merely the excuse that a policy of terror would break popular morale and bring about a quicker end to the war than orthodox, legal operations. This assumption proved mistaken in the short term as regards Strasbourg, whose Alsacien commander, General Uhrich, held out until his ammunition was exhausted; while in Paris the immediate effect of the bombardment was to provoke the starving, desperate populace to demand an all-out *sortie torrentielle* to end the torment. Unfortunately, as even French generals admitted, military governors were seldom able to resist for more than twenty-four hours the pressure of the civil authorities to surrender once the bombardment began.[19]

Extreme ruthlessness seemed to pay military dividends and to confuse the moral issue. Bombarding the unfortified civilian quarters of towns was not a German monopoly. British admirals displayed an unedifying propensity to bombard enemy ports at the least excuse throughout the nineteenth century. One admiral, Dundas, was accused by the press of 'mawkish sentimentality' for confining his attack on Odessa during the Crimean War to the military installations, but since most of these incidents took place in what would now be called 'the Third World', such as the destruction of Alexandria in 1882, Britain suffered less criticism than the major land powers. But it should be remembered that the French *Jeune École* navalists of the 1880s made ruthless attack on (British) civilian property on land and at sea a major point in their programme and would surely have bombarded coastal towns had there been an opportunity.

By far the most sensitive area of controversy however concerned the rights of an occupying power on the one hand and of non-regular military resistance on the other. The extreme occupier's view made no concession whatever to the rights of partisans or guerrillas; rather it expected absolute docility and obedience from the defeated enemy population in return for a guarantee of a minimum of law and order. Even in the rare case where complete acquiescence was obtained, there remained the even more delicate issue of positive assistance pejoratively known as 'collaboration'. Given the imperfections of logistical arrangements and the determination of most armies anyway to subsist wherever possible at the enemy's expense, there could be no amicable compromise. As for the other side of the coin, the Germans were unprepared for French irregular warfare in 1870–1 and tended to react with extreme severity. Partisans wearing a recognizable uniform, bearing arms and subject to some sort of discipline could be treated as legitimate enemies, whereas at the other extreme even the more legally minded French condemned undisciplined, garishly dressed gangs who were simply bandits and whose depredations were more feared in some districts than the methodical exactions of the Germans. [20]

The real problem, of course, was how to regard resisters who fell between these extremes? French guerrilla activity was widespread from the very beginning of operations in 1870. German cavalry crossing the Moselle in mid-August were frequently fired on by villagers and by way of reprisal hanged the culprits – or suspects – whenever they caught them. The roads between Sedan and Paris were haunted by *francs-tireurs* who were treated as murderers. When Favre complained to Bismarck that German civilians had done the same in 1813, the chancellor grimly replied, 'That is quite true; but our trees still bear the marks where your generals hanged our people on them.' In the later stages of the war some 60,000 *francs-tireurs* were active in all but the most thoroughly patrolled districts, their motley companies swelled by foreign sympathizers of every kind. [21]

As mentioned above the German high command took a harsh view of *francs-tireurs* from the start, Moltke ordering that they be allowed no belligerent rights and that where individuals could not be punished entire villages might be destroyed. In mitigation and even justification, however, it must be noted that the German invaders were as disciplined, moderate and sober as any army Europe had ever seen. By contrast, as even some fair-minded Frenchmen admitted, their own troops straggled, looted and drank in the traditional fashion. In the early stages the German authorities severely disciplined their own troops for the slightest damage to property, such as burning vine posts, but gradually murders, burning and mutual hatreds escalated. Humane German officers deplored this brutalizing effect on their own men and prayed that the war would end. From German headquarters General Sheridan chided the occupiers for their leniency. The French people, he urged, 'must be left nothing but their eyes to weep with over the war'. By the end of hostilities this deplorable attitude had inflamed not only the bulk of active participants but also large sectors of the civil population. Mutual hatreds and stereotypes of the enemy as barbarian were engendered which would find even fuller expression in the First World War.

It is only superficially a paradox that at precisely the time when warfare was spilling beyond recently established standards of restraint and humanity, the international peace movements reached the zenith of their efforts to limit and humanize war. Rather it seems likely that the prospect of a new plunge into barbarism caused the peace party to redouble its efforts.

One of the few enduring achievements of the peace party was widening international recognition of the Red Cross, originally established at the Geneva Convention in 1864. It was a great step in principle, however flawed the practice, to agree that once wounded a soldier ceased to be a combatant and became simply a suffering individual, and also that all involved in caring for the wounded should enjoy neutral status. The battlefield implications of the neutrality of Red Cross personnel were not properly anticipated and both sides were irritated in 1870 by what Professor Best calls 'the cool assumption by cosmopolitan do-gooders that they only needed a Red Cross label to get them the freedom of the battle-zone'. Worse still was the abuse of the symbol to secure immunity for buildings or vehicles which were not run by the Red Cross at all. Finally, in the years after 1870, the national societies tended to become paramilitary organizations which enabled those unable or unwilling to bear arms to 'do their bit' by caring for their own fighters.[22]

Earlier, by the Declaration of Paris in 1856 following the Crimean War, the first important steps had been taken to clarify what was legally permissible in maritime conflicts. Privateering was abolished, and blockades, in order to be binding, had to be 'effective'; that is, they must be permanently enforced by ships capable of preventing exit and entrance to ports and not just nominal or paper declarations.

It was further declared that enemy goods on neutral ships were free from seizure unless they were contraband, and also that enemy ships did not make forfeit neutral goods carried on them unless they were contraband. These clauses were naturally welcomed by commercial and neutral interests, and there was even the prospect that enemy private property (i.e., not warlike goods and material) might be allowed to proceed peacefully in war.

This vision would appear Utopian after the First World War, but it testified to the almost mystical value which was attached to the free exchange of goods in the mid-nineteenth century. The great drawback to these declarations for the major maritime powers such as Britain, France and the United States was that limitations which suited them as neutrals would handicap them as belligerents. They also had to gauge how far a tough belligerent policy at sea would affect their relations with neutrals. Britain, above all, was wary of further international discussions and none in fact took place for the remainder of the century. It is worth mentioning here that the outstanding example of successful arbitration in this period concerned war at sea; namely Britain's acceptance of responsibility in 1872 for the damage done to Union merchant shipping by the British-built Confederate raider *Alabama*. It was very exceptional then, and has remained so since, for any sovereign state to admit responsibility *vis-à-vis* another, let alone to make reparations.

Lastly there was the intractable problem of trying to reach international agreement on the definition of combatant status in land warfare. From the Brussels Conference of 1874 there emerged four criteria for the laws, rights and duties of war to apply to regulars, militiamen and volunteers: they must be commanded by a responsible officer, have a fixed distinctive badge or uniform recognizable at a distance, carry arms openly, and conduct their operations in obedience to the laws and customs of war. A second article added that inhabitants of a territory not yet occupied who spontaneously took up arms to resist invaders without having had time to organize themselves in accordance with article one, should still be regarded as belligerents if they carried arms openly and respected the laws and customs of war. [23]

These stipulations were better than nothing but of course their terms were open to legal dispute. For example, from precisely what distance would insignia have to be visible to qualify? More seriously, these and other legal restraints were ultimately dependent on the

31

commanders' determination to implement them and punish transgressors on their own side. There were many scrupulous, honourable and humane generals in this period, but with the best intentions they were often thwarted by a variety of conditions covered by the term 'military necessity'. How far, in short, could or should a commander risk the loss of his soldiers' lives or the failure of his mission in order to respect some principle which the enemy might anyway ignore? 'Military necessity' was allowed to cover a multitude of breaches of the rules; indeed even the rules themselves were qualified with such phrases as 'so far as possible'. It is hard to escape the pessimistic conclusion, that valiant and well-meaning as these international conventions were, they exerted only a marginal effect in moderating international disputes and mitigating the horrors of war. Then, as now, there was no international body powerful enough to enforce the rule of law on sovereign states unwilling to accept it. As Professor F. S. L. Lyons summed up the impasse:

> There was no permanent international league. There was no compulsory arbitration. There was no agreement on disarmament. Instead there were empty phrases, ambiguous gestures of friendship . . . and a steady preparation for war by the professional militarists.[24]

Between 1871 and 1914 nearly every continental European state – as well as Japan – adopted some form of conscription following Prussia's successful example. Compulsory military service was first and foremost regarded as a vital component of national security, but it was also seen in some countries as an instrument for developing social cohesion and political docility in the masses. Armed forces now enjoyed a period of enhanced popularity as nation-builders and, even, as the guardians or repositories of national virtues. A fair amount of idealism was now invested in the revived concept of the nation in arms. Even before the Franco-Prussian war the Bavarian statesman Hohenlohe was struck 'by the interest manifested by the lowest of the people in things military' at a Berlin parade. 'No traces', he said, 'of the former animosity against the military which used to be noticeable among the lower classes.' The military profession acquired a new reputation for general versatility, ability to cut red tape and get things done. In France the Republic's revised regulations for obtaining commissions attracted a higher social class of officers, though this in time created resentment among the less well off. Also, in the bitter aftermath of defeat, the French army became for a time the focus of national aspirations for unity and revival. Military service became a sort of secular religion in which officers took over the role of priests. A decade after defeat, 'on aperçoit nettement la notion d'une éducation de style spartiate, tout entière tournée vers l'exaltation patriotique et où l'école devient l'antichambre de la caserne'.[25]

Yet even in this halcyon period for armed services, social and political problems were never far distant. As European states became increasingly more industrial, and expanding cities drew in a new proletariat from the countryside, tensions inevitably developed. In some countries, such as Britain, the officer corps gradually adapted itself with only minor inconvenience, but in others, notably Germany, the army found itself increasingly at odds with the urban interests and its representatives in parliament. Viewed from another angle, the very prestige and political power which armed forces had acquired in the mid-nineteenth century rendered them difficult to control politically in subsequent decades. Finally an era of rapid technical and social change provided a severe test for the military mentality to adapt traditional notions of strategy, tactics, organization and style of leadership to new weapons, new combat conditions and a better-educated, more politically conscious rank and file. The tactical revolution and the peak period of late nineteenth-century 'militarism' will be fully examined in the next chapter, but this one may conveniently conclude with a brief look at how the leading European countries began to adapt to the military lessons of the mid-century wars.

The victorious German army's popularity was secure for at least a decade after 1870. The possession of a reserve commission was eagerly sought by the middle classes as the surest method of enhancing their social standing. Even in Prussia, however, conscription was never universally popular. Professional men, for example, resented the peremptory way in which they were called to the colours at short notice. More resented still was the exclusion of soldiers committing civil offences from the civil courts. These irritations, however, were as nothing compared with the friction between the army and society on the political plane. Bismarck was never entirely able to remove the army from the political debate, but managed to preserve a large amount of military autonomy by gradually withdrawing military matters from the war minister, who was responsible to the Reichstag, in favour of the military cabinet which answered to the emperor. Since the army received about 90 per cent of the federal budget, the frustration of the left-wing opposition was understandable. In 1874, as mentioned earlier, Bismarck secured a fixed establishment without further debate for seven years – a truly incredible emasculation of democratic rights. Four years later Bismarck ended his association with the national liberals in favour of an alliance with the East Prussian *Junkers* and the conservative Ruhr industrialists. Thus in the closing years of the century the gulf between the Reichstag and the imperial army was widening.

In 1867, as a direct result of its defeat by Prussia, the Hapsburg empire was divided into the two constituent parts of Austria-Hungary for administrative purposes. The regular armies of the empire remained under the central control of the imperial war ministry, and were subjected to drastic reorganization on the Prussian model. The traditional army commands were replaced by territorial commands with a view to linking regiments more closely with the districts from which they drew their recruits and reservists. In recognition of the changing nature of battle the famous white Austrian uniforms were replaced by a less conspicuous dark blue. In contrast to Prussia, however, Austria did not introduce general conscription for equal periods of colour and reserve service. Instead the annual contingent was split into two different systems: one group served for three years with the colours, seven in the reserve and two in the *landwehr*, while the other group served twelve years in the *landwehr*. Again in contrast to Prussia, the Austrian and Hungarian *landwehr* remained quite distinct and responsible to their respective ministries of national defence. The latter's *landwehr* (the *honved*) developed its own unique organization reflecting Magyar aspirations for their own permanent army entirely recruited from and commanded by Hungarians.[26]

French military politics in the 1870s revolved around the problem of reconciling the idea of the nation in arms with the preservation of internal and external security. The legislature in the early years of the Republic was dominated by conservative republicans and monarchists so, despite the introduction of universal liability to military service in 1872, the army remained a conservative institution. Some deputies looked to the army as a moral antidote for anarchy and as a solvent of social discontent. Nevertheless, the old faith in high-quality professionals produced by long service died hard and, rather surprisingly, there was wide agreement that French recruits, lacking German habits of obedience and discipline, required more than three years' training to become good soldiers. Clearly France could not afford to make long service obligatory for all young men so the old lottery system was revived: a 'good number' meant from six months to a year's duty, but a 'bad number' entailed five years' colour service. Even the latter was too short for Thiers who complained that this obsession with the nation in arms was tantamount to 'putting a gun on the shoulder of every Socialist'. Thiers secured the adoption of two extremely controversial amendments to the 1872 law: educated and well-off young men could enlist for a single year only (as in Germany); and those intending to follow a 'liberal career' in education or the church were totally exempted. Despite continuous controversy the 1872 law survived until 1889 after which no one was conscripted for more than three years. In the 1870s, for the first time since the early years of the century, nearly every French family became acquainted with the nature of army life. According to numerous memoirs, military service was extremely popular with many conscripts. The darker aspects of barrack life were pushed into the background: what mattered above all was to prepare for the imminent war of revenge against Germany. Officers marked in black the frontiers of the lost provinces on maps of France, and soldiers ending their service often presented a bust of 'Alsace in tears' to their company commanders. For twenty years, according to Girardet, the army was sacrosanct and placed above party politics:

L'institution militaire était devenue, dans les consciences françaises, la représentation même de la patrie amputée et vaincue mais toujours vivante.[27]

Despite its leading role in the unification of the country, the Italian army suffered a decline in popularity in the later 1860s and its military reputation was hardly enhanced by the farcical incompetence displayed in expelling the small French garrison from Rome in 1870. In seeking to emulate the Prussian army Italy was badly handicapped by relative poverty: she possessed very little coal or iron ore and was largely dependent on foreign capital to construct her railways. The military share of the budget fell from 40 per cent in the early 1860s to a nadir of less than 20 per cent in the early 1870s. Nevertheless General Ricotti Magnani carried out a thorough reorganization between 1870 and 1876. In 1875 he reduced the period of conscript service from four years for the first contingent to three. The second served for nine years in the reserves and a third category was introduced to ensure that most young men received some elementary training. However substitution was still allowed so there was a serious anomaly in that many men were obliged to serve who were refused the right to vote. Ricotti also introduced the Prussian system of one-year service for educated volunteers. These measures established a standing army of 224,000 which could be swelled to 800,000 on mobilization – an impressive number in view of the country's poverty. The army was organized in ten, and later twelve corps, but unlike Prussia these formations were not based on regions but rather drew their recruits from all over Italy. This imposed serious handicaps on mobilization but was deliberately adopted as part of the solution to the critical problem of the kingdom's intense regionalism. In short, social and political considerations were given priority over purely military ones. Ricotti also pushed through a complete re-equipment of the infantry and artillery with modern weapons, and initiated an extensive building programme of new fortifications and barracks.

The Italian monarchy was even less inclined than the French Third Republic to encourage revolutionary, egalitarian concepts of a people's army, but as in France there was a strenuous effort in the 1870s to project the image of the army as the embodiment of national virtues as well as the defender of internal and external order. A recent historian of the Italian army (Dr John Whittam) doubts whether the service itself displayed much enthusiasm for this propaganda, whereas for the middle class the army was regarded more as a necessary evil than as a focus of sentiment and loyalty. Despite the growth of antimilitarist literature and politics and a tendency, particularly marked in the south, to avoid military service, the left-wing parties actually accepted an enlargement and strengthening of the military establishment in 1876.[28]

Military reform in Russia received its initial impetus from defeat in the Crimean War, but it was Prussia's victories in the 1860s which gave the great war minister Milyutin (1861–81) the necessary impetus to effect really drastic changes. The obstacles facing him were formidable. The Russian army had won few laurels since 1815;

its prestige was low; and its officer corps had little cohesion or sense of professionalism. Nor was modern organization and training helped by Russia's poverty, vast sparsely populated country with poor communications and lack of a substantial armaments industry. Worst of all, the people were politically passive, lacking any real sense of nationalism. Until 1864 the army was composed largely of peasant conscripts who served for life under officers drawn mostly from the aristocracy who lacked much in the way of education or specialized training. In 1864 Milyutin reduced the normal period of service to fifteen years, but with provision for furloughs after eight years or so depending on proficiency and education. All classes were henceforth liable to service in principle but substitution was freely available to the wealthier classes. Mass illiteracy prevented the adoption of anything closely resembling the Prussian system, but in 1874 Milyutin reduced the basic period of service to six years. As in France and Germany there were special provisions for well-educated and wealthy young men who could serve for as little as a year or even six months. Milyutin abolished the more degrading forms of corporal punishment and took the first cautious steps towards making life in the ranks an honourable patriotic duty as distinct from a form of penal servitude. Supported by a modernizing group of general staff officers, he also improved military education at all levels. Unfortunately the general staff itself remained largely untouched. Composed largely of military bureaucrats without combat experience, its numbers enjoyed preferential treatment and accelerated promotion which made the whole institution deeply unpopular.

In purely numerical terms Russia's inflated standing army and seemingly inexhaustible reserves gave her a formidable reputation as a leading military power. Even her inept performance in nearly every respect in the war against Turkey (1877–8), including clumsy mobilization, weak logistic arrangements, a divided command and obsolete tactics (notably in repeated costly assaults during the siege of Plevna), did not destroy her awesome reputation as the 'steamroller'.

In reality the prestige of the army in Russia actually declined. The nation-in-arms ideal could not be pushed very far for fear of encouraging political unrest. Officers' commissions lost some of their attraction as Milyutin's 'democratic' reforms had the effect of reducing the numbers and influence of the nobility. On the other hand a new generation of more professional regimental and staff officers felt themselves to be impeded and derided by titled and ignorant seniors. Novels might convey a sense of the brilliant and colourful social life at St Petersburg, Moscow or Warsaw, but service for the majority of officers and their families in remote and impoverished garrisons was monotonous and badly paid. Milyutin's twenty years of heroic endeavour achieved some immediate improvements in military efficiency but were largely thwarted by Russia's poverty, political backwardness and administrative weaknesses.[29]

Britain has been left to last because her army was not such an important or controversial political institution as those of the continental powers, thanks to her well-developed democratic constitution, immense industrial and commercial wealth and dominant navy. As in Russia, the British military reform movement, which had briefly revived but then faltered after the Crimean War, received a powerful boost from Prussia's spectacular victories. Britain however was debarred from adopting the vital ingredient of conscription for two quite different reasons. It was politically unthinkable and also militarily impractical due to the need to garrison an expanding, worldwide empire. In particular it is only a slight oversimplification to say that the British army existed to garrison India (which required a permanent force of some 70,000 white troops after the crown's assumption of direct authority from the East India Company following the Mutiny in 1857), and the possessions which safeguarded the route thereto.

Within these limits, and allowing also for the fact that parliament imposed a rigorous curb on service expenditure, Edward Cardwell as war minister (1868–74) implemented a cluster of reforms designed collectively to usher the army into a new era. Terms of service were made as short as practicable (six years with the colours followed by six in the reserves), with the twin aims of improving recruiting figures and building up a trained reserve. Other reforms designed to make the army more attractive in a more competitive labour market included abolition of corporal punishment on home service, improved barracks, food and leisure activities, and the association of regular battalions with the auxiliaries (militia, volunteers and yeomanry) in brigade districts. Perhaps best known of all, in 1871 Cardwell ended the well-established system of the purchase and sale of officers' commissions in the infantry and cavalry regiments. This opened the way for more professional attitudes, but did not of itself deeply affect the social composition of the officers corps since it was almost impossible to hold a commission on home service without considerable private means. The post-Cardwellian army performed reasonably efficiently in its almost unbroken series of imperial conflicts, but – in complete contrast to the world supremacy of the Royal Navy – it was simply not in the same league as the major continental powers. Pressures to gain admission to this league, with all their social and economic ramifications, only began to be seriously felt after 1900.[30]

This chapter has described the waning prospects for peaceful cooperation as a consequence of the mid-century wars which threatened a new era of aggressive nationalism. Nevertheless internationalism remained a force to be reckoned with in the 1870s, while Bismarck made determined efforts to preserve the status quo by a system of alliances. Despite extreme advocacy of military coups on the one hand and of people's militias on the other, moderate conservatives whether operating under monarchs or republics kept a firm grip on military power. Nowhere were armed forces allowed to take over the direct control of the state. In the next chapter we shall examine the emergence of a more strident form of militarism which was accompanied by radical developments in the means and methods of waging war.

2

THE ARMING OF NATIONS, c. 1880–1900

The German army had introduced a new era in 1871 and fear of provoking that mighty machine again remained a basic, if latent, consideration in European diplomacy for the next thirty years. Nevertheless, for all its tensions, arms races and war scares, this was essentially a period of peace, progress and prosperity in Europe. Indeed, even the chronicler of militarism, Alfred Vagts, allowed that the period was 'full of prejudice against violence', and witnessed very little overt application of military force as a pressure in politics:

> the military accepted the governments as frameworks within which their interests could be secured, often by identifying them with those of the governing groups.[1]

Without too much exaggeration the final quarter of the century might be called the climax of materialism. This period witnessed the virtual completion of the European railway network, with over 100,000 miles of track constructed mainly in Russia, Austria-Hungary and the Balkans. By the mid-1870s submarine cables permitted direct communication from Europe to North and South America, India and the Far East. By the end of the century Marconi's wireless telegraph had 'bridged' the Channel, and in 1901 the first message was sent across the Atlantic by wireless. This invention greatly improved communications in land warfare, but at sea its implications were truly revolutionary because it freed ships from the constriction of visual signalling. Material progress was most spectacularly evident in the growth of the population of Europe. In the last thirty years of the century the population increased by almost 32 per cent or nearly 100 million people, and this despite the 'loss' of 25 million emigrants, mostly to North and South America. Great Britain's population rose from 31 to 41 million; Germany's from 41 to 56 million; and European Russia's from 77 to 103 million. Only France was out of step, her rate of increase being scarcely more than half a million per decade – from 36 to 39 million.[2]

Moreover, France alone failed to experience an increase in the number and size of large cities. In Germany, for example, cities with over 100,000 inhabitants rose from 8 to 41. These statistics of urban expansion at the expense of rural areas indicate a period of agricultural depression and heavy industrial growth. In Germany, for example, coal production increased from 34 to 149 million tons and steel production from 0.3 to 6.7 million tons between 1870 and 1900. The spread and speeding-up of mechanical manufacture and transport yielded immense accumulations of material wealth. There was more to eat, more goods to wear and enjoy, and more money to invest at home and overseas. Despite periods of hardship in the mid-1870s and mid-1890s, the generation of 1870–1900 could view with optimistic satisfaction 'a steady access of wealth, of corporate business enterprise, of material well-being, and of that precious golden metal by which all things were measured and treasured'. On the debit side, however, the greater internal stability and prosperity of the leading European states was accompanied by intensified nationalism. In Professor Hayes's words:

The more nationalistic a state was and the more ambitious for colonial dominion (and of course the heavier its armaments), the greater was its claim to international prestige and to the rank of great power.[3]

One of the most disturbing manifestations of national competitiveness was the widespread institution of tariff barriers in the last quarter of the century.

Inevitably such civil inventions as the telephone, typewriter and colour photography were matched in the military sphere. The most important development was the adaptation to military uses of the Swedish inventor Alfred Nobel's nitroglycerine. Combustion in the new explosives was virtually complete which meant that the size of ammunition could be reduced, ranges doubled and the traditional smoke and 'fog' of war abolished. An improved propellant and smaller projectile also permitted a lower trajectory and increased lethal effectiveness; while magazine loading greatly improved the rate of fire. The French army led the way with the new Lebel rifle in the mid-1880s, and by the end of the century all the great powers had adopted magazine rifles which could kill at 2000 yards. Such weapons exercised a truly paralysing effect on movement in the zone of fire when first employed on a large scale in the South African war.

These developments in small arms would have negated the superiority of artillery, so important on the Prussian side in 1870, had not the latter arm also made enormous strides in the late nineteenth century. After years of dispute between the rival merits of bronze and iron cannon, both were supplanted by steel which could withstand a greater explosive force. Smokeless powder and improved high-explosive shells here again permitted an increase in muzzle velocity and range. Equally important was the invention of recoil-absorbing carriages which did not need to be manhandled back into position after each round. By the end of the century quick-firing field guns like the excellent French 75 mm were in service in all the major armies with effective ranges of between 3000 and 6000 yards. Simultaneously Germany lead the way in constructing monster siege guns, howitzers and mortars with great penetrative powers and ranges of 10 km and more. Early types of machine guns such as the Gatling and the *mitrailleuse* had already appeared in the American Civil War and the Franco-Prussian war respectively but these were large, cumbersome pieces operated by a hand crank. The British inventor, Sir Hiram Maxim, devised the first truly automatic machine gun in 1885 in that his weapon used its own recoil energy to load itself, fire and eject its own empty cases. So long as the gunner squeezed the trigger the Maxim would rattle off ammunition from mechanically fed canvas belts each containing 250 rounds. In the South African war, the British employed a Maxim of field-gun dimensions fed by 25 belts containing 37-mm shells and familiarly known as 'pom-poms'.

Just as guns had to be improved to offset developments in small arms, so the science of fortification was transformed after the French experience in 1870–1 to counter the greater range and penetrative power of guns. Masonry was replaced by concrete and steel with forts being pushed out ever further (to ranges of 18 km) from the central bastion. It was fittingly an engineer from repeatedly invaded Belgium, General Henri Brialmont, who pioneered the replacement of fortresses by vast fortified areas. Guns were placed in revolving turrets, protected by concrete and earth, which would rise up out of subterranean pits to fire. A labyrinth of trenches and tunnels linked the gun emplacements, housing not only magazines but also barracks for the garrison and mechanics. Antwerp, Verdun, Lemberg and other historic fortresses were converted into fortified areas covering hundreds of square miles.[4]

In contrast to these enormously costly defensive systems, a notable lesson of the American Civil War seemed to be that a cheap and effective answer to improved firepower lay in improvised entrenchments. This tactical development was impressed on a larger European public in 1877 by the Turks' heroic defence of Plevna in Bulgaria against a larger Russian army advancing towards Constantinople. So long as their supplies lasted, Osman Pasha's defenders held out against repeated assaults, inflicting heavy casualties – as many as 18,000 out of 60,000 Russian troops in one attack. By the end of the century armies were already setting the scene for the First World War in their routine use of entrenching tools, picks and shovels.

In the maritime sphere the last quarter of the century also witnessed a second technical transformation following the revolutionary conversion to steam-driven ironclads between the 1830s and the 1860s. A new era in warship construction was signalled by the British *Devastation* in 1873 which was the first battleship to abandon sails altogether following the capsizing of the top-heavy *Captain*. As in land weapons, improvements in explosive powders led to a revolution in naval ordnance. After 1881 all new naval guns had composite barrels made of steel. Breech loading, dropped after experiments some twenty years earlier, was now firmly adopted. One historian of military technology describes the changes in naval guns between 1860 and 1885 as 'fantastic'.[5] The maximum weight of British naval guns rose from less than 5 tons of the 68-pounder smoothbore to 111 tons of the 16.25-inch rifled gun. The latter fired an 1800-pound shell (solid shot having been replaced) which could penetate 34 inches of wrought iron at 1000 yards. Guns were increasingly housed in revolving turrets and their recoil mechanisms were steadily improved. There was no corresponding improvement in accuracy, however, because both fire-control instruments and ability to observe and report the fall of shells were lacking until well into the next century. These improvements in naval firepower stimulated a desperate search for countermeasures in the way of stronger and thicker armour. After centuries of extremely slow change, warships could now be obsolescent on completion. Between 1860 and 1880 armour at the water line increased from 4½ inches to a maximum, never since surpassed, of 24 inches. Different processes were applied to the composition of armour: wrought-iron gave way to nickel-steel armour in 1893 and by the end of the decade this too was being superseded by Krupp's 'new process' armour.

After a long and chequered history, marked by farcical failures and self-destructive successes, the submarine was also becoming an effective instrument of naval warfare by the end of the century. In 1884, for example, two Britons, Campbell and Ash, built a submarine propelled by two 50-horsepower electric motors with a 100-cell storage battery. Its effective range was however only about 80 miles. The United States navy's *The Plunger* was completed with the vital addition of a periscope in 1900. In the short term automatic torpedoes and anchored mines made an even bigger impact on naval thinking, by threatening to put an end not only to close-action combat, but also to close blockade of enemy ports. The breakneck speed of technological innovation with its alarming corollary of obsolescence for a time rendered the relative status of great naval powers remarkably fluid. In the 1890s the United States made a bid to join the three leading naval powers, Britain, France and Russia; Italy and Germany laid the foundations of modern navies; and by judicious purchases Japan and Chile also aspired to membership of the top league.

As regards the production of gunpowder and armaments, France alone relied predominantly upon public factories. Elsewhere the firm opposition of liberals to state industry, including even arms factories, generally prevailed. In Britain, for example, a government committee chaired by the distinguished liberal politician and man of letters, John Morley, advocated giving more orders to private firms on the grounds that this would stimulate competition among inventors and producers while also widening the area of production. Subsequently, proposals to manufacture all the government's arms in Woolwich and other state-owned arsenals were rejected on the grounds that it would wreck the (private) arms trade in Birmingham. Arms supply also took on an increasingly national character without the services apparently foreseeing the dangers of technical stultification and inflated prices. Consequently, as arms supply became heavily 'nationalized', much of the stimulus of international competition was lost. Indeed the leading arms and munitions firms such as Armstrong, Creusot and Krupp shrewdly safeguarded their interests by arranging 'rings' which enabled them to share foreign markets, thereby showing 'a fine disregard of the narrow chauvinism they sometimes exhibited at home'. In 1886, for example, Nobel established the first international trust (the Dynamite Trust Ltd) with subsidiary monopolistic companies in Britain, France, Germany, Sweden and the United States. Schneider-Creusot in France, Skoda in Austria-Hungary and, above all, Krupp in Germany practically monopolized the supply of armaments to their own forces.[6]

According to Vagts, the services rather surprisingly preferred these arrangements, so much so that they positively discouraged competition within the home market. Less surprisingly, serving, but more especially retired, officers developed close personal contacts as advisers, shareholders and even salesmen with the great arms firms. This clearly had sinister possibilities in that influential soldiers might advocate armaments contracts out of personal interest irrespective of the firm's suitability to execute the order. Moreover, lavish entertainment at monstrous baronial palaces like the Krupp's Villa Hügel – or outright bribery – might be used to ensure that particular models were accepted for mass production.[7]

How successfully did the military chiefs adapt their thinking to the technical and, by implication, tactical challenges of the late nineteenth century? Vagts states unequivocally that the services remained out of step with the technological progress of the times. They were not, in short, willing to adopt 'the most modern machinery or to advocate the purchase of the maximum amount of destructive apparatus'. He makes the interesting suggestion that the services' peacetime preoccupation with managing *men* prevented them from thinking clearly about war in a more mechanized age. They felt confident of their control over men and exercised it in mobilization tables, war games and manoeuvres. But the unexplored and possibly uncontrollable implications of new machinery was another matter. In short, they preferred to deal with men and animals rather than explosives and armour. A German staff officer epitomized the unreality of such attitudes when he remarked: 'In peacetime you cannot have enough of light artillery, but in war . . . you cannot have too many heavy guns.'[8]

Closer inspection of particular services confronting specific problems of whether to innovate or hold fast will certainly reveal monumental misjudgements and wilful obscurantism, but in other cases there were inherent uncertainties which should cause the historian to be more understanding, even charitable. One general criticism of the services may be advanced before turning to particular case studies, and it is a tendency still detectable today: namely a predisposition to focus on technicalities and gadgetry to the virtual exclusion of broader political and strategic implications.

The Royal Navy, for example, did an excellent technical job in overcoming successive French naval challenges in the mid- and later nineteenth century, but its theorists were much slower in getting to grips with how these changes would affect naval operations, not to speak of the subtler exercise of maritime power. It was only in the 1880s that the concept of 'imperial defence' was developed by such British writers as the Colomb brothers and J. K. Laughton; and the full distillation of the doctrine of 'sea power' had to wait until the 1890s for elaboration by an American naval propagandist, Captain (later Admiral) A. T. Mahan. Teaching and publishing in the 1900s, Julian Corbett was at pains to instil some sense of maritime principles and concepts into Royal Naval officers to offset an unreflective Nelsonian obsession with seeking out and destroying the enemy's battle fleet in a decisive action. Corbett was not opposed to such heroics in principle, but he correctly anticipated that an inferior fleet might refuse to play.[9]

Although a great outpouring of professional military literature after 1870 suggests a keen, enquiring spirit in a minority of officers, it is hard to deny that a lack of realism was again becoming evident in tactical manuals and field exercises towards the end of the century. This was doubtless due in part simply to the passing of time: memories of the shambles of 1870 grew dim and a new generation sought to prove its valour in heroic combat for the fatherland. It must be stressed, however, that a profound conflict occurred, not simply between 'progressives' and 'conservatives', but *within* the mind of intelligent officers who saw the trends in warfare very clearly but did not like the prospects.

What was this disturbing vision? It concerned the increasing dominance of fire power which was creating an ever wider 'fire zone' or no-man's-land in which troops could not stand upright and live. Officers would not be able to transmit orders and cohesion would be lost; the infantry advance would break down into a disorderly rabble; both sides would entrench and a stalemate would result. Furthermore, they appreciated that rapidity of fire would create huge logistical problems. It was calculated for example that more than fifty

46

men and fifty horses would be needed to serve a single 75-mm field gun. An able French historian, Jean Colin, deduced even from the Franco-Prussian war the startling conclusion that fronts were inviolable: neither side, even employing superior numbers and tactics, had taken a position by frontal assault. A French official report of 1875 insisted that: 'Troops massed in column, or in line in close order, can no longer manoeuvre, fight, or even remain in position under fire.'[10]

Colin perceived that one partial solution was for the artillery to support the infantry not only before but *throughout* its advance. This had not been done at Plevna and infantry regulations ignored the problem for the next generation. He denounced the French Army Regulations from 1894 onwards which, ignoring recent history, wrote of moving whole battalions in close order and referred to 'decisive attacks' by brigades or divisions in mass. Colin realized that increased 'friction' under fire created a fearful dilemma: considerations of discipline required that the troops be kept in close order for as long as possible, but the ever-increasing range of fire dictated that they be dispersed into skirmishing order at greater and greater distances from the enemy's position. Unlike some of his compatriots, Colin accepted that there was unlikely to be any marked difference in moral qualities or technical skill between European armies. He drew the conclusion that, given approximate equality, the attacker would have no chance of success in a frontal attack.[11]

Colonel Frederick Maurice reached similar conclusions in 1891 in a celebrated essay *War*. He saw that with the huge numbers involved taking up most of the ground, and with the artillery opening fire at about 4000 yards, there would be little if any opportunity for Napoleonic tactical skill in future battles. General Colmar von der Goltz, writing in 1883, also accepted that the rapid victories of 1866 and 1870 could not be repeated due to the ever-growing size of armies. In 1870 the ten German army corps collected on the Rhine covered 120 square miles; now the army would take up more than 200 square miles. More than a decade before Schlieffen began to grapple with the problem, he noted that there was barely enough room on the whole Franco-German frontier for the two armies to deploy. He envisaged a protracted and severe struggle with little scope for movement. The outcome would be the entire annihilation of one party or the complete exhaustion of both. This would take time because enhanced national consciousness would tend to prolong resistance.[12]

At the end of the century the Polish banker, Ivan S. Bloch, described the imaginary, but all too prophetic, subterranean siege war of the future. The outcome would be decided not on the battlefield but by famine and revolution on the home front. Bloch did not say that war was now impossible, but merely described its appalling character and likely consequences. This massive six-volume treatise by a civilian failed in its purpose. The professionals, though sharing many of his assumptions, could not endorse Bloch's grim conclusions. It is significant that Colin, so perceptive about the lunacy of current tactical doctrine, spends the greater part of his book extolling the Napoleonic spirit and strategic methods. The offensive, he thought, 'is more potent in imposing battle and in forcing decisions to one's advantage, for the assailing army occupies the whole theatre of operations and sweeps all away on its passage'. No one, he urged, should be allowed to command armies who is not disposed by nature to take the offensive.[13]

General von der Goltz was not prepared to generalize about the alleged 'cleansing effects of war', but he ended his rhapsody to the nation in arms with a stirring appeal to Germans to prepare themselves for the inevitable struggle. He appealed to national honour and desire for undying fame:

Whoever has a heart, feels it beat higher and becomes enthusiastic for the profession of a soldier. [italics in original] To defend the Fatherland, means also to gain the thanks of the Fatherland, and to knit one's name and one's being together with the name and the fame of one's king, one's captain and one's people.[14]

Thus von der Goltz also allowed patriotic fervour to obscure the unromantic realities of future war which he had sketched in his famous book.

It is appropriate to begin our selection of case studies with an example where a service's deliberate policy was opposed to initiating technical innovation which would entail scrapping serviceable vessels and incur heavy costs for replacements. The Royal Navy's pre-eminence permitted the Admiralty to adopt such a policy through most of the nineteenth century. As a result France gained a brief advantage on several occasions, notably with her construction of the first iron-armoured wooden warship *La Gloire* in 1859, but the Admiralty's confidence in Britain's dockyard facilities, expertise, wealth and determination to 'rule the waves' was well-founded. When Germany mounted a really serious challenge to British naval supremacy from 1898 the Admiralty, in the person of Sir John Fisher, took the extremely bold decision to initiate a new race from scratch by laying down the first dreadnought in 1905. His gamble proved successful: Britain was able to increase her naval expenditure between 1900 and 1914 from £29 million to £47 million, Germany from only £7 to £22 million.[15]

A more complex question of naval conservatism concerns the place of the submarine in maritime theory before 1914. It is certainly true that very few writers had predicted before 1914 its potentially decisive role as a destroyer of both merchant shipping and warships. Even the erudite and open-minded Julian Corbett, writing in 1911, hesitated to offer any firm guidance on the submarine's future role in naval warfare, but believed that its main value would be in inshore defensive operations. Three explanations may be offered for this apparent blindness. First, the range and striking capacity of pre-1914 submarine models were limited, and there were too few of them in being to constitute a decisive offensive force. Secondly, in so far as theorists like Corbett envisaged a German assault on British seaborne trade, they rightly expected it to be conducted by powerful surface raiders such as the *Emden*. Thirdly, with a few exceptions like the aggressive Fisher, most naval thinkers expected – or hoped – that internationally agreed limitations would be observed; they simply could not envisage any 'civilized' nation adopting a submarine strategy of sinking on sight without warning.

It would be easy to portray the Austrian army in the later nineteenth century as a classic example of obscurantist opposition to technological change *per se*, but resistance in reality was often to *the source* from which change was threatened. Innovation tends to be costly and in most armies money is always short. Civilians usually control the purse strings and employ this control to preserve their power over the services. The Austrian army attributed its defeat in 1866 largely to the Prussians' possession of the needle gun. They carried out thorough trials and by the end of the year were about to adopt a new Remington rifle. Then nationalism, encouraged by personal connections, prevailed and an Austrian firm, Werndl, won the order. So far so good, but further technical progress was obstructed by the commander in chief, the archduke Albrecht, who valued morale and the military spirit above material factors. Even after his replacement the archduke continued to frustrate technical research and innovation. Thus the military reformers' vision of the Artillery Committee as the 'intellectual forcing house' of the army, maintaining high technical standards in every field, was not realized. It degenerated into a research institute cut off from the realities of military life. The moral here appears to be that the Austrian army lacked neither progressive officers nor the technical capacity for innovation but was blocked by a reactionary at the top.[16] This case study suggests that more attention needs to be paid to the precise nature of the innovation being resisted and the reasons for it than is usual in denunciation of military conservatism by writers such as Vagts.

All the European armies, however, may justly be charged with underrating the potential of machine guns right up to the First World War. This mistrust and neglect was mainly due to the weapon's early technical flaws (including the celebrated jamming of the Gatling gun at Abu Klea in 1885), and heavy consumption of ammunition. There was moreover uncertainty as to its tactical role: was it an artillery piece or an infantry support weapon? There was less excuse for suspicion after the adoption of the Maxim in the late 1880s, and machine guns played an important part on both sides in the Russo-Japanese war. Yet, writing in 1912, Colin refers only once to machine guns, in discussing operations in Manchuria. Military conservatism in this instance remains puzzling.

In retrospect no aspect of the nineteenth-century conservatism is easier to ridicule than the survival of horsed cavalry and the emphasis persistently placed on its traditional role: the close-order charge with lance or sabre. Certainly supporters of the *arme blanche* continued to make extremely foolish – and highly quotable – statements in its defence well into the twentieth century. But even here the issues were not as clear-cut before 1914 as they now seem. For one thing the role of cavalry in reconnaissance and liaison duties was actually enhanced in the period between the introduction of rifles and machine guns and the full development of the motorcar. Secondly, as the American Civil War had shown, cavalry could play an important function in deep raids to cut enemy communications; a role which remained feasible on the eastern front in the First World War. Thirdly, provided it was prepared to carry firearms and fight dismounted, cavalry in the guise of mounted infantry could be a valuable instrument of mobile fire power. Admittedly, the cavalry as the arm

50

of great social prestige and aristocratic associations also had a tremendous emotional commitment to its past glories. Thus sensible tactical innovations were bitterly opposed as tantamount to a threat to a whole way of life. The author has discussed this fascinating case study more fully elsewhere.[17] What is surprising, however, is that even progressive-minded non-cavalry writers such as Colonels Frederick Maurice and G. F. R. Henderson hedged their bets in the cavalry versus mounted infantry debate. Maurice, for example, accepted that cavalry could not succeed in a frontal attack on unbroken infantry and artillery, yet he still expected great results from sudden, surprise flank assaults. He remained totally opposed to musketry practice for cavalry:

> Every hour devoted by cavalry to shooting which subtracts anything from training in their own proper work, or which leads them to compete with the other arm in that way, weakens them.

The success of the charge depended essentially 'on the impetuous power and moral effect of the man and horse, glued to one another as though they together formed the old ideal of the arm, the centaur'.[18]

There was not much point in drawing attention to the extreme vulnerability of the charging horse to those who believed in centaurs! Rather one finds in this case the unedifying spectacle of committed parties ransacking distant and recent history for supporting evidence while ignoring, or dismissing as 'untypical', evidence which told against them. Thus the undistinguished performance of cavalry in the Russo-Japanese war was attributed variously to poor training, low morale and unsuitable terrain. The British army sensibly abandoned the lance and the *arme blanche* role in the South African war and converted the cavalry to mounted infantry. Then, under the influence of French and Haig, the lance was reintroduced in 1907 and retained in service for another twenty years by which time its sole practical use seems to have been for pigsticking in India.

Lastly may be mentioned another case in which tradition and faith in morale spectacularly triumphed over practical considerations. The deadly power of rifles and heavy artillery put a premium on concealment and camouflage. The British army recognized that gaudy uniforms were equivalent to death warrants and by the South African war had entirely abandoned its traditional red coats in combat. The troops dressed in khaki, buttons and buckles were dulled, and officers dispensed with conspicuous evidence of rank. Drabness was all-important on the modern battlefield. Yet through a combination of thriftiness and emotional commitment to *élan*, the French *poilus* attacked in 1914 wearing red pantaloons and dark blue tunics. This, to adapt a well-known comment on the charge of the light brigade at Balaclava, was magnificent but murderous in modern warfare.

There were remarkably few large-scale wars between 1871 and 1914 and none at all between major European powers if the Russo-Turkish war of 1877–8 is excluded. Bismarck's brilliant diplomacy deserves much of the credit for the period up to 1890 in that he contrived to paper over Russia's hostility towards Austria-Hungary and so deprived France of any prospect of success in a war of revenge. Shortly after Bismarck's dismissal in 1890 Russia became an ally of France, but their likely opponent for the next few years was Britain rather than Germany. In Europe a precarious balance of power was preserved but the quest for greater 'security' was unending.

Certainly there were several serious war scares, such as those of 1875 between France and Germany and 1885 between Britain and Russia, but in none of these did the armed forces get out of control. A rapidly expanding reading public was also periodically titillated with the imminent prospect of war by a new fashion for alarmist war literature set off by Sir George Chesney's invasion story, *The Battle of Dorking*, first published in 1871.[19] Yet despite the fragility of the diplomatic safety net and a remarkable number of predictions of an approaching Armageddon, there was not in reality before 1900 quite that feeling of teetering on the edge of a precipice which prevailed between about 1908 and 1914.

In the military sphere however the main lesson of 1870–1 exerted a far-reaching influence; namely that henceforth national readiness for war in peacetime was not just important but crucial. One manifestation of this persistent anxiety was the phenomenon of 'arms races' more clearly defined and intense than ever before. These were made possible by improved communications and industrial capacity; i.e., information about the rival's arms programme could be obtained through open or clandestine methods, and shared technical know-how made a speedy response feasible. Arms races could be quantitative, qualitative or (more usually) a combination of both. The changing relationship between production time (longer than in the past) and usefulness in service (shorter) added new impetus to qualitative competition.[20]

Anglo-French arms races in the nineteenth century were basically naval and qualitative since Britain never contemplated rivalling France as a land power, while the latter had little hope of winning a quantitative competition with Britain in capital ships. As already mentioned, French technical challenges in the 1850s and 1860s had been fairly easily countered, but in the 1880s France initiated a new phase by flirting with an unorthodox strategic concept. This was the doctrine of the French *Jeune École* whose leader, Admiral Theophile Aube, was minister of marine in 1886. Its thesis was that torpedo boats and cruisers had rendered the battleship obsolete and in doing so had exposed the hollowness of the traditional aim of winning 'command of the sea'. The *Jeune École*'s trump card against an England now dependent on imported food and raw materials was to be commerce destruction. The Royal Navy need not be defeated in battle; it would simply be unable to provide adequate convoy escorts and so would be powerless to prevent a breakdown in the economy in an all-out *guerre de course*. Britain responded with massive additional expenditure on capital ship construction in the Naval Defence Act of 1889 and instituted a building programme designed to give the fleet a 'two power standard' of equality with France and Russia combined. Whether the *Jeune École*'s strategy had the remotest prospect of success against the greatest commercial power of the day will never be known because the movement was ephemeral. Its credibility was further undermined by the publication of Mahan's *Influence of Sea Power Upon History* (1890) with its derogatory views of the *guerre de course*.

France and Germany were involved in an arms race almost continuously between 1871 and 1914 though there was a brief lull in the later 1890s and early 1900s. This was a competition that could hardly be ended peacefully so long as Germany retained Alsace-Lorraine, though that is not to say that it directly caused the outbreak of war in 1914. Despite a growing obsession about being outwitted by technical inventions (and it is significant that the Dreyfus case had its origins in the betrayal of French artillery secrets to the German embassy in Paris), the Franco-German arms race was predominantly one of military manpower. This meant first and foremost the standing armies available at any moment of crisis, and secondly the numerous classes of reservists who would be recalled to service in the first six weeks or so after the order for mobilization. General staffs did not think much beyond that, nor did they truly grapple with problems of national economic mobilization much before 1914. There was evidently something unrealistic in the obsession with numbers, analogous to the quest for air 'parity' in the 1930s, and both sides committed the customary mistake of exaggerating the enemy's strength. Neither contestant moreover carried its belief in 'the nation in arms' to anywhere near full capacity. Not only would this have been exorbitantly expensive but also there was some appreciation of the military problem that 'armed hordes' would tend to overcrowd the theatre of operations and render a decisive battle impossible. Even by 1900 armies on the move resembled 'the most stupendous emigration of peoples'.[21]

In different ways domestic politics affected the size of the armies: in France the republican left advocated universal liability but very short colour service, whereas conservative regular officers and parties of the right preferred longer service and a smaller, better-disciplined standing army. In Germany the main opposition to an increase in the number of conscripts likewise came from conservative officers who feared dilution of the ranks with socialists and the swamping of the officer corps with undesirables from the middle class. France's smaller and almost stationary population put her at a disadvantage in 'the numbers game', but she bridged the gap temporarily by calling to the colours a higher percentage of available young men than Germany – as many as 83 per cent against Germany's 53 per cent in 1911. The alliance with Russia from 1892 was another countermove since Russia was rich in manpower but desperately in need of financial backing for industrialization which France supplied. Britain's commercial, financial and naval power could have tipped the scales either way, but before 1900 it was far from clear that she would join France against Germany.

Neither of these arms races ended in war, though it must be said that they did nothing to further international harmony either. Britain and France resolved their colonial conflicts between 1898 and 1904, while the Russian threat to the British empire virtually disappeared as a result of her defeat by Japan in 1904–5.

The Franco-German rivalry in land forces temporarily abated from 1898 as the latter put her major financial and industrial effort into creating a great fleet. German naval expenditure nearly tripled between 1900 and 1911 (from approximately £7 million to £20 million per annum), while military expenditure increased by only a quarter

(£34 million to £41 million). In this period the German standing army increased by only 25,000 men and there were even fears that France was gaining a numerical advantage. This led to renewed emphasis on military expenditure and increased numbers between 1911 and 1914. Germany's endeavour to enter the ranks of the great naval powers virtually from scratch posed a direct challenge to Britain. The resultant arms race did in a sense prove fatal in creating mutual tensions and antagonism which could not be solved peacefully without a radical change of policy by one of the contenders. [22] This subject will be more fully explored in the next chapter but here we should look at one issue concerning the origins and purposes of the German naval programme.

Some recent studies of Wilhelmine Germany have reached the conclusion that Tirpitz's naval programme must be viewed at least as much in social and political as purely strategic terms. Naval armaments, they claim, were a means of solving the manifold internal and external problems confronting the monarchy and the ruling classes. The conservative bureaucracy and military establishment owed their allegiance to the kaiser rather than the Reichstag and maintained close social and political ties with the landed aristocracy. Since the contribution of agriculture to the nation's wealth was declining, this important group, the *Junkers*, needed their privileged political position to be shored up. According to this historical school's interpretation, a great battle fleet was preferred to a *coup d'état* as a means of drawing the aristocracy and bourgeoisie together. The idea was apparently that the conservatives would vote for naval armaments which suited the bourgeoisie, while in return the latter would support increased agricultural tariffs. Moreover, both groups hoped to curb the growth of socialism, and a powerful navy would effect this by appealing to the patriotism and material interests of the workers. Yet somewhat at odds with this last aspiration, Tirpitz sought to remove control over naval finance entirely from the control of the Reichstag – hardly a way to conciliate the growing left-wing parties. [23]

If the building of the German battle fleet was inspired 'primarily by political and economic considerations', it failed to deceive socialist leaders such as Liebknecht, Bebel and Parvus. Liebknecht regarded it as a clumsy attempt to divert the workers' attention away from the need for constitutional and social reforms. Moreover the socialists perceived that the naval programme would impose a crippling tax burden on generations of ordinary Germans. The fleet doubtless remained a focal point for German patriotism, but in so far as it was designed to remedy internal class conflict, it was patently failing by 1900. As for its strategic justification, Tirpitz's long-term vision may have worked in ideal circumstances, but the odds of geography and naval power were against it. For Germany it would be strictly a 'luxury' fleet, whereas for Britain naval dominance in the Channel and the North Sea was of vital importance. As Tirpitz might have foreseen, the immediate effects of his early naval bills were that Britain sought allies and embarked upon a determined shipbuilding programme.

Armed services and armaments imposed serious though not crippling financial burdens on the wealthier European states. Ivan Bloch estimated that between 1874 and 1896 the total expenditure on defence of the principal European powers had increased by more than 50 per cent. Germany set the pace with an increase of 79 per cent, followed by Russia (75 per cent), Britain (47 per cent) and France (43 per cent). Less wealthy states had to make a greater defence effort in proportion to their national income: by 1914 the figures were Russia (6.3 per cent), Austria-Hungary (6.1 per cent), France (4.8 per cent), Germany (4.6 per cent), Italy (3.5 per cent) and Britain (3.4 per cent). A. J. P. Taylor calculates that between 1880 and 1914 German arms expenditure more than quintupled, British and Russian expenditure trebled and France had not quite doubled. These figures provide a fair indication of the changing power relationships between the major powers. They resemble a football league table except of course that each power did not have to 'play' against every other. Austria-Hungary was slipping towards relegation whereas Italy had barely achieved first division status. Here the analogy breaks down because Britain, though a negligible military power in continental terms, was easily the premier naval power. Germany was the greatest military power but had weakened herself by a naval competition with Britain. France, who had matched herself against the German army and the Royal Navy, was feeling the strain badly. Only Russia could rival Germany as a land power. Thus, by 1914, Russia, Germany and Britain stood out as the dominant European powers. Russia was the least developed but potentially the strongest. Parliaments grumbled and opposed increases in the defence budgets with varying degrees of stubbornness, but everywhere they gave way and voted most of what the services demanded.[24]

The armaments competition not only contributed to international tensions but also exacerbated domestic conflict particularly in the less industrialized countries which could not stand the pace. In the 1880s for example, the Italian government attempted to lay the foundations of an arms industry based on a consortium of foreign and domestic banks and linked to Schneider and Armstrong. But nationalist rhetoric and an ambitious colonial policy could not for long conceal Italy's economic weakness. In the early 1890s there were serious cuts in the military budget and in contrast to all the other major powers Italy's defence expenditure actually declined during the decade 1890–1900.[25]

The Ottoman empire was even less able than Italy to respond to the armaments competition, but from the late 1890s she was propped up by massive German investments. France performed a similar service for her ally Russia, but by 1898 the finance minister Count Witte reached an impasse over the lack of money to procure the most modern quick-firing artillery comparable to the French 75 mm for which the French parliament had voted 30 million francs the previous year. He therefore hit on the ingenious idea of summoning a disarmament conference to approve a ten-year 'holiday' in the arms build-up. The resulting Hague Conference of 1899 disappointed these expectations.[26]

Although Europe became notably more nationalistic and militaristic towards the end of the nineteenth century, it was also a period when antimilitary and peace movements became more vocal and determined. Outright pacifist movements flourished mainly in the United States and Britain, geographically secure and predominantly naval powers where 'militarism' was little feared. European groups also championed arbitration in international disputes and the perpetuation of peace through the unrestricted distribution of the growing industrial wealth. Influential and wealthy individuals lent their names to the cause of peace; including Alfred Nobel, the Swedish dynamite manufacturer, Andrew Carnegie, the American steel tycoon, bestselling antiwar novelist Bertha von Suttner, Ivan Bloch and the British publicist, W. T. Stead.

Another impressive phenomenon was the steady growth of the antimilitarist German social democratic party despite the tremendous efforts of Bismarck and his conservative successors to muzzle or destroy it. In 1877 the social democrats won 500,000 votes and 12 seats in the Reichstag; by 1890 they had trebled the vote and secured 35 seats; while by 1912 they had become the largest party with 4½ million votes and 110 seats. This was all the more impressive in that German class barriers were rigid and it was extremely rare for a worker to enter the bourgeoisie – a class which was itself strongly influenced by aristocratic and military values.[27]

Armies could on occasions evoke patriotic sentiments but they were far from universally popular. Many potential conscripts avoided military service by the drastic resort to emigration. This escape route was most prevalent in Italy, but this was not the only state which vainly attempted to stem the flow of young men by legislation. Russians (especially Russian Jews), Greeks and other Europeans poured into the United States and Britain in the late nineteenth century to avoid the call-up. Socialists were among the bitterest critics of conscription and some Marxists, including Engels, hoped that the ruling classes were preparing their own demise by simultaneously antagonizing and arming the workers. This expectation was proving illusory long before the collapse of socialist international solidarity in 1914. On the one hand armies proved remarkably adept at instilling obedience and patriotic values; while on the other, workers' living standards were rising, even in Germany, encouraging greater reliance on orthodox political and trade union activities.[28]

'Militarism' is such a vague and elastic term that it might be as well to dispense with it completely, but it is possible to isolate several specific aspects for discussion.[29] One of the most obvious aspects is the irresponsible influence of service chiefs or military cliques on policy-making, thereby usurping or bypassing the proper authority of elected representatives and governments. The best-known example, that of Wilhelmine Germany, has been so fully described by Craig, Ritter, Kitchen, Demeter and other authorities that it would be tedious to treat the topic here at great length. The essential points are that between the 1860s and 1900 the Reichstag lost the right even to discuss the military budget for as long as five or seven years; that the war minister became a figurehead with no real authority over the army; and that actual authority steadily accrued to the kaiser who looked for advice mainly to his own military cabinet and to a lesser extent to the general staff. These tendencies increased dangerously after 1888 under Wilhelm II, described by Craig as 'a kind of perennial Potsdam lieutenant' who preferred military companions, military manners and military advice to any other; so much so indeed that he encouraged his chief of staff Count Waldersee to believe that a *coup d'état* was contemplated.[30]

Coordination of planning between the politicians, diplomats and service chiefs, which would have required far more ability and dedication than Wilhelm II possessed, was completely lacking. Army leaders took an exaggerated view of their rights to interfere in domestic issues where military matters were even marginally concerned. This could be irritating but it was in foreign affairs that they made a really dangerous impact. The elder Moltke, for example, opened unauthorized staff talks with his Austrian counterpart in 1882 in order to concert war plans against Russia, and when asked what Bismarck's attitude might be, loftily replied: 'My position is such that I do not depend on the Foreign Office.' In 1889 Wilhelm II promised the Austrians that their mobilization would immediately be the signal for Germany's no matter what the chancellor might say. It does not seem fanciful to suggest that German military planners, by persistently assuming that France and Russia would be allied against the central powers in the next war, helped to bring that alliance into being soon after Bismarck's restraining influence was removed.

To his credit, the elder Moltke did not become swollen-headed as a result of his great victories, but on the contrary grew increasingly sceptical about the prospects of victory in a two-front war. His successor but one, Count Schlieffen, was more willing to gamble, and concluded – contrary to Moltke's order of priorities – that France must be decisively defeated first. To what extent, if at all, the general staffs should be criticized for what is now coolly known as 'contingency planning' may be debated; but it is abundantly clear that no chancellor after Bismarck ensured that such plans were subordinated to and wholly consistent with state policy.[31]

In other countries, such as France, the army's hold on the reins of political power was less firm than in Germany, but occasionally they were dragged willy-nilly into political controversy by individuals such as General Boulanger; or actively intervened because they believed their autonomy threatened, as in the later stages of the Dreyfus affair.

During the first thirty years of the Third Republic the senior ranks of the French army were strongly Catholic and monarchist in composition. Such men had no love for the Republic but they were prepared to live and let live. By the 1890s the agricultural depression was forcing more and more sons of the nobility to seek security in the army, and the numbers from a religious background (i.e., Catholics) also increased. By the time of the Boulanger and Dreyfus affairs the army was about the only refuge open to the nobility and to monarchist families. Boulanger happened to be a junior general who became minister of war, but his was not a military movement as such and the army showed no interest in supporting a *coup d'état*, as even the socialist Jean Jaurès admitted. By the time the Dreyfus case began, the Republic's political leaders had become so confident of the army's loyalty that they allowed it a greater degree of autonomy in its own affairs than had any previous regime in the nineteenth century. For their part the generals took pains to keep the army apart from civil life, even to the point of regarding the minister of war (invariably an active general) as their representative with the civil power.[32]

The evidence presented to the court martial in 1894 that Captain Dreyfus was the general staff officer guilty of selling military secrets to the Germans was, to say the least, flimsy. But as a cold, unsympathetic character, a wealthy industrialist's son and a Jew – the only one on the general staff – he was ideally cast for the role of traitor. Whether he was guilty or not seemed of secondary importance, but if General Mercier (the minister of war) and other high-ranking officers believed in his guilt, that was good enough for the army. The ironies of the case are numerous: Dreyfus was in many respects himself a militarist, and remained uncritical of the service despite its gross injustice towards him. It was well said that Dreyfus himself would not have been a *Dreyfusard*. On the other side, Jews and socialists (often identical) seemed more enthusiastic about attacking the French army and military institutions generally than exonerating the victim.

By 1898 it was becoming clear that the evidence on which Dreyfus had been convicted was false, but in reaction to scurrilous attacks in the press, the army's leadership now took the view that Dreyfus's innocence or guilt was irrelevant compared to 'the honour of the army'. Military justice was clearly not the same as other kinds of justice. At the second court martial at Rennes in 1899, General Mercier was in effect on trial as much as Dreyfus, hence the incredible verdict that the latter was guilty 'with extenuating circumstances'. The real issue had become the army's effective autonomy within the state, and when forced to the point the army could not get its way without staging a coup. At no time during the affair did even a significant minority of officers contemplate such a drastic course. The army thus emerged from the affair with its public image badly tarnished and vulnerable to a republican backlash in the early 1900s.[33]

Italian politics were dominated for almost a decade from 1887 by a 'civilian militarist', Francesco Crispi, who became both prime minister and foreign minister in that year. Crispi believed that a successful war would erase the unhappy memories of the 1860s and add to Italy's international prestige. After a visit to Bismarck, Crispi signed a military convention with Germany in 1888 committing Italy to send five army corps and three cavalry divisions to fight on the Rhine should the Triple Alliance go to war with France and Russia. How they would get there and be supplied was to remain a staff officer's nightmare. By 1890 Italy's military expenditure was almost double that of a decade earlier; and Crispi took a direct interest in technical matters, urging for example that mobilization should be put on a territorial basis like Germany's. Crispi's grandiose foreign policy and emphasis on the military offensive by a larger army helped to cause his fall in 1891, and the military budget was immediately reduced.

In March 1896 Italy suffered a humiliating blow when an army of 16,000 troops under some of the best-known generals was routed at Adowa by a far larger force of Ethiopians under Menelik (many of them using Italian or French firearms). This was widely regarded as the Nemesis of Crispi's militarism and a reflection of Italy's economic weakness and social disunity:

the metropolitan army was split between colonialists and anti-colonialists, and capitalists were divided over the relevance of imperialism.

In the period of scapegoat-hunting and breast-beating that followed Adowa, the fragile Italian state was threatened by a surge of antimilitarism, republicanism, socialism and peasant risings against the southern landowners. A military coup seemed likely, but as in France, the army showed no desire to assume political power. Italy emerged from this 'militarist' phase with her monarchy and parliamentary institutions shaken but intact.[34]

Russia in this period was an autocracy supporting a huge army in relation to her weak industrial base, but she was not 'militaristic' because the officers were lacking in both prestige and political influence. The majority of officers, though monarchist and chauvinistic in outlook, were professional soldiers without political ambitions. True, Russia had her equivalent of Boulanger in the 1880s in the vainglorious swashbuckler General Skobelev but, like the Frenchman, he was unable to secure military support for his warlike speeches against the central powers and quickly disappeared from the stage. The Russian government and generals alike were too acutely aware of their military inferiority to Germany to provoke a war. Moreover, as Ritter stresses, 'society' in late nineteenth-century Russia embraced only a tiny segment of the population. The government was so isolated and so terrified of anarchist attacks that even the officer corps was under surveillance by the secret police. Tsar Nicholas II, though even less able to coordinate strategic and foreign policies than Wilhelm II, was also less of a militarist and not so inclined to listen to military advice.[35]

Britain was very little exposed to 'militarism' in that her constitution was extremely stable, with political control by parliament firmly established. Moreover the service leaders were mostly drawn from the same social strata as the ruling class and therefore did not feel threatened, as for instance the French Catholic military elite did by republican socialist governments. Not least important, British service leaders enjoyed great social prestige (note the number of public statues raised to them and inns named after them), and the more successful ones were lavishly rewarded with titles and estates. Even so, Britain's relative decline as a world power (indeed *the* world power) towards the end of the century did generate anxieties as to whether the politicians were sufficiently committed to maintaining increasingly costly defences. Here perhaps lies part of the explanation of the ageing Wolseley's diatribes against politicians, the aggressive posturing of Admiral Jackie Fisher and the scathing indictments of all and sundry by Henry Wilson. The general staff's clandestine contacts with their French opposite numbers from 1905, though known only to a few ministers, were mildly disturbing but hardly amounted to sinister militarism. The involvement of a very small segment of the army in the Curragh incident of March 1914 was more alarming, but it is clear that the cavalry officers were forced into a political crisis which they would rather have avoided. Thus Vagts's reference to '*Junkers* from the western hinterland of London', though amusing, is really wide of the mark.[36]

Another meaning of the term 'militarism' is the excessive permeation of civil society with the military outlook and behaviour values. This phenomenon was most strikingly evident in Wilhelmine Germany where it has been exhaustively studied. Here we will look at just a few of its causes and manifestations. First, the German army enjoyed unique prestige for, as Ritter concisely put it, 'in western Europe the military were considered a necessary evil, whereas in Germany they were the nation's pride'. He also stresses that this was a new strain not derived from the aristocratic Prussia of Frederick the Great; rather it was the bourgeoisie who were now perverted by patriotic pride and free citizens who were captivated by a sense of power. In other domestic issues they might be quite critical of government policy. Indeed it was the educated middle classes, considerably influenced by academics, who were particularly prone to swing full circle from strident antimilitarism to idolatry after 1870 because they were most keenly aware of Prussia's historical achievement. For a generation after 1870, German patriotism was strongly nostalgic. Middle-class society (particularly in northern Germany) generally continued to show tremendous respect for the officer's uniform. Famous statesmen such as Bismarck, Bülow and Bethmann Hollweg encouraged this fashion by appearing in uniform on every possible occasion. The reserve officers, who excluded a wide range of 'undesirables' such as socialists, peasants, artisans, shopkeepers and Jews, became more militaristic than the regulars, aping and exaggerating their manners and vices such as gambling, drinking and brawling.[37] Hence a sort of 'pecking order' arose even in civil life and the very status of civilian came to be widely despised by these prigs in uniform.

The German officer corps was seen at its worst in its prejudice against Jews. This attitude was so prevalent that Jews could be virtually excluded from the officer ranks by consensus without the need for any specific anti-Semitic regulations. Exclusion was easy since a commission in the army was dependent on approval by the regimental officers who could simply refuse to elect Jews to the mess. The other gambit was to refuse Jews promotion from the ranks on the vague grounds of 'weakness of character'. Ingrained beliefs that Jews were physically different from 'true' Germans could not of course be substantiated. Equally implausible was the prejudice that involvement in financial speculation, trade and shopkeeping deprived Jews of the 'martial spirit'. In vain did Jewish spokesmen protest that Jews were on average as physically fit as other German town dwellers and, more to the point, that they had fought with distinction in all Prussia's nineteenth-century wars. By 1878 there was not one Jewish officer in the Prussian army and that remained the case in 1910, though by the latter date there were over 2000 Jews in the Austrian-Hungarian army, including a field marshal. Morever, 16.4 per cent of reserve officers were Jewish although the Jewish population in the Dual Monarchy represented only 5 per cent.[38]

The German army waged an equally determined campaign against social democrats and other baneful civilian influences. The army fought a successful rearguard action to prevent civil offences by military personnel being tried in civilian courts. The vain struggle to prevent social democratic literature and ideas from infiltrating the army was carried to ridiculous lengths. Among many other examples, Kitchen cites the case of a soldier in Hanover who was sentenced to fourteen days' close arrest for saying in public 'Long live Social Democracy'! By the 1890s the war ministry had become so paranoid that it suspected perfectly harmless dances of being pretexts for secret socialist meetings. In 1896 an order was published not only banning soldiers from having any contacts with the social democrats, but also binding them to denounce any comrade suspected of doing so. This, and many similar orders, proved as ineffective as trying to stem the tide. As Kitchen sums up, many officers simply could not grasp the motive force behind social democracy; their opposition to socialism was understandable, but it was also blind and uninformed.[39]

Armed services had long since found representatives and supporters of their interests in civil life in the form of veterans' associations, but a new phase may be traced from the 1890s with the foundation of numerous pressure groups and leagues with a high proportion of civilian members designed to inculcate service values and lobby for particular policies. They were closely followed by the formation of numerous paramilitary youth movements. Such paramilitary bodies were symptomatic of a much wider proliferation of movements to combat supposed national weaknesses. The British and German Navy Leagues set the fashion in the 1890s, the latter especially serving as an innocent publicist for a new service lacking traditions. By the 1900s army leagues were flourishing in most European countries including the *Wehrverein* in Germany, the

National Service League in Britain and the *Ligue pour la service des trois ans* in France.

In the period covered by this chapter the activities of the British and German naval leagues are most significant. The British Navy League was launched in the mid-1890s following a major dispute over the naval estimates. By 1901 it had only 14,000 members but the subsequent naval race with Germany swelled the number to nearly 100,000 by 1914. Its presiding committee comprised retired admirals, aristocrats and civilian apostles of greater naval preparedness such as Spenser Wilkinson, Sir Charles Dilke and Rudyard Kipling. It had no official tie with the Admiralty which indeed viewed it with mixed feelings, welcoming its stimulating effect on public interest in the navy but deploring some of its claims and proposals – such as Wilkinson's hobby horse of the need for a naval staff on the lines of the German army's general staff.

The German Navy League, founded in 1898, enjoyed the support of the Ruhr industrialists and was much more closely in touch with the Naval Bureau. Its propaganda campaign far surpassed the British Navy League's, as did its membership figures which had topped 300,000, not counting at least twice as many more supporters in corporate bodies, by 1914. Both bodies fostered and in turn benefited from the tensions generated by the Anglo-German naval race, and both suffered from internal feuds and threatened secessions. These leagues provided a platform for hyper-patriots who shared a belief that their countries' defence policies were being mishandled. Also, as Paul Kennedy shrewdly notes, their aggressive posturing only imperfectly veiled a good deal of anxiety and even pessimism about their respective nations' prospects. It was ironic that each nation's patriots tended to see in the other a model of those heroic virtues such as discipline, class solidarity, and healthy recreations which its own country lacked.[40]

The most important instrument of militarization – namely the 'nation in arms' policy so widely adopted after 1870, has been left until last. Marxist critics correctly stress that conscription must be viewed as far more than a military method of preparing for war. Victor Kiernan, for example, perceives a close association between the spread of conscription and of industrial capitalism. Mass armies provided buttresses for the status quo as year by year young men from the peasantry and working class were 're-educated' to support the conservative establishment. In Kiernan's words:

Like the often painful initiation rites of tribal life . . . a spell with the colours became the introduction to manhood and membership of the community.

Military service not only improved townsmen's health and so extended their potential working life; it also accustomed them to minimal pay, regimentation and unquestioning obedience to orders. In theory at least, all classes met under the colours, 'like well-chaperoned young men and women at a ball'. Engels, Jaurès and other left-wing critics who hoped that radicalism would survive or even be furthered by the repressive aspects of military service clearly underrated the influence of the drill square, barrack room and regimental mythology. Tolstoy had a deeper insight into the taming effect – even the infantilizing impact – of compulsory service on young men of stunted mental development like the East Prussian or Russian peasantry. It would be a mistake, however, to overemphasize the negative conditioning of military service. Many ex-national servicemen of a more recent vintage would endorse Kiernan's remark that 'it is hard for the individual to go on feeling at odds with the life around him, and the more so when this is as close and all-enveloping as an army's'. One learns not merely to accept what must be endured but even in some cases to hug one's chains.[41]

Before accepting Kiernan's brilliant analysis *in toto*, it would be necessary to subject certain generalizations to rigorous scrutiny to see if the pattern varied in different countries. How conscious, for example, were the military authorities of the need to produce disciplined 'factory fodder' as distinct from 'cannon fodder'; and did military indoctrination wear off quicker in some countries than in others? Is it possible that in some countries, Russia perhaps, military service did promote radical activism? At least one anomaly looms large; namely that in several cases the military leaders shared the left's opposition to the thorough implementation of universal service, though obviously for different reasons. Neither French nor German military leaders wanted their rhetoric about the 'nation in arms' to be interpreted literally, for to do so would be only to pile up millions of semi-trained men whose military skills and endurance were doubtful. France was unusual in subjecting nearly three-quarters of its available manpower to a period with the colours by 1914.

The meaning and connotations of the concept of the nation in arms underwent kaleidoscopic changes in France between 1870 and 1914.

By the 1890s a new generation of bourgeois recruits was unimpressed by the myths of 1870 and cared less and less about risking their lives to recover Alsace and Lorraine. Military life, to all but a minority of idealists, was dull and even degrading. Educationalists began to attack the army's wrong scale of values, while several writers, including Emile Zola in *The Debacle* (1892), undermined the heroic legends of 1870. The counterattack was launched by the then Captain Hubert Lyautey in a celebrated article published in *La Revue des Deux Mondes* in 1891. Lyautey accepted the charge that the officers had entirely failed in their social and educational roles. Indeed many of them knew their horses much better than their men. His plea for a new style of military paternalism was at first ridiculed but then enthusiastically taken up under General André's war ministry in 1901–3. Indeed conservative generals protested that civic education was now getting in the way of military training. France would acquire a nation in arms but she would no longer possess an army. Regimental libraries and other barrack entertainments could not fully cater to the soldiers' off-duty interests; while officers could not hope to overcome their troops' reserve merely by casually asking after their families or whether they liked the soup. At best these educational efforts had some marginal benefit in preparing conscripts for civil life.[42]

For General von der Goltz the enigma to be solved by the nation in arms policy was:

> how to completely fuse the military life with the life of the people, so that the former may impede the latter as little as possible, and that, on the other hand, all the resources of the latter may find expression in the former.

The paternalistic strain ran strongly in the traditional German officer corps with its sense of *noblesse oblige*. Franz von Papen doubtless spoke for thousands when he recalled nostalgically of his early regimental experience in the 5th Uhlans that 'although discipline was strict, a human relationship was built up that lasted all our lives'. Some officers, however, interpreted their main educational mission as being to cure the conscripts of the 'disease' of social democracy. The darker side, which has been fully documented by Kitchen and others, is that the German army had by 1914 acquired an unenviable reputation for rudeness and even physical maltreatment of civilians and of frequent cases of brutality and cruelty to rankers. In 1892 a royal corps commander publicly condemned the ill-treatment of privates, and in 1914 General von Falkenhayn, then minister of war, deplored recent episodes which had sullied the army's name.[43] By this time, however, as among the other major powers on the brink of war, a narrower concern for trained soldiers had largely submerged the paternalistic, educational aspect of the nation in arms.

Britain and the United States scorned any measure of compulsory military service before the First World War, but all the European states felt compelled to make at least a gesture towards a nation in arms policy. In Spain selective conscription, with substitution allowed for those who could afford to pay, was restored with the institution of a republic in 1874. Regional separatism was far too strong for the army to serve as a unifying agent – as it did with remarkable success in the Hapsburg monarchy – and in the absence of external enemies the Spanish army was viewed as the bulwark of internal law and order.

Earlier generalizations about the power of regular military forces to subdue and mould conscripts into obedient, unthinking automata do not hold good for Russia. She could hardly attempt to introduce the more idealistic 'civic' aspects of the nation in arms when these principles had made such little headway in civil society. Worse still Russia lacked an officer corps capable of fulfilling such an educational role: she possessed neither a large middle class whence France drew most of her officers, nor a genuine military aristocracy which gave the German army its tone even if middle-class officers were dominant numerically long before 1914. With discontent endemic among the peasants and spreading to the cities before 1914, there was little prospect of officers and conscripts meeting on idealistic terms. The pre-1914 Russian army was a nation in arms in numerical terms only.[44]

The armies of the Hapsburg monarchy represented the last refuge of the old imperial spirit of blind devotion to the dynasty. Given the insuperable problems of the polyglot empire, and the inability to raise the military budget, the Hapsburg armies were a considerable success up to 1914 and it was not a military collapse that brought about the downfall of the dynasty. The common army of Austria-Hungary (as distinct from the Austrian *landwehr* and Hungarian *honved*) was supranational, owing direct allegiance to the emperor. Its officer corps was comparatively free from nationalist intolerance and a rigid class outlook. Between 1867 and 1918 about 90 per cent of general staff officers were of middle- or lower-middle-class extraction, and several of the most important generals in the First World War derived from humble origins. The officer corps was however overwhelmingly German in character (79 per cent of regular and 70 per cent of reserve officers in 1910) and German was the language of command. Within each regiment, however, the languages of the men were used and officers had to acquire them (sometimes three or four) within three years or accept dismissal. This worked amazingly well in peacetime but it was another matter in war: mobilization posters had to be printed in fifteen languages; and as casualties mounted reserve officers had to be accepted who could not (or would not bother to) understand their men, having to resort in some cases to English as a *lingua franca*. Well before 1914 the German character of the army brought protest and acts of indiscipline from some minorities, particularly Czechs and Ruthenes, but even so antimilitary propaganda had no serious effects until the Russian revolution. The outbreak of war in fact inspired a remarkable display of imperial unity.

The great weakness in the monarchy's constitutional structure since 1867 was that measures affecting military organization had to be ratified by the Hungarian parliament as well as in Vienna, and Magyar chauvinism persistently rejected bills which would have increased the common army. According to her population Austria-Hungary should have been able to field many more divisions in 1914. Moreover, scarcely half the young men available received any military training, and for financial reasons colour service was in practice only two rather than the statutory three years. By 1914 the monarchy trained only 29 per cent of its manpower whereas even Italy inducted 37 per cent. On the outbreak of war the monarchy's maximum military strength was 2,265,000 whereas France could mobilize nearly 4 million from a population smaller by 10 million.[45] The reckless policies and strategies of the monarchy's military leaders will be discussed in the next chapter.

There is no need here to describe in detail the varying forms of compulsory military service introduced in nearly all the European states from Turkey to Norway between 1870 and 1914. Everywhere the tendency was to combine comparatively short periods of colour service for as high a proportion of the young men available as the economy would permit, followed by obligations to militia and reserve training of up to twenty years. This meant of course that by 1914 even thinly populated states such as Greece, Montenegro and Sweden could in theory mobilize tens of thousands of reservists more or less fit for active service. As a corollary, most countries adopted some variant of the German territorial organization in army corps areas with the emphasis on the speediest mobilization of maximum numbers for war rather than for peacetime political control.

Another noteworthy phenomenon in these years is the 'export' of military advisers to new or modernizing states. Japan, the recipient of German military and British naval assistance, lies outside the scope of this study, but the Turkish army was reformed by a German military mission under the same General von der Goltz whose impassioned writings were quoted earlier; Bulgaria and some other Balkan states received Russian military tutelage; and Greece was assisted by France. The Balkan states generally put a very high proportion of their manhood into uniform in relation to their small populations and poor economies. This enabled them to present a formidable facade of armed might but, as the First World War was to show, their efficiency varied greatly. Finally, the Belgian case is of special interest for two reasons: her neutrality had been internationally guaranteed in 1839, and there were (and remain) profound differences between her Flemish and Walloon populations. When mobilization against possible invasion during the Franco-Prussian war revealed glaring deficiencies, the military leaders mounted a political protest by all refusing to take over the portfolio of the ministry of war – a gambit more frequently practised in Japan. Even this act of non-cooperation failed to persuade a succession of antimilitary Flemish Catholic governments to introduce conscription, and it was not until 1909, with a Franco-German war appearing imminent, that Leopold II signed a law instituting eight years' colour service (with certain exceptions) and five years in the reserves. Thus by the outbreak of war even a small and unmilitary state like Belgium could rapidly put over 100,000 troops into the field.[46]

This chapter has examined some aspects of the remarkable development of military power in the last quarter of the nineteenth century founded upon an expansion of population, industrialism, material wealth, communications and overseas possessions. Larger standing armies backed by even more impressive echelons of trained reserves both reflected international tensions and made them harder to resolve. General staffs, now regarded with awe rather than contempt, planned for possible confrontations more systematically than ever before, but they remained more or less subject to political control. Military experts conceded that the greater strength of the tactical defensive would pose formidable problems, but they drew comfort from the hope that the attackers would still succeed through the employment of railways, by intensive training and by superior morale. Great faith was placed in moral and spiritual factors as against material obstacles.

Yet despite the jingoistic parades, chest-thumping and aggressive speeches, it would be a mistake to assume that the inevitability of a general European war was widely accepted by 1900. On the contrary, faith in material progress and optimism about the future of European civilization remained buoyant for another decade. How these hopes were undermined by internal and international tensions will be examined in the next chapter.

3

*THE APPROACH
TO ARMAGEDDON,
c. 1900–14*

Shortly before the outbreak of the First World War Colonel House reported on the atmosphere in Europe to his political chief President Woodrow Wilson: 'The situation is extraordinary. It is militarism run mad.' Many historians have commented on the fact that the declarations of war were greeted with an outburst of popular enthusiasm which had been brewing for a long time. The diplomats and businessmen may have made desperate last-minute efforts to avoid the plunge into warfare, but they were powerless in face of the emotions of a generation which had been physically and mentally prepared for this supposedly inevitable clash between the nations. The aim of this chapter is to trace the development of this militaristic mentality; to examine the diplomatic and military arrangements which speedily transformed a limited Balkan conflict into an all-out European war; and to explain why a protracted war of attrition occurred despite the predictions of virtually all the experts.

The vital point to remember is that there was a widespread fascination with war before 1914, and that numerous public figures uttered pro-war sentiments which would appear sinister or 'sick' after the experience of 1914–18. Many of these eminent men, such as the last commander in chief of the British army, Lord Roberts, were authoritarians who regarded war as a necessary tonic and conscription in peacetime as the only antidote for 'the mass of human rottenness that threads the thoroughfares of any of our large industrial cities'. For hundreds of thousands of ordinary citizens, however, an idealized notion of war offered romantic and vicarious excitement as a complete contrast to their humdrum working lives. Philip Larkin has captured the carefree spirit in which these young men rushed to volunteer in his poem 'MCMXIV':

> Those long uneven lines
> Standing as patiently
> As if they were stretched outside
> The Oval or Villa Park,
> The crowns of hats, the sun
> On moustached archaic faces
> Grinning as if it were all
> An August Bank Holiday lark;
>
> . . .
>
> Never such innocence,
> Never before or since,
>
> . . .
>
> Never such innocence again.[1]

Behind this innocence, however, zealous patriotic pressure groups and leagues had been working for a decade or more to inculcate a military spirit and a belief in the impending, inevitable conflict of nations. In the previous chapter we noted the pace being set in the 1890s by the German and British Navy Leagues, but many other movements sprang up after the turn of the century.

One of the best known of these pressure groups was the *Alldeutscher Verband* (Pan-German League). Its membership was quite small – only about 22,000 in 1900 – and did not increase much thereafter, but it was vociferous and influential, particularly in the right-wing parties and in the world of business and education. Its main theme was that Germany must expand from being a mere continental power to a world power, if necessary by means of war. Non-German elements in the Reich and the Danubian basin were to be 'Germanized', and German elements everywhere supported. A 'Greater Germany' was to be created initially by economic and commercial links, from Berlin to Baghdad. Central to the League's propaganda was the call for a great navy to protect Germany's expanding overseas trade and to win British respect. Several well-known ex-soldiers, including Generals Liebert and Keim, were prominent in the League's activities. Many of the League's policies were half-baked, indeed it was viewed with suspicion and even hostility by the war and navy ministries. The League, in short, was an ultra-nationalist opposition faction which bitterly condemned the government whenever it appeared to fall short of the League's high standards. Hence its disgust at the kaiser's apparent attempt to mollify Britain during the Boer War; at the moderate nature of the Naval Bill in 1906; and at Germany's humiliation in the two Moroccan crises.[2]

Another nationalist league, the *Wehrverein*, was founded in 1912 mainly to campaign for greater preparedness for an imminent continental war. Within a year it had recruited 78,000 members and some 200,000 corporate members. Its main platform was to denounce even the large army increases introduced from 1911 as utterly inadequate. General Keim and other members of the Pan-German League played a leading part in its activities and by the outbreak of war it had acquired an extremely strong public position.

The nearest British equivalent to these German pressure groups was the National Service League, founded in 1902 to counter the military – and national – weaknesses as revealed in the Boer War. Its fundamental aim was to secure the introduction of some form of compulsory military service in peacetime, say a year's training for every able-bodied white man in the empire. Its pamphlets and journal (*The Nation in Arms*) stressed that military service would follow the democratic Swiss rather than the autocratic Prussian model. Like the Swiss militia its main role would be home defence against invasion. The League was slow to make an impact and had only about 2000 members by 1905. Then it received a tremendous boost when Britain's most famous soldier, Lord Roberts, resigned from the CID to assume its presidency. It also throve on the Anglo-German naval competition and the torrent of invasion-scare literature which this spawned. By the outbreak of war the League claimed a total membership of over 200,000, including many famous people such as Milner, Curzon, Kipling and Wolseley, which was a remarkable achievement in antimilitarist Britain. It was not, however, despite considerable support in parliament, within sight of its goal of compulsory military service.[3]

Paul Kennedy offers some penetrating reflections on these ultra-patriotic leagues. First, that despite the emphasis on their non-party nature, their political support was in fact drawn overwhelmingly from right-wing parties. Thus, for example, the National Service League claimed to have well over one hundred MPs as members, but only three were liberals. Similarly it was virtually impossible for a left-liberal to subscribe to the tenets of the Pan-German League. Secondly, the various leagues' claims to be 'non-political' were widely held to mean that they put national interests above party politics; but it could also denote a more sinister contempt for party government.

There were certainly individuals who held such authoritarian beliefs in the German Navy League and the Pan-German League. Thirdly, the leagues in both countries made their major appeal to the working classes, for example, by painting a lurid scenario of what would happen to ordinary families if their country was invaded, defeated in battle, or subjected to a long blockade. A fourth point which deserves special emphasis is the determined efforts made to 'militarize' youth. Many of these movements, like the most famous of them all, the Boy Scouts, arose after the Boer War in part from a high-minded desire to improve the nation's health by a new interest in outdoor life and activities. But a militarist undertone was detectable from the start. Thus youthful readers of *Scouting for Boys* were urged to avoid the example of the Romans who lost their empire because they became 'wishy-washy slackers without any go or patriotism in them'. The Boy Scout motto was not merely a vague admonition: Baden-Powell exhorted members to 'BE PREPARED to die for your country . . . so that when the time comes you may charge home with confidence, not caring whether you are to be killed or not'.[4]

The Boy Scouts alone had over 150,000 current members in 1913 and there were numerous similar organizations including the Boys Brigade, the Church Lads Brigade, the British Girls Patriotic League and the Lads Drill Association. By no means all their activities were overtly militaristic in purpose, but their emphasis on patriotism, loyalty and comradeship undoubtedly laid secure foundations for the real thing.

At the heart of the National Service League's campaigning was a belief that Britain was suffering from moral decay which could easily be remedied by instilling discipline in the nation's youth through the imposition of compulsory military service. Lord Roberts's speeches on this issue are filled with references to moral training, character reform, self-discipline, patriotism and the evils of urban life.[5]

The Royal Navy, incidentally, needed such youthful imitations rather less because its recruits in those days were all schoolboys, future officers and ratings alike. Even so the Navy League sent Admiral Sir Charles Beresford and other speakers to the public schools to lecture and provide lantern-slide shows on service life. Trafalgar Day celebrations and potted lives of famous naval heroes were also used to foster schoolboy patriotism. By 1910 more than 150 schools and several universities had formed officer training corps to encourage drill, discipline, rifle-shooting and practice camps.

In Germany some of the youth movements were closely linked with the army and were generously funded by the ministry of culture. Such adult pressure groups as the *Wehrverein* and the *Kriegerverein* set up militarist youth movements in a deliberate effort to counter the pacifistic youth organizations supported by the social democrats. In 1911, for example, General von der Goltz founded the *Jungdeutschlandbund*, a semi-military, nationalist organization, precisely for this purpose. All its officials were regular or reserve officers and it took part in annual military exercises, including training in putting down a revolt by social democrats which was expected to occur in the event of war. The *Jungdeutschlandbund* received fervent support not only from the army and government, but also from the churches. Its official journal the *Jungdeutschland Post* devoted much of its space to war propaganda, with what must strike modern readers as an unhealthy emphasis on the beauty of war and the glory of dying for the fatherland. When the fateful hour came, one exhortation of January 1913 concluded,

> it will be more beautiful and wonderful to live for ever among the heroes on a war memorial in a church than to die an empty death in bed, nameless . . . let that be heaven for young Germany. Thus we wish to knock at our God's door.[6]

By the turn of the century the popular press, feeding upon an expanding semi-literate readership, was playing an increasingly significant role in fanning the flames of self-righteous jingoism. Contrary to what contemporary critics alleged, both German and British governments lost what little control over the arch-patriotic press they had ever enjoyed. In Germany the popular press was literally *plus royaliste que le roi*, claiming to speak for the Hohenzollerns in denouncing every sign of moderation towards Britain and her foreign policy. Similarly the British right-wing press found its main target in the liberal government, but also became increasingly irritated with the conservatives, led by the aloof and philosophic Balfour, for failure to grapple with internal and external enemies. Even *The Times*, then and subsequently regarded as a semi-official government organ, refused all threats and blandishments designed to modify its consistent Germanophobia in the 1900s. It seems fair to conclude that the right-wing popular press played a significant role in publicizing international conflicts and preparing their readers for the impending crisis which could only be resolved by war. Liberals like Lord Bryce were surely justified, at the height of newspaper jingoism during the Boer War, to feel apprehensive about an England 'intoxicated with militarism, blinded by arrogance [and] indifferent to truth and justice'.[7]

In the short space available we can only touch lightly on the influence of military literature in preparing the European nations for the inevitable war. In Britain an extremely popular genre was the spate of invasion and war-scare stories started in 1871 by *The Battle of Dorking* by Sir George Chesney. In the late nineteenth century these stories had generally provided support for improvements in the Royal Navy, but after 1900 Lord Roberts and other famous public figures adapted them as a polemical weapon for strengthening the land forces both regular and auxiliary. Such sensational books as William Le Queux's *The Invasion of 1910* (1906) did not make a serious contribution to the debate on national defences, but they did fill the public mind with the fear of invasion by a stereotyped enemy 'the Hun', and in so doing paved the way for the xenophobia of the early months of the war. In Le Queux's highly moral tale, brave but ill-prepared Englishmen narrowly defeated evil but well-armed Germans. Lord Northcliffe, who initially published Le Queux's work in the *Daily Mail*, shrewdly caused the invaders to pass through an improbable number of large southern towns in order to attract the maximum number of readers.

In this instance fiction exercised a remarkable, tragicomic influence on reality in that Le Queux's (and other alarmists') references to what would later be styled German 'fifth columnists' in Britain created an outbreak of spy fever. Letters poured in telling the authors and editors of suspicious behaviour by German waiters, barbers and tourists which presented an almost exact mirror image of Le Queux's book. A cabinet committee, set up under Haldane's chairmanship in 1909, solemnly concluded, despite the dearth of evidence, that German spies were active in Britain. In 1911 a new Official Secrets Act was passed which put the onus on the accused to prove that he was not guilty of endangering national security. A handful of bizarre cases were brought to court with disappointing results, but on the outbreak of war thousands of innocent aliens were imprisoned or deported. By mid-September, 10,500 Germans living in Britain had been interned, and there might have been more arrests had not the War Office complained to the Home Office that there was nowhere else (not even derelict factories) to put any more prisoners.[8] In the first six months of the war the pre-war stereotype of the evil and ubiquitous 'Hunnish' spy was transferred to the entire German nation.

There was a further ironic twist to the saga of invasion stories and the associated spy fever. British interest in imaginary German invasion preparations were not confined to what would happen when the enemy actually landed. In the realm of fiction Erskine Childers's famous book *The Riddle of the Sands* (1903) graphically described the enemy's invasion plans and preparations in the creeks and inlets of the East Frisian islands. In real life the newly formed British Secret Service encouraged discreet spying in German ports by Englishmen living there, and by naval officers sent over for the purpose. These efforts necessarily proved futile though at least one agent profitably concocted stories of German invasion forces. A number of arrests were made, and Anglophobe alarmists like General Bernhardi were confirmed in their opinion that Britain, in league with France and Russia, was deliberately plotting Germany's encirclement.[9]

Friedrich von Bernhardi was an extraordinarily able officer whose radical views on the writing of official military history cost him his place on Schlieffen's general staff and who retired from the army in 1909. Three years later he published *Germany and the Next War* which Gerhard Ritter calls 'a best seller and a political disaster', because it created the impression that the general staff was sedulously fostering war with a view to making Germany the principal world power. The author did indeed give many hostages to fortune in arguing vehemently that the Germans were far too peaceable and legalistic and must be stirred up in readiness for the approaching life-and-death struggle. In Bernhardi's world where peace appeared 'amost as a state of depravity', a statesman's stature was measured by his willingness to strike in time, even if there was no certainty of success. On the other hand he correctly concluded that external circumstances were unfavourable at the time of writing in 1911. Moreover he was deeply pessimistic about the outcome of a naval war with Britain.[10]

Bernhardi was probably the ablest but by no means the only bellicose German writer in the 1900s. In 1908, to cite just one more example, we find von der Goltz, whose general view of war we have seen to be anything but romantic, arguing that the German nation needed to engage in a long and bitter struggle for survival in order to restore its 'health'. This would bring about a return to the simple, wholesome life style of the previous generations. As Ritter comments, such political literature creates an impression that the cultured elements of Europe were weary of peace and yearned for the challenge of war (chillingly referred to as 'a plunge into the bath of steel') to destroy the comfortable complacency of middle-class life. It does indeed seem likely that the middle classes were more receptive to such literary propaganda designed to appeal to nationalism, armed might and the spirit of self-sacrifice.

A general increase in chauvinism, accompanied by a belief that a great war was imminent, was noticeable after the Moroccan crisis of 1911. A new spirit of self-confidence was evident in France where the superiority of Frenchmen over Germans was continually stressed in books, newspapers, plays and schoolrooms. This heady atmosphere was especially evident in France in the impassioned debate on the bill to increase military service from two to three years in 1913. Schoolboys petitioned the president in their eagerness to sacrifice three years of their youth for France; plays on a patriotic theme enjoyed a great success; and the prestigious dailies such as *Figaro*, *Le Matin* and *Le Temps* joined the nationalist papers in urging a return to the longer term.

The passage of the three years' law, which was a remarkable event, given the leftward trend in military legislation in recent years, was explicable only in terms of a great upsurge in patriotic nationalism. In France antimilitarism had never been so muted nor a spirit of national unity so evident as in the years immediately preceding the First World War.[11]

In Austria-Hungary the approach to war brought not so much national unity as the almost complete disappearance of political agitation for greater autonomy or independence by the separate nationalities. On mobilization the polyglot peoples of the Hapsburg monarchy responded with quite unexpected enthusiasm; even the Czechs, though hostile to the privileged German minority in Bohemia, gave no cause for complaint. Similarly Austria-Hungary's socialists abandoned their internationalism in support of the war. Antimilitary propaganda made no real impact in the monarchy until after the success of the Russian revolution. As Norman Stone comments, the behaviour of the peoples of the monarchy in uniform suggests that their alienation from the dynasty was by no means as pronounced as extremist politicians claimed.[12]

Nothing did more to foster national animosities and the military spirit than the propaganda surrounding competition in armaments. The most spectacular example of this after 1900 was the mutual suspicions and hostility engendered by the Anglo-German 'naval race', whose origins were discussed in the previous chapter. Up to 1905 Tirpitz's daring programme enjoyed some success, both in terms of warships built and in the device of financing them out of the Reich's revenue without tax increases. But then Britain's decision to build dreadnoughts drastically altered the rules. Henceforth Tirpitz had not only to continue the numerical competition in his effort to achieve a 2:3 ratio, but also to improve *quality* since it was useless to attain the numerical goal if German warships were outclassed in armour, speed and fire power. The development of the Royal Navy between 1905 and 1909 showed that the German service chiefs had underrated both Britain's economic strength and her determination to maintain a clear-cut lead. The strain was most obvious in rising costs. Between 1900 and 1914 Britain's naval estimates increased by as much as 74 per cent. It is also noteworthy that the Royal Navy now became more expensive than the army: in 1905 their respective shares of the budget were 46 per cent and 54 per cent, whereas by 1914 the percentages were 64 to 36.

Between 1905 and 1914 the German defence budget as a whole rose by 142 per cent, while over the same nine-year period the naval estimates rose by 105 per cent (as against 28 per cent for the Royal Navy). By 1910 most German political leaders, though not the kaiser, recognized that such a huge and rapidly increasing naval expenditure could not be met by indirect taxes on consumer goods – no matter how much beer and brandy were consumed. The conservative and agrarian interests reluctantly agreed to an inheritance tax but strongly opposed any further increase in direct taxation. A capital gains tax was finally passed in 1913 by which time Germany was devoting 90 per cent of her income to defence. Tirpitz strove to conceal the fact that his long-term programme was in ruins, but opposition to his building plans grew steadily, not least from the navy which realized that virtually every aspect of efficiency, including a balanced fleet, was being sacrificed in the obsession with capital ships.

So, far from uniting the parties and augmenting the power of the Reich, naval armaments became a divisive force which contributed decisively to Germany's isolation. The social democrats had by 1912 become the largest party; the bourgeois parties were at loggerheads over the ruinous finances; the navy had ceased to be the cynosure of national unity; and the crown's glitter had been tarnished by a series of diplomatic reverses. Britain had outbuilt Germany in capital ships without financial disaster and the Royal Navy continued to rule the North Sea. Most humiliating of all, in 1912 Tirpitz was forced to accept that the German army must again be given priority in armaments and strategic planning. The failure of Tirpitz's overambitious programme caused a crisis in German domestic and foreign policy. For constitutional as well as strategic reasons the kaiser and his advisers felt that desperate risk-taking was now justified. A victorious land war against France and Russia would tilt the balance of power in Germany's favour while at the same time solving domestic class conflict which was threatening to get out of hand. The Anglo-German naval race did not 'cause' the First World War, but it played a significant part in preparing an explosive situation which was detonated elsewhere.[13]

After 1918 it was widely believed that the build-up of armaments had itself somehow 'caused' the war and, more specifically, that the great arms manufacturers had deliberately exploited international tension with a view to filling their order books for personal gain. As is suggested later in this chapter, there was a vestige of truth in the former belief in the sense that by 1914 the balance of military forces had become so delicate and future projections so uncertain that there was a temptation to strike before conditions worsened. On the second and more serious charge, however, economic historians have not merely undermined the 'merchants of death' image, but have argued that arms technology offered unique advantages in what is now called 'spin off'. Just five points must suffice to illustrate these contentions.

First, it was not in the general interest of armaments firms either to stimulate war or to become involved in customers' internal politics. Stable governments offered the best customers, not turbulent areas such as the Balkans. Before 1914 arms manufacturers reasonably believed – though they were eventually proved wrong – that their products had served as effective deterrents to war. Their utter unpreparedness to meet the enormously increased demands after the outbreak of war in 1914 does not accord well with the charge of warmongering. Secondly, while it is true that competition *between* arms firms was declining through the employment of combinations and 'rings', this resulted mainly from the firms' need to protect themselves against unfavourable market conditions where they were dealing with monopolistic customers, i.e., nation states, who would do little to alleviate their problems in lean periods when international tension was low. Thirdly, the charge that arms manufacturers indulged heavily in bribery is true, but as more recent business representatives have discovered, 'the greasing of palms' is endemic in some parts of the world as a preliminary to *all* deals, not just armaments. In the 1900s this was generally the case in Russia and the Far East. Such illicit payments were essential to *obtain* contracts – they did not *create* new orders. Fourthly, and much more important, the early twentieth-century arms industry tended to lead the way in thoroughness of research, willingness to innovate and the superb qualities of finished products. In Britain, for example, armament research and technology between 1890 and 1914 played an important part in aiding the development of civil technology. Rifle manufacturers such as BSA were able to convert their expertise in modern industrial practices to profitable production of bicycles, motorcycles and motorcars. Vickers similarly found that the principles involved in specialized engines and gearing systems originally developed for submarines were also applicable to motorcars. The possibilities of such 'spin off' benefits to the civil sector were appreciated by numerous industrializing countries before 1914, including Russia, Spain, Italy, Japan, Canada and Turkey. Although the immediate purpose in importing superior technology (and technologists) was to secure up-to-date defence equipment, more than one government evidently appreciated the chance of infusing 'a technology far more advanced than anything in current use within its own frontiers', in such areas as metallurgical, machine-tool and heavy shipbuilding practice.

Finally, there is the charge that such 'spin off' benefits were obtained at exorbitantly high cost; in other words that equivalent amounts spent directly on non-military projects would have produced greater benefits less wastefully. Such a proposal is anachronistic in that it falsely assumes a wide range of outlets in expenditure on social services and public facilities which were not as yet regarded as government responsibilities; and to which, moreover, there was entrenched ideological resistance in certain countries. In other words, in the period concerned there is a strong probability that the only alternative to heavy expenditure on armaments was simply reduced total expenditure. In addition, it seems to be simply untrue that civilian concerns could have emulated, let alone replaced, the armaments experts in industrial research and development. It is hard to see how developing countries could have acquired high-grade technologies by any other means than the 'spin off' from imported armaments.[14]

A mistaken assumption, which was to exercise a dominating influence not only on military preparations before 1914 but also on the course of the ensuing conflict, was that a great war would necessarily be short. Schlieffen's strategic planning, for example, stemmed from the belief that a modern industrial country simply could not afford the economic costs of protracted warfare. Ivan Bloch's military analysis led him much nearer to true prophecy: the strength of the tactical defensive would ensure a long attritional struggle; civilian steadfastness under hardship would count for more than military excellence; whichever side 'won' there would be social convulsions. It is often overlooked, however, that Bloch's economic views were narrowly orthodox and so far less perceptive. He anticipated that war would cause rapid dislocation in trade and commerce but had no inkling of the tremendous economic mobilization and state interference in the private sector which would be achieved in the course of the First World War. Ironically, he believed that Russia's self-sufficiency in food supplies and comparative lack of industrialization would afford her greater staying power in a long war. In France Lt-Col. Henri Mordacq was among the few soldiers who challenged the prevailing view that war would not last more than a few weeks. But although he doubted that governments would quickly run out of funds, even Mordacq thought that the disruption of industrial, economic, commercial and agricultural life would limit the war to a year at most. French economists likewise paid lip service to the adage that 'money is the sinews of war', but they had no notion of how in practical terms an economy could be geared to military purposes in wartime. On the whole they endorsed the soldiers' view that the outbreak of war would cause such economic disruption that hostilities could not last more than three months. Even at the beginning of 1915 one distinguished economist, Paul Leroy-Beaulieu, still argued that the war would not last more than a year and anticipated the imminent collapse of the German economy.[15]

In mitigation it must be said that none of the belligerents of 1914, including Germany, were any better prepared to introduce a war economy. With a few honourable exceptions military writers and general staff officers went badly astray in their notions about the nature of combat in the coming war and how it would be resolved. This was certainly not for want of effort because recent wars, such as those in Manchuria and South Africa, were studied assiduously, indeed almost obsessively. What was absent of course was detached objectivity capable of grasping and then accepting unpalatable lessons. In any case it was not that simple. The Russo-Japanese war lasted just over a year and then ground to a halt with stalemate on the Mukden front, Japan financially exhausted and Russia on the brink of revolution. True the South African war was made more protracted by untidy guerrilla operations, but conditions on the veldt, it could be argued, were even more untypical and abnormal than in Manchuria. An able young German general staff officer, Max Hoffman, found tactical conditions in the Russo-Japanese war very different from what orthodox instruction had led him to expect, but his truthful reports were treated with derision in Berlin. In 1911 a German military handbook specifically stated that long-drawn-out frontal battles and siege warfare such as had occurred in the Far East were most unlikely to occur in a European war.

Several officers called attention to the increasing importance of trench warfare but this was not welcome news either. Entrenching tended to be neglected in peacetime partly because it ruined uniforms and partly because it was thought to be detrimental to 'the offensive spirit'. One French colonel wrote after the Russo-Japanese war: 'The combatants had to have recourse to the movement of vast masses of earth; they have disappeared from the battlefield.' The Russian commander in chief, Kuropatkin, also complained of the invisibility of armies, yet this phenomenon would cause a shock when it recurred early in the First World War.

The prevalent mentality, which attached far more importance to morale and spirit than material factors such as bullets, found appropriate lessons in recent foreign experience. The devastating effect of Boer marksmanship had briefly shaken some soldiers' faith in the offensive, including the value of the bayonet, but it was restored by Japanese successes in 1904–5. Superior Japanese morale and determination to advance had usually carried positions defended by modern firearms though at a high cost in casualties. In Britain the War Office was only too well aware of the heavy casualties likely to be suffered in crossing the fire zone, and perhaps for this very reason training manuals exaggerated the virtues of the final assault, close combat, and the bayonet. The 1914 edition of *Infantry Training* contained the laconic statement: 'The main essential to success in battle is to close with the enemy, cost what it may.'[16] Professor Tim Travers raises the interesting speculation that the Edwardian army authorities were apprehensive about the loyalty, patriotism and determination to win of the city-bred masses and consequently tended to emphasize the intangible, moral causes of success rather than the material. He also argues that preoccupation with the moral factors and the offensive spirit inhibited the development and full acceptance of machine guns even though the weapon's critical importance was generally accepted in principle. In other words the technological challenge was perceived but the solution was sought in the alteration of human behaviour rather than in radical technical and tactical changes. This approach may have been conditioned by the Edwardian attitude of mind which tended to see problems of society in individual and moral terms. Army officers in particular may have felt that their professional ideals and their social status were under threat. These ideals could be encapsulated in the value-charged term 'character'. If new conditions of war required fire power and technical skills rather than character, then their whole way of life seemed endangered.[17]

We may conclude that in all the major armies there were perceptive individuals who drew more or less accurate lessons about the nature of future warfare from the experience of the later nineteenth- and early twentieth-century operations, but they could make little impression upon official doctrines which supposed that the next great war *must* be short and that it would be decided by the strategic and tactical offensive performed by soldiers whose high morale and unquenchable spirit would enable them to surmount every barrier and hail of lead.

In no European country in the years before 1914 were civil-military relations fully in harmony or defence and foreign policies thoroughly coordinated. It is perhaps in the nature of general staffs to encroach upon strictly political matters unless rigorously briefed and controlled. Such control was notoriously inadequate in certain countries such as Germany and Austria-Hungary. As regards Britain, there is still disagreement among historians as to whether the general staff's secret negotiations with their French opposite numbers from 1905 entailed a 'moral commitment' on behalf of the British government to assist her Entente partner in 1914. It should be said that certain key ministers knew of these talks from an early stage, and also that the government did not in fact feel morally bound to go to war in August 1914. What is noteworthy, however, is that despite the creation of the Committee of Imperial Defence in 1902, army and naval strategies were completely at odds until 1911 and even after that were never fully coordinated.[18]

In France the army had little respect for ambassadors and foreign ministers because it regarded peaceful diplomacy as too weak an instrument where questions of national interest and honour (such as the recovery of Alsace-Lorraine) were concerned. Indeed a substantial sector of the French officer class was crudely antidemocratic, and would have been glad to see the country freed from the 'parliamentary yoke'. In Italy too there was not merely no close understanding between politicians and service leaders, but even a good deal of mutual contempt. Neither party seemed to realize that it was impossible to wage modern war at short notice without prior consultation and arrangements for the supply of weapons and equipment. This was borne out in 1911 when belated orders from the prime minister to send an expeditionary force to seize Libya from Turkey found the army completely unready. The navy went into action without waiting for the expeditionary force and the latter suffered inevitable early reverses which led to a steady build-up to 100,000 men. This fiasco not only exposed Italy to a possible Austrian attack, but also made it virtually certain by 1912 that she would be unable to fulfil her military obligations to the Triple Alliance. In August 1914 there was general relief when Italy opted to remain neutral, but the chief of staff, Cadorno, was dumbfounded. Soldiers and politicians, having learnt nothing from the experience of 1911, still displayed a remarkable ignorance of each other's techniques and difficulties.[19]

To the Hapsburg monarchy falls the dubious distinction of providing the arch-militarist of the pre-1914 decade in Baron Franz Conrad von Hötzendorf. Conrad (for that was his surname) should not be taken lightly as a military buffoon. He was a formidably industrious, able and ambitious soldier who had completely mastered seven languages. He believed passionately that the monarchy must strike down Italy and Serbia in a pre-emptive war before they grew strong enough to pose a real danger to the empire. As chief of staff from 1906 Conrad repeatedly advocated war. In 1907, for example, he sought to take advantage of the Messina earthquake to attack Italy and again proposed a surprise attack in 1911 when Italy was at war with Turkey. In 1908 Archduke Francis Ferdinand wrote to his adjutant:

> Please restrain Conrad . . . he must stop this warmongering. It would be tempting to strike down the Serbians . . . but what use are such cheap laurels when we might risk the impossible war on three fronts? Then it would be the end of the song.[20]

Conrad was in fact restrained by the Jewish foreign minister, Count Aehrenthal, but he died in 1912 and his successor Count Berchtold eventually succumbed to Conrad's arguments. In the event the monarchy got the worst of both worlds because Berchtold allowed himself to be bullied into a preventive war against Serbia, but frustrated Conrad's plan for an immediate invasion by insisting upon the diplomatic preliminaries.

Although neither the Triple Alliance nor the Triple Entente were in any sense monolithic or unbreakable, their very existence clearly restricted and to some extent shaped diplomacy in the years immediately before 1914. It was only from the 1890s, with the Franco-Russian Alliance confronting Germany and Austria-Hungary, that the urgent need arose to concert military plans between allies in peacetime on the assumption that speedier mobilization and deployment would literally decide the outcome in war. In general, soldiers favoured making the military arrangements with allies as definite and detailed as possible, whereas diplomats were reluctant to sign away freedom of action to an ally who might be unduly keen to go to war. In each camp the party better armed and prepared for war (i.e., Germany and France) lost a large part of the initiative to its ally (i.e., Austria-Hungary and Russia respectively) who was less well-prepared but readier to risk going to war. Yet in neither alliance was the coordination of war plans anywhere near adequate. France and even more Russia acted initially on the outbreak of war with a view to meeting the mutual needs of their partner, but little thought had been given to forging institutional or even geographical links. A combined Russo-French high command and staff never was achieved but, more surprising, the only port through which France could ship vitally needed supplies, Archangel, had not been equipped to receive them. Doubtless this was partly due to the cultural obstacles to concerting arrangements with Russia in any period, but it must be admitted that there were also grave doubts among French generals before 1914 as to whether Russia would honour her agreement, and if so with what degree of commitment. Foch told Henry Wilson in 1913 that he favoured war in the near future because, the *casus belli* probably being Balkan, Russian involvement would be assured. Paradoxically the French army seemed to rely more on the nation that refused an alliance (Britain) than on the nation treaty bound (Russia). Britain did indeed refuse to be politically committed in advance and it is impossible to say with certainty that she would have entered the war in 1914 had not Belgian neutrality been flagrantly disregarded.[21]

The failure to reach agreement on military plans between Berlin and Vienna was far more serious since it was from the latter capital that the initiative for war was always likely to come. A salient feature of the Schlieffen Plan was that it made only minimal provision for German troops on the eastern front, thus, by implication, taking no account of Austria-Hungary's need in the opening months of a two- (or more) front war. The younger Moltke and Conrad were in frequent contact from 1909 about joint war plans, but the nominal agreement made in that year only papered over their completely different preoccupations. Eight-ninths of the German army were to attack France because Moltke believed the entire war would be decided on the Seine. Conrad, by contrast, was anxious about how his armies could attack superior Russian forces across the Narev at the outset if he was already heavily committed against his principal enemy, Serbia. In March 1909 Moltke surprisingly promised that his Eighth Army in East Prussia would join in the opening offensive against Russia but reneged on it in August 1914. In the resulting crisis for Austria-Hungary, Conrad took an enormous gamble, on the assumption that Russia would not begin operations against Galicia immediately, by sending his crucial reserve of twelve divisions ('B-Staffel') to Serbia. When it became clear that his army would have to fight virtually alone against the Russians Conrad belatedly recalled B-Staffel (on 6 August) with disastrous results: it neither stayed long enough to inflict a defeat on the Serbs nor reached Galicia in time to avert a defeat there. Both allies had attempted to exploit or deceive the other and both their offensives collapsed: on 11 September Moltke would begin his retreat from the Marne and Conrad his from Galicia.[22]

There is no need to discuss the Schlieffen Plan in any detail. Its main features, which were endorsed and eventually implemented by the younger Moltke, were to seek a decision in the west rather than the east; to destroy the French (and any allied) forces by a great envelopment sweeping through neutral Belgium and – on the extreme right – along the Channel coast; and to pre-plan the whole operation which was to be completed in six weeks. Comment will be confined to just two aspects of this remarkably ambitious military plan. Moltke inevitably bore the brunt of post-1918 criticism for the failure of the 'master plan' which had apparently cost Germany the war. In some respects this was deserved (and ironically by respecting Holland's neutrality Moltke increased his logistical difficulties), but in general the charge that Moltke ruined a perfectly feasible plan by 'watering it down' does not stand up to investigation. Schlieffen was very much the technical, drawing-board strategist; in some ways his plan was immensely detailed but he took no trouble to see that adequate manpower was available (it was not), and even more surprisingly he largely ignored logistical arrangements. Recent research has shown that as Schlieffen left it the plan simply could not have worked: the right wing could not have been fed and could not have marched to the Seine and around Paris in the tight schedule set without complete exhaustion. Even in the modified form actually implemented there were serious delays and shortages; the men kept moving and largely fed off the country, but there was an acute shortage of ammunition and the horses were largely sacrificed for lack of fodder. A recent study of the logistics of this campaign concludes that the German armies were so exhausted and overstretched by the time they reached the Marne that they probably could not have continued the advance even had they been victorious there.[23]

The most serious charge against Schlieffen, Moltke and the general staff is that they formulated a purely military plan which ignored the political dimension. Schlieffen certainly gave military needs complete priority: if France were to be defeated in six weeks armies of a certain size were necessary; if they could only find room to deploy by passing through neutral Holland and Belgium, so be it. Schlieffen was aware that this blatant violation of neutral states was likely to bring Britain into the war, but calculated that her forces would be too late and too small to save France from defeat. What remains truly astonishing is that Schlieffen (and even more Moltke) formulated and retained a plan without alternatives which committed Germany to an immediate all-out attack on France no matter where or how the war began. During Moltke's time as chief of staff it became increasingly likely that war would begin in the Balkans, but France still had to be attacked, whether she wished to enter the war or not.

Although the general staffs were certainly culpable for military deficiencies in their plans (such as the underestimation of rail and road transport requirements), and more generally for their narrowness of vision, it can hardly be disputed that their political masters were even more to blame for not laying down clear political guidelines and ensuring that war plans were subordinated to foreign policy. Moltke notoriously complained at the eleventh hour that his strategic movements to the west could not be reversed; Conrad caused chaos in trying to modify his; and Britain and France both implemented the only mobilization scheme which each had devised. It seems clear in retrospect that these plans need not have been so rigid had not the politicians abdicated from their responsibilities. This was no sudden failure of political nerve in a crisis for as early as 1900, on hearing that Schlieffen did not propose to be bound by international agreements, Privy Councillor Holstein had replied ('after a long, brooding silence'):

> If the chief of staff, if a strategic authority of Schlieffen's stature, considers such a position to be necessary, it is the duty of German diplomacy to adjust to it and prepare for it to the degree that this is possible.

In trying to exculpate himself after the war had been lost, Bethmann Hollweg wrote:

> During my whole term of office there was never any kind of council of war in which politicians intervened in the pros and cons of the military debate.[24]

In sum, Germany had nothing but a plan for a military offensive, whose rigid timetable robbed her diplomacy of all freedom of manoeuvre. A. J. P. Taylor's verdict is severe but just:

> Schlieffen first created the Franco-Russian alliance; and then ensured that Great Britain would enter the war as well. The Germans complained that the war could not be 'localized' in 1914; Schlieffen's strategy prevented it. He would be content with

nothing less than total victory; therefore he exposed Germany to total defeat.[25]

It is ironic that this myopic usurpation of political responsibility by the German general staff was supposedly carried out under the revered authority of Clausewitz who in fact had counselled precisely the opposite; namely that there is no such thing as a purely military plan. Of course it is tempting to assume that greater political concern with the military plans would have meant more moderation and restraint, but the grim possibility has to be faced that – as regards the central powers anyway – politicians may have shared the soldiers' fatalism and belief in war as the only solution for unbearable tensions.

The short war illusion had important effects on attitudes to manpower and training. What seemed to matter most in the years immediately before 1914 was to have the maximum number of trained soldiers available on or soon after mobilization together with the means to convey them to the frontier for the supposedly decisive battle. Thus, for example, French war plans in 1914 affected a large sector of the national economy but they nevertheless lacked scope and depth. Industries producing war goods were valued almost entirely for the assistance they would provide prior to and during the initial mobilization. Moreover it was assumed that with a little help from private businesses, war could be fought to a conclusion from existing stockpiles. Another remarkable assumption was that when war broke out and the army took control, all normal commercial and passenger traffic would inevitably cease. Tremendous efforts were devoted to solving problems of initial troop concentration by rail, but thereafter it was assumed there would be little for the railways to do. As regards manpower, the long debate on the French Three Year Service Bill in 1913, in contrast to all previous ideologically coloured debates on the terms of compulsory service, was almost entirely concerned with making more men immediately available on the outbreak of war. Less reliance was placed than previously on any but the most recently trained reservists, and virtually no interest was shown in building up reserves of arms and ammunition.

As mentioned above, scarcely any thought was given to the possibility that the state might have to take over important sectors of the economy and private enterprises in order to wage a long war of material. This attitude resulted in a *cause célèbre*, namely French failure to defend the all-important Briey basin, but it should be stressed that the other belligerents made equally bad though less-publicized errors. In Britain, for example, the CID had at least studied some aspects of wartime organization and had produced a useful 'War Book'. But the outbreak of war found the liberal government and its advisers still imbued with the philosophy of *laissez-faire* epitomized by the slogan 'business as usual'. To give just one example of obsolete thinking, ammunition expenditure (and hence reserves) were calculated on the basis of the South African war.[26]

The Briey industrial area, actually within range of the German guns in Metz, fell to the enemy almost without fighting in the first week of August 1914. In 1913 the Briey area had produced 15 million out of a national total of 21 million tons of iron ore (about 75 per cent), and it also produced the bulk of France's pig iron. With the loss of this area France was deprived for the whole war of some 75 per cent of her coal resources, 80 per cent of her iron production and 70 per cent of her facilities for producing regular-grade steel. People began to wonder why Briey had been lost without a fight and an investigating commission was set up while the war still continued. This enquiry uncovered the remarkable fact that no responsible member of the high command or the government had foreseen that a region producing the bulk of France's iron ore and finished iron goods would be of any strategic value in the prosecution of a war.[27]

Modern students of the pre-1914 military mentality, such as Douglas Porch and Tim Travers, have shown that the cult of the offensive had complex causes and was not simply due to a professional overemphasis on a particular tactical doctrine. In British military thinking, for example, it was supposed that success in battle was not predetermined by material or environmental factors, but by the exercise of human qualities directed by the willpower of individuals. The word *decisive* was reiterated in the manuals like an incantation: thus *decisive* offensive, assault, attack, result, victory and so on. There was also a preoccupation with the *weight* of attack, measured before the war largely in terms of manpower or 'bayonets' but during the war with the addition of artillery and material generally. What emerges from these studies is that pre-war military thought was in some critical respects unwilling to face the full implications of mass, industrial war.

Moreover, the belief that the war would be decided by moral qualities rather than physical force provided a self-fulfilling logic for

THE APPROACH TO ARMAGEDDON, c. 1900–14

the human attrition of trench warfare. Victory would go to the army that had been trained to die rather than to avoid dying.[28]

The cult of the offensive was most evident in the amazing revival of *arme blanche* cavalry doctrine despite the disappointing performance of that arm in both South Africa and Manchuria. The lessons of these wars were brushed aside as irrelevant to European conditions. One polemicist even argued that the Boer mounted infantry would have fared better if they had been equipped with lance and sword. At the core of cavalry resistance to change was a wealth of social tradition embodied in the 'rider spirit' which held that putting a foot on the ground was tantamount to disaster. This tradition, as Vagts put it, 'sees in horsemanship an aim whereas it is only a means'. The cavalry's faith in its 'moral superiority' was impervious to arguments about the devastating effects from modern fire power. As a British cavalry general argued in 1910:

> What we should seek in war is to produce moral rather than material effect; indeed, the only object of material effect is to produce moral effect on the enemy, and to get his nerves . . . into such a state that he will acknowledge defeat.[29]

In accordance with their social prestige, self-confidence and glamour, cavalry played a spectacular role in manoeuvres which bore no relation to their actual duties in war. European manoeuvres traditionally concluded with a stirring cavalry charge past the assembled dignitaries. The younger Moltke clinched his appointment as chief of the general staff by his bold criticisms of the 'kaiser manoeuvres' with their ridiculous cavalry battles and the regular enveloping of armies of half a million men in only a few days. But no amount of peacetime discussion could radically change such a well-established institution as the *arme blanche* cavalry: only prolonged exposure to industrialized modern warfare could do that.

The final point to mention in pre-war preparations is the extreme difficulty of assessing the real military strength of the rival camps in the decade or so before 1914. To take just a few aspects, Russia seemed to have been virtually eliminated as a land and sea power as a result of her humiliating defeats in 1904 and 1905 exacerbated by revolutions at home. Yet within a few years she had begun a remarkable recovery and by 1914 was again regarded as a formidable 'steamroller'. Italy, by contrast, was the least prepared for war of the major powers. Her poor performance in the Libyan operations in 1911 and 1912 demonstrated the weakness of virtually every aspect of her military organization, including shortage of money and armaments, poor training and a command system riven by political controversies. Well before 1914 Germany regarded Italy as a very uncertain ally, while Austria (in the person of Conrad) was eager to attack her. France, as we have seen, had by 1911 got over the worst of the bitter civil-military conflicts of the early 1900s and by 1914 appeared to be near the peak of national unity, confidence and military strength. Britain's participation in a general European war was not counted upon by either potential allies or enemies. Her mighty navy and the kind of influence which its power could exert on the continent through blockade were not taken seriously given the general expectation of a short war. Foch was supposed to have shown French appreciation of Britain's military *potential* when he remarked to Henry Wilson that it would suffice to send one 'Tommy' and he (Foch) would ensure that he was killed, but very few people imagined before 1914 to what an amazing extent Britain and her empire would mobilize that potential manpower and commit the bulk of it to the western front.

Thus in the summer of 1914 the balance of military power seemed to be so even, and with so many imponderables, such as how the war might begin and who would participate, that each side could believe itself to be ready and the other about to attack. In view of the outcome the decisions which led to general war would appear to be acts of criminal folly; they were certainly an enormous gamble by those soldiers and statesmen (notably in Vienna and Berlin) who took the initiative.

It is only necessary to mention briefly how war came about. In the summer of 1914 Germany could still have averted catastrophe by abandoning her rivalry with Britain and making peaceful overtures to France. This would presuppose however that Germany was a satiated power and that was far from the case. Despite all her weaknesses Austria-Hungary was essential to German ambitions to dominate the Near East. Consequently Germany's political and military leaders made a deliberate decision to maintain Austria-Hungary as a great power and to support her in a limited Balkan war. In May 1914 Moltke told Conrad in a meeting at Karlsbad that they could not compete with Russia in manpower; further delay would lessen their chances of victory. On 5 July both the kaiser and

Bethmann Hollweg gave Vienna the crucial assurance of unqualified support should Austria-Hungary decide to declare war on Serbia. It seems likely that both men thought that Russia was not ready for war and that she would accept the humiliation of Serbia's elimination after ineffectual protest. If, however, Russia *did* opt for war they were more confident of victory now than at a later date. Even after the receipt of this blank cheque Austria-Hungary might still have got away with a limited war had she acted promptly. But the ultimatum to Serbia was not sent until 23 July and although, despite Serbia's accommodating reply, war was declared on 28 July the armies would not actually be ready to crush her for another fortnight. Russia's precautionary decision to mobilize on 30 July set up a chain reaction due to the rigid requirements of the Schlieffen Plan. Germany demanded that Russia arrest all war measures and when she refused declared war on her on 1 August. Germany had no real reason for war against France but her military plans made it imperative that this occur and it duly did on 3 August. Complex issues of latent war aims, 'war guilt' as defined in 1919 and the intricacies of the mobilization arrangements which triggered off a general war should not be allowed to blur the obvious fact that the initiative came from Vienna and Berlin. Certain Austrian leaders (notably Berchtold and Conrad) wanted war against Serbia, but they would not have forced the issue unless assured of Germany's support. Germany did not plan for a general war in August 1914 but she welcomed it when the opportunity occurred. By contrast none of the Entente powers wanted a great European war, nor was there any real harmony between their foreign policies. Despite German allegations, the 'ring' around them was far from solid. As A. J. P. Taylor has pointed out, the likelihood is that the Entente would have weakened over the next few years had war not occurred, and Germany's industrial strength would have brought her the mastery of Europe which she sought instead by war.[30]

Thus soldiers and statesmen opted for war with a mixture of trepidation and fatalism. In most of the belligerent countries, excluding Britain, the service leaders (or 'brasshats') forced the issue, and everywhere politicians willingly surrendered a large amount of political responsibility to them. The soldiers (and sailors) were, after all, the technical experts and the reins of authority could be resumed after the decisive victory had been speedily won.

This attitude suggests a remarkable spirit of complacency on the part of the ruling classes: the actual fighting would doubtless be horrible but it would not last long and might incidentally stave off their social and political problems. Few imagined that it could cause a social catastrophe. Grey, a most unwarlike statesman, exemplified this complacency when he told the House of Commons on 3 August: 'If we are engaged in war, we shall suffer but little more than we shall suffer if we stand aside.'[31]

It would be absurd to attribute the outburst of enthusiasm which greeted the declaration of war in the principal cities of all the belligerents solely to the propaganda of a hard core of militarists. On the contrary it has to be accepted that the ecstasy was widespread, genuine and long nurtured by the competitive nationalism of the past generation. Many of the hordes of eager young men who flocked to volunteer and 'do their bit' before the fighting ended must have had some experience of military life, if not of actual warfare, but innumerable diaries and letters testify to an idealism which briefly blinded them to the inevitable hardship and misery inseparable from warfare. Caroline Playne, in the concluding summary of her book *The Neuroses of Nations*, captures something of the mental attitude of 1914 as crowds everywhere rejoiced:

At last! At last! We get what we want! We *can* do and *die*! And they felt, in their hearts, intense relief that there was to be no more negotiating, no more thinking, no more heeding, only rushing on, on, gloriously, splendidly on, all traces kicked over, all bridles thrown away![32]

More recent scholars such as Eric J. Leed and Paul Fussell have deepened our understanding of the attitudes of 'the community of August' by their sensitive analysis of the literature produced by soldiers who were already, or were to become, famous authors. Leed in particular makes an important contribution to our understanding of the 1914 mentality by showing that many volunteers had a vision of what they were escaping to as well as what they were fleeing from. His concept of a desire to escape from modernity and industrialization seems appropriate for the central powers, whence he draws much of his evidence, but less so to Britain where the trauma of the industrial revolution was long since past. Carl Zuckmayer, Magnus Hirschfeld, Stefan Zweig and others expressed a widespread feeling of euphoria at escaping from the problems of industrial society into a sphere of action governed by authority, discipline, common purpose and, above all, comradeship. This last quality was most valued for, as Rudolf Binding expressed it, at the outbreak of war men '*were* equal. No one wished to count for more than anyone else. On the streets and avenues men looked each other in the eye and rejoiced in their togetherness.' All soldiers had accepted a common fate and 'a kind of anonymity of obligation in which the conventions of social class no longer seemed to identify individuals'. Paradoxically, Zweig and others expressed a longing to escape from burdensome privacy; they longed to throw off a too narrow and confining identity. Ironically, too, military life seemed to promise an escape from boredom: war would signify 'real living' with never a dull moment. War in other words seemed to offer the antithesis of materialism and mechanization from which countless middle-class sons desperately wished to escape.

Of course those who sought a rigidly structured, communal life were not wholly deluding themselves in seeing the army as a haven. It did indeed offer an antidote to the civilian malaise consisting of indecision, aimlessness, and loneliness. T. E. Lawrence and Robert Graves were among those who celebrated service life for these reasons. Leed acutely notes that it was precisely the militaristic features such as training and drill which appealed to such men. For many German intellectuals and members of the middle-class professions, war seemed to offer the complete liberation from the constricting bourgeois world of comfort, profit and security which had only been partially achieved by the youth movements. Britain was conveniently seen to represent these despised qualities: 'The enemy – bourgeois society – was externalized and impressed upon perfidiously commercialized Albion.' Divisive internal economic class conflict could now be transformed into a real external conflict which would call forth national solidarity.[33]

One of the most striking, and in restrospect ironic, illusions shared by so many of the men who described their early notions of the coming war, was the concept of a pastoral world greatly preferable to urban, industrial society. War embodied a return to a healthy open-air life and to simplicity as well as discomfort and danger. As Paul Fussell points out, the pastoral illusion was only to be expected in British writers since this had been a dominant (perhaps *the* dominant) theme in poetry for several hundred years. But in central Europe, where some of these young men were escaping from real and not simply poetic clutter:

> August liberated many a bourgeois youth from shelves lined with
> carved cocoanuts, arcadian porcelains, gilded lilies of plaster,
> rooms stuffed with upholstery and damask draperies and sprinkled
> with handicrafts enjoying the patina of time.[34]

Not least of Fussell's achievements is to provide a sample glossary of
the euphemisms which testify to the prevailing innocence of mind –
or wilful self-delusion – in 1914. In this linguistic garden there were
no noxious weeds and a spade was never called a spade. Thus a horse
is a *steed* or *charger*, a soldier is a *warrior*, legs and arms are *limbs*, dead
bodies constitute *ashes* or *dust*, and the blood of young men is
(according to Rupert Brooke) '*the red Sweet wine of youth*'.[35]

To enter the first 'total' war of industrialized nations with these
idealized expectations and images was to invite a traumatic shock for
which irony, disenchantment and disillusionment are inadequate
terms. Instead of escaping the soul-deadening mechanization of
modern society, this generation – or at least its literary elite, which
is an important distinction – discovered that the tyranny of
technology was even more omnipotent in war. There was little scope
for individual chivalry on battlefields where the domination of the
machine was carried to its most extreme form. In the First World War
'technology' soon came to embrace not simply the accumulation of
weapons and equipment, but also the organization of material and
men. The real dehumanization of soldiers was mirrored in the official
jargon as they were increasingly referred to as 'effective rifles' or, in
abstract banking terms as 'drafts', 'balance', 'deficit' – in short they
were treated as commodities.[36]

The ingredients for a catastrophe in the event of a general European war had been in existence for a decade or so before 1914. A few
military writers, in addition to the civilian Bloch, perceived this
dreadful possibility – of stalemate, attrition and social upheaval –
more or less clearly but they had little or no influence on policy or
strategy. First, armies had become too large and cumbersome to
stand much chance of winning a decisive 'Napoleonic' victory. If the
initial offensive failed the chances of achieving another Austerlitz,
Sadowa or Sedan would virtually disappear, provided that nations
remained united in their war effort. This they were to do to an
astonishing degree even in the Hapsburg and Ottoman empires and

Russia. Secondly, mass involvement of nations in the war effort with their xenophobia whipped up by propaganda militated against a compromise peace without victory. So too did the ambitious war aims cherished by Germany and to varying degrees among all the European belligerents. Thirdly, the politicians nearly everywhere willingly surrendered their authority to the generals on the assumption of a short war. Finally, we have seen that despite a good deal of theorizing, there was scarcely any practical pre-war preparation for a mass industrial conflict requiring drastic state control of manpower, industry, transport and commerce. Thus when the great opening battles in eastern and western Europe failed to bring a result there was bound to be a long delay while the belligerents mobilized for total war. So a strange combination of psychological preparedness and material unpreparedness set the scene for the Armageddon which was to prove longer and more destructive than even Bloch had imagined.

4

ARMAGEDDON,
1914–18

In retrospect the worldwide conflict between 1914 and 1918 was widely regarded as a disaster for European civilization. Approximately 10 million men were killed and twice as many seriously wounded; there were 5 million widows, 9 million orphans and 10 million refugees.[1] Not surprisingly many people were shocked when, in 1920, Colonel Repington entitled his account of these events *The First World War* because it presupposed another. Yet in 1914 the coming of war had been greeted in European cities in a spirit of euphoria, even of ecstasy. Statesmen like Sir Edward Grey may have regarded the plunge into war as the catastrophic breakdown of a system, but for many more people it promised excitement, fulfilment and escape. Nationalism as the expression of popular loyalty, though soon to be enflamed by propaganda and manipulation by the ruling elites, was nevertheless genuine and profound. How else can one account for the willing self-sacrifice of hundreds of thousands of young men in the opening months and their persistent, dogged enthusiasm which only began seriously to flag in 1916?[2]

This chapter is concerned not so much with military operations as with the relationship between warfare and the societies (soon to be termed 'home fronts') which both supported and endured it. Four broad stages may be discerned, though of course their timing and duration did not coincide precisely in all the belligerent countries.

The first phase, characterized by the initial war of movement which had been generally expected, lasted until the spring of 1915. Every country at war, including tsarist Russia, experienced a sudden surge of patriotism and sense of national unity; in Russia, for example, there was a marked decrease in strikes and everywhere there was an agreed truce in party conflict. In terms of industry, commerce and manpower, however, soldiers and statesmen alike were slow to appreciate the demands of total war: 'business as usual' with a minimum of state interference was the prevailing policy. Again, on the assumption of a short, decisive war, generals everywhere were given wide and ill-defined powers exceeding their immediate professional needs.

Between the middle of 1915 and the end of 1916 the conflict spread as new belligerents like Italy and Rumania became involved; it also reached a peak of intensity in campaigns such as Verdun and the Somme. Governments were now forced to take drastic measures to harness all their resources, human and material, to the war effort. There were early signs of political opposition to the war and disquiet over its inept conduct and, more ominously, stirrings of discontent on the part of soldiers and sailors.

In 1917, the penultimate phase, the strain of total war was evident on the home and military fronts in the form of strikes, food riots, increased desertion and mutinies. The French armies were badly affected by mutinies in the spring, while in the autumn the Italian forces were routed at Caporetto; but by far the most spectacular and momentous event was the Russian collapse in revolution. By now statesmen were struggling to reassert the authority earlier ceded to the generals. In France, in the person of Clemenceau, they were successful, but in Germany Generals Hindenburg and Ludendorff had become virtual dictators. By insisting on the resumption of unrestricted submarine warfare against Britain they brought the United States into the war in the spring of 1917. This, in effect, assured the Entente of eventual victory, if Britain and France could hold out for another year or so, and countered what otherwise might well have been the fatal defection of Russia at the end of 1917. In what proved to be the final year of the war, 1918, the crucial question was whether Germany could win the war in western Europe before her allies collapsed and before the United States's great potential military power was translated into fact. In the last phase war-weariness was universal and in countries facing defeat there is a clear connection between military reverses and disintegration on the home fronts. In general, however, the front-line armies preserved their cohesion and discipline almost to the end.

With the benefit of hindsight it has become difficult to understand why so few pre-1914 students of war recognized – or accepted – that the development of magazine rifles and machine guns had given the defensive a marked advantage. Sir John French, the mercurial commander in chief of the British forces, plaintively summarized the generals' bewilderment:

> No previous experience, no conclusion I had been able to draw from campaigns in which I had taken part, or from a close study of the new conditions in which the war of today is waged, had led me to anticipate a war of positions. All my thoughts, all my prospective plans, all my possible alternatives of action, were concentrated upon a war of movement and manoeuvre.[3]

By the end of 1914 the west European battlefield had congealed in continuous trench lines from the Channel to the Swiss frontier, thus setting the stage for a protracted siege. Fire power and barbed wire ruled out mobile cavalry operations and rendered unsupported infantry attacks suicidal. Henceforth increasing reliance was placed on artillery to prepare and support the attack, but that arm was mainly equipped in 1914 to fire shrapnel shell at bodies of troops in the open. Medium and heavy guns firing high-explosive shells to smash barbed-wire entanglements and strong points were needed in numbers undreamt of in 1914; and even when they became available the expenditure of ammunition far outran supply. A French battery firing at maximum rate would exhaust its entire supply in 1914 in a quarter of an hour; within a few weeks of the opening of the war the British Expeditionary Force had nearly exhausted its supply of ammunition which had been calculated on the basis of expenditure in the South African war. Ceremonial sharpening of officers' swords and the French infantry's red trousers were symptomatic of the profound failure to grasp the realities of modern combat which resulted in the hundreds of thousands of casualties in the first few months of the war.[4]

Contrary to popular antimilitary writing, there was a steady development of tactics even on the superficially unchanging, stalemated western front, but innovations such as poison gas (first used in the west in 1915) and the tank (1916) were either ineffective or were quickly countered before they could prove decisive.[5] Logistics, hitherto dependent on railways and horses, were transformed by the appearance of tractors and lorries on a vast scale: in 1914 for example, the British army went to war with 100 lorries, but ended it with 60,000. Advances in medical science and food processing made possible a truly remarkable achievement in the First

World War: it was the first conflict in which the main combatants suffered more casualties by enemy action than by disease.

From the outset this was a war on an unprecedented scale. The Entente powers in Europe (excluding the British and French overseas empires), out of a population of 256 million, put approximately 200 divisions into the field while at sea they possessed 44 of the latest warships. The central powers and Turkey, from a population of 137 million, put some 136 divisions into the field and possessed 27 modern warships. The Entente's apparent numerical advantage was in reality greatly reduced by the low standard of training and equipment of the enormous Russian army. Russia did remarkably well to mobilize 5 million troops in the opening days and took the field unexpectedly quickly on the Polish and East Prussian fronts in order to confront Germany with her strategists' nightmare of a two-front war. But deficiencies, mismanagement and the resultant suffering on a colossal scale brought the possibility of a speedy collapse. As early as December 1914 the chief of staff, Yanushkevich, feared that lack of munitions would force his armies to surrender. There was an acute shortage of officers.

Many men have no boots, and their legs are frostbitten. They have no sheepskin or warm underwear, and are catching colds. The result is that in regiments which have lost their officers mass surrenders to the enemy have been developing, sometimes on the initiative of war-time officers. 'Why should we die from hunger and exposure, without boots? The artillery keeps silent, and we are shot down like partridges. One is better off in Germany.'[6]

In 1914 Germany's army was by far the most formidable, with able staff officers, the largest trained reserve and the best modern equipment and weapons. Germany was handicapped by the weakness of her Austrian ally but, unlike Britain and France in their efforts to aid Russia, had the advantage of good communications on internal lines. By the end of 1914 the Royal Navy dominated the surface of the seas and British merchant shipping was not yet endangered by submarine attacks on a large scale. This did not seem to count for much as long as notions of a short war prevailed. Britain sought to impose a rigorous naval blockade on Germany from the outset but the effects would take several years to bite. The crucial war theatres appeared to be on land where Germany's initial advances brought lasting advantages. In the west the Schlieffen Plan, though failing to achieve its full objective of a French collapse, had left the German army in occupation of most of Belgium and an industrially valuable sector of north-eastern France. This obliged the Entente to attack a well-entrenched defender over the next three years while Germany sought, ultimately successfully, to knock out Russia, against whom she had won resounding victories in 1914. Fortunately for the Entente, Russian fortitude, encouraged by periodic successes against the Hapsburg armies, kept the fluctuating eastern front in existence until the end of 1917.

In all the belligerent countries national unity and sense of togetherness found expression in 1914 in similar forms of truce in domestic politics. On 2 August in Germany the state of *Burgfrieden* (literally, fortress truce) was proclaimed whereby employers and trade unions agreed to suspend all labour strife for the duration of the war. The social democrats, committed through the Socialist International to disrupt the capitalists' war by obstructing mobilization, in the event reneged on their pledge and supported the war almost to a man. In the Reichstag the party voted *en bloc* in favour of granting war credits to the government. In France the *Union Sacrée* provided a patriotic umbrella under which socialists, anarchists, militants and revolutionaries went gaily to war. Individual dissenters went in danger of lynching. Emergency measures against anarcho-syndicalists were suspended in return for the trade unions' (CGT's) unanimous rejection of a general strike. In Britain the outbreak of war only served to mitigate not eliminate the unprecedentedly bitter relations between the liberal and conservative parties. However, Asquith's appointment of the non-party proconsul, Lord Kitchener, to the War Office provided a suggestion of national government, while the conservatives allowed their criticism of the conduct of the war to be modified by patriotic restraint. Two liberal ministers resigned on the declaration of war, but only a handful of labour politicians, led by Ramsay MacDonald, risked public obloquy by open opposition to the war.[7]

In the Duma only a handful of left-wing deputies, including Mensheviks and Bolsheviks, opposed the war and towards the end of the year five of the latter were arrested and exiled to Siberia. Even in tsarist Russia popular enthusiasm for the war was briefly triumphant. From August 1914 until the spring of 1915 there was a steady decline in the number and scale of strikes. Similarly in Vienna, where mobilization was smoothly carried out, the multilingual armies went to war with astonishing ardour. Indeed 'the pessimists must have marvelled at the unanimity of feeling in every race and class, and felt almost persuaded that their emergency decrees had been a needless insult to a really loyal and patriotic nation'.[8]

Italy was exceptional, both in delaying her entry into the war until May 1915 (and then initially only against Austria-Hungary), and also in having to bear the burden of an antiwar party in the form of 75 socialists, not counting the extreme conservatives who had always been averse to intervention. Nevertheless the declaration of war temporarily united the nation: the conservatives declared their loyalty; socialists agreed not to disrupt the war effort; and most bishops urged their flocks to cooperate with the secular government even against a predominantly Catholic enemy. This 'sacred enthusiasm' did not survive intact for more than a few months.[9]

At the outset of war military leaders everywhere were invested with quasi-dictatorial authority while the popular press bestowed on them heroic attributes. This was conspicuously so in France where parliament not merely placed Joffre in absolute command of a loosely defined war zone but also, on 4 August, adjourned itself indefinitely. A month later, with Joffre's encouragement, the deputies and government fled for safety to Bordeaux. During Joffre's ascendancy, after he was credited with the victory on the Marne, not even the war minister was a welcome visitor to the forward areas. Similarly Hindenburg's and Ludendorff's victory at Tannenberg earned them an inflated reputation as 'saviours of the fatherland'. Thereafter the Reichstag, though it still met, had even less power to influence the kaiser and his ministers than before the war. In Britain the heroic mantle fell not so much on the field commanders as on the physically impressive person of Kitchener, summoned to take over the War Office on the outbreak of war, but in reality treated as a generalissimo whose laconic decisions were never questioned by mere civilians.

The Reichsrat in Vienna, aptly described as 'a babel of obstructionism' where orators in nine vernaculars harangued one another across the house, was dissolved in March 1916 and did not meet again for three years. Count Stürgkh, the Austrian minister president, reposed his trust in the bureaucracy and in the authoritarian chief of staff, Conrad von Hötzendorf. Curiously in Russia the Duma's activities and prestige increased in the first phase of the war. The tsar reluctantly delegated command in the field to Grand Duke Nicholas, a moderately competent commander, but under constant pressure from the tsaritsa, he eventually made the fatal mistake of taking on the supreme command in person in August 1915. By the end of the first phase of the war the fallibility and bewilderment of all these military titans was becoming obvious to their nominal political masters, but the latter would everywhere experience difficulty in recovering the authority they had so lightly surrendered in August 1914.[10]

The patriotism of 1914 had its idealistic as well as its ugly side. An ironic outcome of allowing thousands of volunteers to rush to the colours to 'do their bit' in the opening weeks was that vital war industries were deprived of skilled labour. In Britain, for example, almost a quarter of the employees in the chemicals and explosives industry had enlisted, and over a fifth had gone from coal mining. Consequently, after a strenuous propaganda campaign at the start to get men *into* the trenches, spasmodic efforts were made to keep certain key workers *out* of the trenches, followed by a final desperate 'combing out' of the reserved occupations in face of the acute shortage of soldiers in the last year of the war.

The distasteful and deplorable manifestations of rabid patriotism were encouraged by soldiers and civilians alike in 1914, though as the war dragged on it was the civilians who tended to utter the more loathsome 'militaristic' nonsense. Alas, the arrogance epitomized by the phrase '*Gott mit uns*' had its equivalent in all languages. Minorities and aliens were persecuted in the name of national unity. The Russian high command not only treated Jews with notorious brutality, but also forcibly depopulated vast front-line areas in a foolish endeavour to create a wasteland comparable to 1812. Anti-German hatred was rampant in Britain, exacerbated by a widespread but largely false belief in the ubiquity of spies. Under emergency legislation enemy aliens of military age were interned, the others repatriated. Racial hatred, far exceeding what the government wanted, was whipped up by the popular press. The *Daily Mail* was a flagrant offender with such prominent advice as the following: 'Refuse to be served by an Austrian or German waiter. If your waiter says he is Swiss ask to see his passport.'[11] Even more deplorable than this nonsense was the successful campaign to oust Haldane from office because of his alleged pro-German sentiments, and the enforced resignation of the First Sea Lord, Prince Louis of Battenberg, because of his German origins. As Battenberg's political chief, Winston Churchill, remarked in accepting his resignation:

This is no ordinary war, but a struggle between nations for life and death. It raises passions between nations of the most terrible kind. It effaces the old landmarks and frontiers of our civilization.[12]

All the belligerents displayed an understandable reluctance to abandon the policy of 'business as usual' in favour of a strictly controlled and regulated war economy. Germany took the lead in the first phase of the war, partly because in her encircled position she quickly experienced serious shortages, but also because she had far-sighted industrialists such as Walter Rathenau and Alfred Hugenberg who realized that a large measure of 'state socialism' was unavoidable in a total war. Thus bread cards for rationing were issued as early as January 1915, followed by cards for meat and fats. From October 1915 two meatless days per week were legally enforced. In the course of 1915 beer production was reduced to a quarter of its pre-war level. In response to intense agitation by the trade unions against rising prices, price controls were introduced early in 1915. The establishment of a War Wheat Corporation in November 1914 set the pattern for cooperation between big business and the government which was taken much further in the second stage of the war.

On the face of it Austria-Hungary was much better adapted to endure an economic siege than Germany since the industrial cities of Austria complemented agricultural Hungary. Indeed in peacetime the empire was normally self-sufficient. Unfortunately for Austria, the 1914 Hungarian harvest had been largely ruined by bad weather, while in 1915 the Russian invasion devastated alternative sources in the wheat-producing provinces of Galicia and Bukovina. In 1915 the Hungarian minister president, Count Tisza, exploited his advantage by closing the frontiers; henceforth Hungarian wheat was exported to the starving Austrian townsfolk only when Hungary herself wanted goods. The Austrians were powerless to break this stranglehold because the Hungarian Diet was completely independent. It must be said, however, that the Austrian response to this and other economic problems was much less vigorous than Germany's. The people as a whole took the government – and the war itself – less seriously than the Germans; they were 'morally unprepared for hardship on a national scale'. It is symptomatic of the Austrian attempt to muddle through that a universal system of food rationing was never introduced. The farmers felt themselves to be a race apart and did not exert themselves to ease the sufferings of the townsfolk.[13]

In August 1914 the Russian government did something which no country had ever done before in time of war; namely renounced its principal source of revenue. This took the form of a complete ban on the sale of alcohol which cost the treasury some 7000 million rubles per annum, or a third of its revenue. Nor did the measure achieve its desired end because peasants turned cheerfully to manufacturing their own home brew, leaving them money in hand to buy up scarce food supplies. Another anomaly was that Russia's vast increase in war expenditure was not covered by new taxes; instead the ministry of finance relied upon loans and the issue of paper money. This brought steep inflation which was to play a vital part in undermining Russia's very considerable war effort. Russia practised her own version of 'business as usual' until the military reverses of the spring of 1915, accompanied as they were by an appalling shortage of munitions, boots, uniforms and all military supplies, and the disorganization of transport. Under pressure of public opinion, a real effort was made to mobilize industry and bridge the gulf between front and rear. In the summer of 1915 four Special Councils were created, for national defence, transport, fuel and food supply. It appeared for a few months as if the country was making a successful attempt to achieve national unity with all its resources geared to the war effort.[14]

Britain in 1914 was the home of 'business as usual' in its purest form, the three sacred principles being free trade, free currency and free enterprise. The phrase itself was coined in a letter to the *Daily Chronicle* on 11 August 1914 and popularized by Harrods in an attempt to combine patriotism with profit. Asquith's government, strongly supported by the business community, was strongly opposed to interference in the free play of the market, or indeed of government action of any kind once the initial spate of emergency measures had been introduced. These, however, provided an ominous foretaste of things to come. In August 1914, for example, the government took control of the railways and pegged the shareholders' profits to the 1913 level. At the same time an export ban was placed on all materials used in manufacturing explosives. By the end of the year, however, it was becoming clear to a few economists that the only way to ensure that factories got the necessary materials at reasonable prices was for the government to take responsibility for purchase, supply and distribution. Early in 1915, when there was an acute shortage of sacking for sandbags, the government intervened to requisition available stocks at generous prices. Another scarce commodity which the government was forced to purchase was sugar. Nevertheless Asquith showed the greatest reluctance for government interference to check rising prices. Frequent government interventions in the financial field were regarded as short-term emergency measures. Astonishingly, until well into 1915, a determined effort was made to continue peacetime accounting by allocating limited sums to particular tasks.

The event that caused the first major break in the government's 'business as usual' policy was the shell crisis following the British army's heavy losses in its first offensive battle at Neuve Chapelle in March 1915. This crisis, accompanied by another over the conduct of the Dardanelles campaign, brought into office a coalition government of all parties under Asquith, one of whose first acts was to create a ministry of munitions. The real boost that the coalition gave to the forces of collectivism was 'that as an all-party ministry, and manifestly a war ministry, it could with much greater impunity pass measures which were in violation of beliefs previously firmly held by most Liberals and Conservatives alike'.[15]

Even so the government moved slowly along the route to wholesale nationalization, and important measures like food control were still only being contemplated when Asquith resigned in December 1916.

The campaigns of 1915 raised the central powers to the peak of their military fortunes. The tsar's armies were routed and rolled back into Russia; Poland and Serbia were overrun. A succession of British and French offensives in the west between May and October, culminating at Loos, were everywhere checked with heavy casualties. Italy, a newcomer to the Entente side, launched four fruitless attacks on the Isonzo front. The one significant Entente attempt to exploit superior sea power by opening up a new war theatre failed tragically at the Dardanelles. The Turks also defeated the British forces in Mesopotamia and besieged Kut, where an Anglo-Indian army capitulated in April 1916.

But there were no encouraging signs, not even from Russia, to suggest that the Entente was prepared to accept a compromise peace. Consequently Falkenhayn, the German chief of staff, faced a strategic dilemma for 1916: should he concentrate on trying to knock out Russia or strike a major blow on the western front? He decided to launch an attritional attack on the fortress of Verdun in the expectation that the French armies would 'bleed to death' rather than yield a prize of such strategic and emotional value. In defiance of Falkenhayn's wishes, Conrad prepared a great offensive against the Italians in the Trentino rather than play the subordinate role of holding the eastern front against a possible Russian revival.

The year 1916 probably witnessed the most terrible fighting of the whole war. The armies were now tactically experienced but still enthusiastic. The home fronts were still reasonably well-fed, loyal and confident, and industry was now organized to produce the vast amounts of guns and ammunition previously in such short supply. The Entente armies everywhere proved themselves to be still full of fight. Between February and November the French not only retained Verdun but eventually counterattacked to recover lost ground and inflicted approximately equal casualties.[16] Despite suffering nearly 60,000 casualties on the first day of their Somme offensive (1 July), Kitchener's New Armies kept attacking until November. Conrad also failed to achieve a breakthrough on the Trentino, but the greatest Austrian reverse was sustained on the eastern front. On 4 June Brusilov, commanding the south-western group of the Russian armies, broke through the Austro-Hungarian defences in Galicia and in a few days took 200,000 prisoners. This encouraged Rumania to enter the war on the Entente side and to invade Hungarian Transylvania. The Entente forces at Salonika also resumed the offensive. These setbacks caused the fall of both Falkenhayn and Conrad. Hindenberg and Ludendorff assumed command of the German armies and at last the Austro-Hungarian forces were subordinated to German direction. The year ended with the capture of the Rumanian capital, Bucharest, but the overall strategic advantage now seemed to lie with the Entente.

Although the German war leaders were correct in thinking that Russia was the most likely of the Entente powers to suffer an internal collapse, her fundamental weaknesses lay in poor leadership and organization rather than economic and industrial backwardness. Norman Stone, in particular, has demonstrated that by 1914 she was developing rapidly and, in purely economic terms, was capable of sustaining a modern war.[17] Russia, for example, was producing much more coal, iron and steel than France yet her shell output was greatly inferior. In the first quarter of 1915 the Russian armies received less than 2 million shells – hardly a fifth of their minimum needs. Russia's handicaps lay in a variety of non-economic factors: among them lack of foresight before and on the outbreak of war, when some crazy assumptions were made, mistrust between the general staff and the war ministry, mistrust between business and government, rivalry between infantry and artillery and gigantic transport problems. Perhaps most important of all, the Russian people were saddled with a huge international debt incurred for war material which did not arrive when it was needed. Contrary to myth Russian war production made an immense improvement in 1916 but by then other factors were undermining her war effort.

The Russian armies' appearance of demoralization and imminent break-up as a result of the retreat from Galicia in 1915 derived mainly from sheer excess of numbers. By July 1915 no less than 9 million men had been called up. Over a million prisoners of war were lost that year alone, and the rate of sickness was alarmingly high with nearly half a million men invalided out of action in 1915. The armies included millions of untrained, ill-equipped territorials, the bulk of them illiterate peasants who had no idea what they were fighting for. The gulf between officers and men was much greater than in western armies and widened throughout 1915. There was also an acute shortage of NCOs who could link officers and men. Stone and Florinsky cite tragicomic examples of military incompetence and lack of trust: telegraphs would stop working because the men had chopped down the poles for firewood; cavalry and artillery abandoned their own infantry and in some cases deliberately fired upon them; treatment of the wounded remained primitive and callous. Not surprisingly troops surrendered in droves and in some cases fought their own Cossacks who tried to rescue them. Increasing polarization between officers and men was to constitute a fatal weakness in the long run.[18]

Brusilov's great offensive in June 1916 testifies not only to the Russian armies' resilience and endurance, but also to more efficient organization of the country to wage total war. Even so Brusilov was still critically short of shells – 300 rounds per gun in some units as against a French standard of 1700 per gun by this time – but paradoxically this very weakness helped him to secure surprise and a breakthrough against an opponent who had committed too many of his troops to the front trenches. Between 4 and 12 June Brusilov demoralized four Austro-Hungarian armies, capturing at least 200,000 prisoners and over 200 guns. Brusilov's advance petered out because his infantry outran their supply lines and because he lacked reserves, especially of cavalry. He had nevertheless dealt his enemy an irreparable blow. Austrian troops had lost faith in their commanders and in fortification of all kinds; henceforth they could not be relied upon to hold any position unless stiffened with German troops. In September the German ambassador in Vienna warned Berlin that Austria-Hungary's continuance in the war could not be counted upon for much longer for both military and economic reasons:

> The reserves of troops are nearly exhausted, and we should expect that next Spring Austria-Hungary will reach the limit of its military potential . . . The people in the suburbs of Vienna are starving; they are driven to despair by long queueing, which often brings no results . . . [19]

As regards the conduct of war and the observance of legal restraints, Liddell Hart confidently asserted that 'the decline of civilized behaviour became steeper . . . there was an appalling growth of brutality towards wounded and prisoners'. But more recent students, such as Geoffrey Best, have been less confident of generalizing on the conduct of different armies on different fronts. Certainly the fighting seems to have been fiercer, limitations more often ignored and the wounded more neglected in the Balkans and on the eastern front than in the west. The Turks have an unenviable record in the war for their cruel treatment of prisoners. Civilians were badly neglected compared with combatants in international laws of war, and suffered everywhere not only from the indirect effects of battle but by deliberate mass expulsions (as in western Russia) and illegal exploitation (as in Belgium). Propaganda inflamed national hatreds and created stereotypes of 'hunnish atrocities' with stories of bayoneted babies, crucified civilians and 'corpse factories', most of which were subsequently proved to be false. Professor Best concludes tentatively that the Red Cross was usually respected; soldiers trying to surrender were usually given quarters if circumstances permitted; and prisoner of war camps on the whole did not disgrace the governments responsible for them. Unfortunately two major developments were making the great recent output of humane conventions difficult to abide by or even interpret; namely the increased destructive and killing capacity of modern weapons, and the erosion of the barriers and distinctions between combatants and others.[20]

Germany had begun the war with a flagrant violation of Belgian neutrality and her subsequent occupation of that small and inoffensive country was remarkably harsh and brutal. The invaders' tendency to imagine that *francs-tireurs* and *saboteurs* lurked behind every street corner and to react with great severity, was probably conditioned by legends exaggerating French partisan warfare in 1870–1. But as Professor Best speculates, deeper religious and cultural prejudices may also have affected German behaviour. The worst reprisal, subsequently shown to have been totally unjustified, was the sacking of Louvain and its famous university library, and the summary execution of many citizens.

Measures arising from 'military necessity' included requisitioning of food to the point where the Belgian population was starving; enforcing huge contributions of money on cities and imposing colossal collective fines for even the slightest offences; imprisoning hostages; and ruthlessly exploiting the country's economy to assist the German war effort. The most notorious aspect of economic exploitation – providing a foretaste of Nazi barbarity in the Second World War – was the enforced deportation of Belgian workers to Germany. In Ritter's words, 'The whole scheme had the appearance of regular slave transports and slave markets.' As there was no medical screening most of the deportees reached the camps in a wretched physical state; many were unable to work. When the deportations were stopped in February 1917 about 62,000 had been shipped off to Germany, of whom nearly one thousand died in the camps and over 13,000 were sent back as too sick to work. The political damage caused by this inhuman and illegal policy vastly outweighed the benefit to German industry.[21]

The conduct of the war at sea was particularly significant in the light of recent attempts to civilize its conduct and protect the rights of neutrals through the Hague Conventions of 1907 and the (unratified) Declaration following the London Conference in 1909. Briefly, the main concerns were rigorously to determine the nature of blockade (it must be effective to be legal) and to allow neutrals to do business with belligerents in all goods that were not war materials, i.e., contraband goods being narrowly rather than loosely defined.

From the outset the Royal Navy's tough attitude was that it would do anything, in the last resort, to ensure national sovereignty. In an effort to make the blockade of Germany as complete as possible Britain put great pressure on neutrals, urging them for example to follow prescribed routes to avoid minefields and submit voluntarily to search for contraband, which was widely interpreted. In effect, neutrals were prevented not only from doing legally permissible business with Germany but also with each other. Hence the rueful German quip that Britannia not only ruled the waves but also waived the rules.[22]

The main mitigating factor in Britain's ruthless naval policy was that it did not normally cost neutrals their lives. Germany, already saddled with a black reputation as the violator of Belgian neutrality, could only counter Britain's increasingly firm stranglehold on merchant shipping by stepping up submarine warfare which inevitably did cost innocent lives. By the end of 1914 Germany's cruisers had all been sunk or interned and her submarines could in practice only be employed for commerce *destruction* rather than capture. Under prevailing laws submarines were required to surface, search vessels for contraband and, if detected, put a 'prize crew' aboard to take the ship to a neutral port for prize adjudication. Not merely were submarines unsuited for these procedures, but they were themselves extremely vulnerable to gunfire (actually carried out by illegally armed merchantmen – the notorious British 'Q-ships') or ramming.

Objectively there was little to choose between Britain's and Germany's attitude to neutrals; indeed legal authorities did in fact subsequently decide that the latter's resort to all-out submarine warfare was justified both as legitimate reprisals and as 'a lawful claim of right'. However, in terms of neutral opinion – above all in the United States – and as a gift to her enemies in the propaganda war, German submarine warfare had the fatal defect of killing British civilians and, more important, neutrals, often in the most shameful circumstances. German propagandists did their best to exploit the fact that the ultimate result of British blockade would be the starvation of 'innocent civilians', but this was a poor card to play as against such an internationally shocking event as the sinking of the great Cunard passenger liner *Lusitania* in May 1915.[23]

Lastly, the First World War witnessed the dawn of a terrible new era with the first significant cases of strategic bombing from the air. Tactical bombing in direct support of army operations at or close behind the front lines did not raise serious qualms on legal grounds, though even in this form civilians were inevitably killed and private property destroyed. But 'strategic' attacks far behind the lines such as German airships and Gotha bombers carried out against English cities from 1915 onwards, and the Royal Naval Air Service against the Ruhr and Rhineland cities, were plainly another matter. In principle a distinction could be drawn between 'precision' and indiscriminate bombing: the former aiming at military targets, broadly defined to cover factories, naval dockyards, airfields and communications centres with a reasonable degree of confidence that they could be located and hit. Civilians and their property would only be injured incidentally and by accident. Given the primitive direction-finding and bomb-aiming apparatus available it was only a short step to the deliberate indiscriminate bombing of industrial areas where military targets were not precisely identified and civilian housing was regarded as a legitimate target, the objects being to undermine civilian morale and divert resources from military purposes.

Resort to night bombing by both Britain and Germany in practice swept aside the last pretexts of precise targeting. Indeed a Gotha crew captured in December 1917 admitted that if their bombs missed military targets in central London it was of no consequence because one of their objectives was to demoralize the civilian population, particularly in the East End. Much depended of course on the *ability* to locate and hit precise targets, but also on the higher directives of governments and air staffs. In the First World War the principle or pretext of precision bombing had not yet been abandoned in favour of a deliberate 'terror' attack on the enemy's cities. One must, however, add as a rather cynical reflection on the moral and legal aspects of long-range bombing that, by the time of the First World War, heavy artillery was already being employed indiscriminately at extremely long ranges against enemy cities. True, reconnaissance aircraft (their principal role in the war) and balloons made the spotting of shellfire well behind enemy lines more feasible than in previous wars, but the problem remains that firing against military targets in cities (for example church spires used as observation posts) inevitably caused widespread damage. Beyond that it must be admitted that such actions as the German 'Big Bertha' siege gun shelling Paris from a distance of 70 miles were a deliberate contribution to newly accepted methods of frightfulness against the civil population.[24]

By 1916 the strains and disruption of all-out warfare were experienced everywhere and all governments were obliged to interfere to a greater or lesser extent in virtually every aspect of national life. Perhaps the most important shortage was of manpower. The armed services demanded more and more men, but so did industry and agriculture. Even Britain was forced to introduce military conscription in 1916. Industrial and agricultural production were adversely affected, not only by shortage of labour but also by other factors such as military destruction of capital equipment, loss of merchant shipping to submarines and denial of essential raw materials by the blockade. The British empire, for example, ended the war with only two-thirds of the shipping tonnage available in 1914. Britain, France, Germany and Sweden all produced less pig iron at the end of the war than in 1913. Germany was unable to increase food production sufficiently to offset losses of imports, and by 1916 the area of land devoted to crops in Britain was smaller than in 1914. America, at peace until 1917, was of course an outstanding exception and her industry gained a lasting advantage from European wartime demands. Indeed American intervention was decisive in economic terms since, despite their ruthless concentration on war needs, the European belligerents could not maintain the production levels of iron, guns and shells into 1918. From 1916 onwards it is not unreasonable to see the war in terms of a conflict of economic systems as much as of armed forces. In such an economic competition the central powers were handicapped by their comparatively small area of supply and lack of access to overseas raw materials. But their problems were exacerbated by Hungary's selfish behaviour towards Austria and by lack of close understanding between Vienna and Berlin. Indeed there was no systematic coordination of resources between the central powers, and their allies Bulgaria and Turkey. Economic cooperation was better among the Entente powers. Conferences were held in 1916 to discuss economic policies in general, and methods of tightening the blockade in particular. Anglo-American cooperation on the north Atlantic trade routes was also improving in the twelve months before America entered the war.

By the end of 1916, then, many pre-war liberal assumptions concerning government interference with finance, manpower, transport, food and fuel had had to be abandoned. The experience of wartime direction of economic life was, in Rathenau's phrase, an 'education in state socialism'. Not only was there a great loss of personal and institutional freedoms, but class divisions were exacerbated by various shortages, above all of food. Some states eventually collapsed under these economic strains.[25]

The Russian home front in 1915–16 merits special attention in view of her collapse in 1917. Norman Stone has argued persuasively that previous historians have been too impressed by superficial evidence of economic confusion and backwardness such as insufficient coal to keep factories working; lack of metals for civilian goods; and above all a chronic shortage of food in the large towns. These deficiencies and muddles certainly in the long run caused revolution, but they were crises of over-rapid industrial growth geared almost entirely to the demands of war. In fact virtually all sectors of the economy grew rapidly between 1914 and 1916. The output of coal and petroleum both rose by almost 30 per cent. There was a vast expansion of engineering and chemical industries, demonstrating Russia's capacity to provide her own in place of imported machinery. Not surprisingly the increase in war goods was most impressive. There was a 2000 per cent growth in output of shell, 1000 per cent in artillery and 1100 per cent in rifles. By 1916 Russia was producing more than 200 aircraft per month and there were five large automobile factories producing lorries. By January 1917 there was a reserve of shell at the front of 3000 rounds per gun and in November the Bolsheviks inherited a shell-reserve of eighteen million. In fact by 1916 the Russian army enjoyed a considerable superiority on the eastern front as a whole not only in manpower but also in war material.

It was Russia's tragedy that this tremendous growth in war production was achieved at unacceptable cost to large sectors of the civil population. At the heart of the problem was the disparity between agricultural production and manufactured goods for the home market. Peasants simply refused to sell their produce for paper money with which they could buy none of the goods they wanted. This unexpected development, coupled with the inadequacy of the railways to provide for the civil population as well as the army, soon led to acute shortages of food, fuel and other commodities in the cities and towns, whose populations were anyway increasing rapidly as a result of wartime industrialization. One authority calculates that on a 1913 basis of 100 the general index number of prices in 1916 was 203, and in 1917, 673. A report of the police department for October 1916 warned that:

the industrial proletariat of the capital is on the verge of despair and it believes that the smallest outbreak, due to any pretext, will lead to uncontrollable riots, with thousands and tens of thousands of victims. Indeed the stage for such outbreaks is more than set . . .[26]

By 1916 hardship and casualties were everywhere beginning to undermine civilian morale. Although the political truces of 1914 such as the *Union Sacrée* had not completely collapsed, individual antiwar spokesmen such as Giolitti in Italy, Caillaux in France and Ramsay MacDonald in Britain began to receive more support. Outspoken opponents of the war in Russia had been imprisoned or exiled, but the appointment of the pro-German Stürmer to ministerial office in February 1916 seemed an ominous sign. In the central powers, socialist support of the war begun to crumble. An antiwar socialist party was formed in Austria, while in Germany Karl Liebknecht's previous isolation in the Reichstag was ended as many SDP leaders denounced the war. Moreover, in 1916 an independent socialist party was formed to oppose the war, though without the backing of the official trade union leadership.

In any case the kaiser's reaction to military failure and loss of the strategic initiative in 1916 was not to give ground to the antiwar opposition but rather, at the end of August, to appoint Hindenburg and Ludendorff to a virtual dictatorship. The latter's ruthlessness and narrow concern for military resources was immediately made evident in the treatment of Poland. Ludendorff ignored the existing policy of German-Polish rapprochement and trampled on the slight remaining hopes of a separate peace with Russia in what proved to be a vain obsession to commandeer Polish manpower for German war purposes on a grand scale. The generals anticipated the Nazis in pressing for the complete militarization of German society. At the end of the year the 'Hindenburg programme' of all-out 'war socialism' was promulgated. A 'Patriotic Auxiliary Service' was created into which all German men not already on war service between the ages of seventeen and sixty were to be drafted. German organization for war reached its peak; for the first time there were systematic attempts to exploit the labour-power of women for war work.[27]

The initial military enthusiasm, evident among all the participants, endured remarkably well into 1916 despite unimagined privations and casualties. By the end of 1916 the French had suffered

3,350,000 casualties, the Germans 2,460,000 and the British forces over 1,000,000. Overt signs of military and naval discontent were now manifest, foreshadowing the large-scale mutinies of 1917 and 1918.

For example, open resentment, indiscipline and desertion were seriously affecting the reliability of the Slav regiments of the Hapsburg empire. Czechs and Ruthenes would doubtless have fought better under their own officers, whose language they could at least understand, but two-thirds of the officers were German and most of the rest Hungarian. Urban and literate Czech soldiers were exasperated by being treated as half-witted peasants; while Ruthene peasants resented fighting Russians whose religion they shared. The high command overreacted to military incidents while its incompetence exacerbated the problem. Ironically the Austrians suffered from their lack of Prussian authoritarianism and failed to make their Slav subjects fight loyally for them. Even more alarming than desertions to the Russians was the failure of their own Slav units to fight resolutely in self-defence.

As early as the summer of 1915 the Russian minister of the interior warned his colleagues that recruiting was causing severe problems: 'The police are unable to deal with the large number of men who are trying to avoid military service. Men are hiding in the woods and in the fields.' By October 1916 conditions in the army had become alarming:

> The behaviour of the soldiers, especially in units located in the rear, is most provocative. They openly accuse the military authorities of graft, cowardice, drunkenness, and even treason. One everywhere meets thousands of deserters perpetrating crimes and offering violence to the civilian population. These express regret that 'the Germans did not arrive', that 'the Germans would restore order', and so on.
>
> The soldiers began to demand peace a long time ago, but never was this done so openly and with such force as now. The officers not infrequently even refuse to lead their units against the enemy, because they are afraid of being killed by their own men.[28]

In the autumn of 1915 there were also grave disturbances among the sailors of the Russian Baltic fleet, the causes of which were military reverses, animosity towards officers with German names, tactless behaviour by officers and poor food. Here were the first signs of the smouldering discontents which were to burst into open revolution in 1917.

Quite distinct from military indiscipline and demoralization, there was also becoming apparent in the middle years of the war the special sense of solidarity shown by front-line combatants. Soldiers felt themselves to be a new class apart, the class of victims. They reacted with increasing bitterness to the 'home front' which, in their eyes, included profiteers, shirkers, ranting politicians, xenophobic clergymen – even in extreme cases their own families who often displayed an utter lack of imaginative understanding as to what the combat zone was really like. This growing antagonism of 'the front' towards 'the rear' would have momentous repercussions at the end of the war and in the early post-war years.[29]

The most obvious evidence of war-weariness in the second phase of the war lies in the numerous efforts made to secure a negotiated peace. Unofficial French and German delegates attended a socialist conference at Zimmerwald in 1915 which denounced the war as an interest only of capitalists. In the same year President Woodrow Wilson made his first attempt to mediate but failed because there was clearly no prospect of American intervention. As late in the war as November 1916 Wilson was re-elected on a peace platform.

Less well-known are German hopes for a moderate peace with Russia. At the height of his victorious advance in the summer of 1915 Falkenhayn proposed that the tsar be offered an armistice, but Bethmann Hollweg believed that a separate peace was unobtainable on any terms acceptable in Germany. Nevertheless the chancellor secretly informed the tsar that Germany was prepared to offer very moderate terms, including a Russo-German condominium in the Dardanelles. Bethmann Hollweg remained hopeful that the Entente's failure at the Dardanelles and on the western front would bring the tsar to his senses. The latter was indeed tired and war-weary but he felt bound to honour his commitments to his allies, and was also persuaded by his military advisers that the loss of Poland and the Baltic provinces was not decisive. On 11 August the tsar and his cabinet resolved that Russia would not even respond to peace offers.[30]

The new Hapsburg emperor, Karl, had promised an early peace to his subjects on his accession to the throne in 1916, and towards the end of the year he took a bold if injudicious initiative to fulfil the promise. Karl used his brother-in-law, Prince Sixtus of Parma, who was serving in the Belgian army, to secure an indirect contact with the French prime minister. Unfortunately for him, the emperor had acted behind the back of his own foreign minister, Count Czernin, and in direct opposition to the latter's pro-German policy. Czernin was working for a rapprochement between the two emperors with the ultimate goal of a general peace proposal, whereas Karl was trying to negotiate a separate peace for Austria-Hungary. This was obviously unthinkable to Germany. The outcome was that Austria-Hungary became even more closely bound to Germany as the inferior partner. On 12 December the German chancellor did in fact announce a peace offer on behalf of Germany and all her allies but the condescending tone was that of an alliance certain of victory. The Entente replied belatedly and unenthusiastically. President Wilson had meanwhile intervened to ask both sides to declare their war aims which at least made clear the unbridgeable gap between them. The Entente governments demanded the evacuation of all territories occupied by the central powers; reparations, and liberation of the subject peoples of the Hapsburg and Ottoman empires. For their part the German generals and admirals pressed on Bethmann Hollweg an extraordinary programme of annexations in eastern and western Europe, and in the Baltic, Mediterranean and Pacific oceans which could only have been realized, if at all, by absolute victories on all fronts.[31]

In 1917 the suffering and war-weariness of all the major belligerents greatly increased while the terrible campaigns of attrition seemed to bring decisive victory no nearer to either combination of powers. Russia experienced revolution and prepared to quit the war; England endured the climax of the submarine offensive and enormous battle casualties; the French armies' mutinies seemed to finish them as an offensive instrument; Germany and Austria-Hungary faced severe shortages and political crises; the Italian armies were routed at Caporetto. In strategic terms, Germany stood on the defensive in both east and west while her military dictators organized industry and manpower for a final effort. In the east the Germans easily beat off what proved to be revolutionary Russia's last offensives. In the west, the new French commander in chief, Nivelle, failed disastrously in his spring offensives east and west of Reims. Haig's offensive at Third Ypres (Passchendaele) began on 31 July with the aim of ending the war that autumn but degenerated into a notoriously ghastly battle of attrition that left both sides exhausted when it ground to a halt in the November mud. The Entente's only unqualified success was the British imperial forces' capture of Jerusalem in December. Only Russia experienced full revolution but the complete breakdown of order on the civil and military fronts seemed a distinct possibility in all the continental nations at war. Even Britain at last suffered real shortages of basic commodities such as sugar, potatoes, margarine and coal but, apart from the worst months of the submarine offensive in April and May, it would be exaggerating to talk of a 'crisis'.[32] Indeed Britain's, and even more so, her Dominions' war efforts reached their peak in 1917. America's entry into the war in April also gave encouragement of eventual victory, a prospect which was not eclipsed by Russia's defection at the end of the year.

Germany's major offensive effort in 1917 was made not on land but at sea: the resumption of unrestricted submarine warfare against Britain. This strategy, carried after many months of agonized discussion, was essentially the work of the 'silent dictatorship'. Admiral Tirpitz had resigned in March 1916 because he had not been allowed to adopt it, but the strategy had remained in favour with German submariners, though less so in the high seas fleet whose role was thereby downgraded. Ludendorff's argument was brutally simple: England was the keystone of the Entente and must be beaten before her blockade strangled Germany. England could be starved into surrender if every ship, combatant or neutral, sailing to or from her ports, was sunk without warning or discrimination. Such a policy would almost certainly bring America into the war but it would take at least a year before her armies could be deployed in Europe. Could Britain be knocked out in the few months available? Technically, recent improvements made it seem feasible, and in fact in April 1917 one in every four large vessels leaving Britain was sunk. But it was a desperate gamble because Germany had only about one hundred submarines available altogether and one critic, Weizsäcker, calculated that no more than 18 large U-boats could be in action at one time. Bethmann Hollweg was never wholly convinced by the generals' arguments; he acquiesced on 9 January 1917 but did not resign.

On 15 March an American ship was sunk without warning and on 6 April she declared war on Germany. This immediately eased the pressure on British trade protection in the north Atlantic, but on a wider view it transformed the nature of the war. What had been hitherto essentially a European conflict now became one of world powers. To the issues of the European balance of power and national aspirations there was added a strong tincture of ideological crusade.[33]

In April 1917 the French armies were crippled by mutinies lasting for several weeks when Nivelle's offensive on the Chemin des Dames failed to achieve the promised breakthrough. The *poilus* simply refused to advance and in some cases insulted or attacked their officers. The movement spread until the majority of units were affected to some degree. A few regimental ringleaders advocated a march on Paris to overthrow the government and proclaim peace. At the time the mutinies were so successfully hushed up that even the British government did not realize their extent, and the Germans opposite them knew even less. Pétain, a hero of the defence of Verdun and a general with a reputation for husbanding lives, replaced the rather unlucky Nivelle, called off the offensive and set about restoring order.

What had been the basic cause of the mutinies? Most of the generals naturally attributed them to pacifist, socialist, anarchist and German-inspired revolutionaries operating insidiously in the rear and disseminating their defeatist propaganda through men returning from leave. Pacifist propaganda certainly did reach the front but recent research, notably by Guy Pedroncini, has revealed a close connection between the incidence of mutiny and the most active sectors of the front during the costly April offensive, notably between Soissons and Auberive. It seems clear that the troops had finally revolted against suicidal tactics in endless futile offensives. Pétain's appointment in itself did not stop the mutinies but they fell off as soon as he abandoned the attack. The mutineers' actions and testimonies support this interpretation: the majority were prepared to do their duty in defending their line and were certainly not pro-German. They were simply fed up with being treated as cannon-fodder by arrogant generals and incompetent staff officers.

The other issues which were far from clear at the time were the number of mutineers and their punishment. On Pedroncini's strict criteria, for example excluding numerous incidents at railway stations, there were only 30–40,000 mutineers. There was also great confusion as to the number of mutineers tried and executed, some sources putting the number of executions as high as 2500. Pedroncini shows convincingly that 3427 sentences were decreed, of these 554 were condemned to death and 49 actually executed. Under Pétain's command the French army made a remarkably rapid recovery and by late summer 1917 was quite capable of holding its long sector of the front while the British attacked in Flanders. But the French government was badly shaken because the mutinies coincided with a period of austerity, a sharp rise in the cost of living, strikes and growing pacifism.[34]

In May 1915 Italy entered the war in the hope of a quick, inexpensive victory against Austria. With morale high and an advantage of 35 divisions against 14, Cadorna attacked the Trentino salient in June but was soon confronted with a trench stalemate and attrition already familiar on the western front. Morale suffered a slump during the hard winter of 1915–16. Peasants in uniform, mostly southerners, found the war in such inhospitable terrain incomprehensible. Frustration found vent in hatred of the *imboscati* or shirkers. For the front-line infantry this meant everyone except themselves, especially all rear units and the general staff. Among detested civilians the munitions workers – well-paid, well-housed, and mostly socialists – were in a special category. In John Whittam's words:

> The peasants in uniform, earning half a lire per day, were fighting for the northern war workers earning seven and a half lire per day, and the southern lower-middle class officers were leading them into battle to make the world safe for industrialists and bankers.[35]

Cadorna remained uncertain as to whether subversive civilians were infecting his soldiers with defeatism or vice versa. By 1916 the euphoria of the previous year had evaporated: there were antiwar demonstrations in several cities, but bitterness was even more evident in the countryside as more and more peasants were drafted, leaving their womenfolk to run the farms. The peasants, subjected to requisitions and forced sales of livestock, also fared badly compared with the cities as regards pensions and state relief.

In mid-1916 the war entered a new and more total phase for Italy with a new government of national unity which promptly declared war on Germany. Military morale had revived by the spring of 1917 partly due to the improved supply of guns and equipment and partly because victory seemed a real possibility by the end of the summer. Even so, there were open demonstrations about appalling conditions and their generals' inhumanity. In 1916, 167 soldiers were executed and 359 in 1917. Civilian spirits, however, experienced no uplift at all. Even the northern industrial workers began to feel the effects of the economic squeeze; coal shortages and inadequate transport caused output in textiles, for example, to fall by more than 50 per cent. There were strikes over wage claims and bread riots. Milan, and even more so Turin, were in a revolutionary mood comparable to Petrograd's, with women and youths playing a vital part in urging the *carabinieri* not to fire on their comrades. Pope Benedict XV denounced the war as a useless massacre, thus encouraging antiwar sentiments among the peasantry. In 1917 there were 20,000 deserters in Sicily alone and nearly 60,000 in all.

When the central powers attacked on the Isonzo on 23 October they had only a slight numerical advantage of 44 divisions (including 7 German) against 41, but they achieved complete surprise using new infiltration tactics. The breakthrough at Caporetto became a rout, the Italians losing 300,000 prisoners and over 3000 guns. Fortunately for them the attackers ran out of steam and the line of the Piave was held.

In response to this disaster a more determined government was formed under Orlando. Cadorna, who tried to blame the collapse on civilian defeatism, was replaced by Diaz. The incursion of the hated Austrians into the homeland enabled the new government to combat defeatism by nationwide propaganda calling for a united war effort. This was implemented by the wholesale takeover of private firms and trade, transport, shipping and agriculture came under state supervision. Some 200,000 women were absorbed into war work permitting an impoverished country to maintain nearly five million men in uniform in the final year of the war. Greater determination and centralization on the home front paid military dividends in 1918. With a stiffening of 5 Anglo-French divisions Diaz attacked on 4 October and won a resounding victory at Vittorio Veneto. The Hapsburg army disintegrated.[36]

The March revolution in Russia was sudden, unexpected and unplanned. In consequence of the Women's Day demonstration and a munitions workers' strike some two hundred thousand men and women surged aimlessly about the streets of Petrograd. There were a few clashes but little bloodshed. Cossacks and reservists fraternized with the crowd and the local commanders lost control. The Petrograd garrison of 160,000 troops melted away and detachments ordered from the front demobilized themselves en route. In the course of a week other cities followed Petrograd's example with little resistance or loss of life. The tsar quietly abdicated, his brother Grand Duke Michael declined the succession, and power was ambivalently shared between a provisional government (replacing the former Duma) and the soviets, forming in all cities from soldiers, sailors and workers.

The provisional government immediately announced a series of liberal reforms including freedom of speech, of the press and of assembly; replacement of the police by a people's militia; and a humane code of civil rights for soldiers. It also called for the election of a constituent assembly. This was a deceptively mild phase of the revolution because the vital questions of peace and land had not been tackled. The provisional government was awkwardly poised between the old autocracy and impending mass revolution: as a representative of the officer class, the bureaucracy and the professional middle classes it had an exceedingly precarious power base. Initially however, its declared intention of moving slowly on the reallocation of land and prosecuting the war with more determination seemed to gain general approval. It certainly reassured Russia's allies. The soviets proclaimed a policy of 'peace without annexations' but it quickly became apparent that Germany was not interested in negotiations: it was a stark issue of German invasion or defence of the homeland. Mensheviks and Bolsheviks alike were thoroughly confused: they mistrusted the provisional government but agreed that the gains of the March revolution must be defended against German imperialism. Lenin, almost alone from the moment he returned from exile in April 1917, advocated all-out class conflict, immediate peace and all power to the soviets. Even many of his Bolshevik colleagues regarded him as a lunatic.

Lenin's revolutionary 'defeatism' was, however, much closer to the mass opinion of peasants and workers than Kerensky's fiery exhortations to the troops to redouble their efforts in a patriotic war. As early as 13 March General Selivachev noted that the sole preoccupation of the troops was whether they would receive additional allotments from privately owned estates and monasteries. Then the terrible thought struck them that the redistribution of land might take place before they could reach home. The army was thrown open to political committees and defeatist propaganda openly disseminated, thus destroying the last vestiges of hierarchical authority. Not that the breakdown of military cohesion should be attributed primarily to the effects of propaganda. Some 15 million soldiers were suffering from immense fatigue, almost uninterrupted reverses, insufficient supplies and lack of belief in the official reasons for continuing the war. Some generals protested that their divisions were in better heart than ever after the March revolution, but General Dragomirov surely spoke for more when he complained privately: 'The fighting spirit has dwindled away. Not only have the soldiers no desire to advance, but their will even to defend themselves has been so terribly shaken that it is a real menace to the issue of the war. All the thoughts of the common soldiers turn towards home.'

Officers who tried to restore discipline were frequently insulted, dismissed and even murdered by their troops. On 1 July Brusilov made a last attempt to revive the glories of 1916 by attacking in Galicia but, after an initial success against Austrian troops, his brittle units met German reserves and retired in disorder. Brusilov handed over to General Kornilov who was arrested soon afterwards for attempting to save the provisional government against its will by setting up a military dictatorship.[37]

In the autumn the revolution began to show its violent side. There was wholesale looting of food shops; peasants seized the land and murdered landlords; and the murder of army and naval officers became commonplace. The reserve forces in the rear areas and towns had long since shown their sympathy with the soviets; now at last the front-line divisions began to suffer from mass desertions. On 7 November, while Kerensky was seeking loyal units at the front to defend his government, the Military Revolutionary Committee proclaimed it to be overthrown and power vested in the Petrograd soviet. That evening the Bolsheviks occupied the Winter Palace after a short bombardment and arrested those of Kerensky's colleagues who were sheltering there. Lenin became president of the Council of People's Committees and speedily implemented his policies of peace and land. On 5 December the Bolsheviks signed an armistice with the Germans at Brest-Litovsk. Despite their confident expectation that this ceasefire would lead to a general collapse of the Entente, the Bolsheviks, in the person of Trotsky, found themselves having to negotiate alone from a position of utter weakness. Trotsky successfully spun out the peace negotiations into 1918 but by then Russia had virtually no organized divisions capable of resisting a German advance. When, early in February, the Germans lost patience and resumed their advance to within a hundred miles of Petrograd, the Bolsheviks were forced to accept humiliating terms. Russia gave up Poland, Lithuania, the Ukraine, the Baltic provinces and Transcaucasia. These losses amounted to a quarter of her European territory, two-fifths of her population and three-quarters of her iron and coal.[38]

Russia's defection from the war and anarchic domestic situation posed serious problems for her allies. The central powers left one million troops in the east to control the spread of Bolshevism, but Germany was able to move forty divisions to the west. Britain and France refused to accept Russia's collapse as final and intervened on several fronts of what now became a civil war.

Although Bolshevik hopes that the Russian revolution would immediately be emulated elsewhere were disappointed, its repercussions were apparent in several countries, particularly in the Hapsburg and Hohenzollern empires where it was now clear that defeat would bring social and political upheaval.

In Germany the Bolsheviks' success greatly encouraged the social democrats who vigorously echoed their demand for peace without annexations or indemnities. Also, following the news of the civil rights guaranteed to Russian soldiers and sailors, there were naval mutinies at Kiel and other Baltic ports provoked by the failure of submarine warfare and harsh treatment by officers. Alarmed by the spread of antiwar agitations the majority of socialists urged Bethmann Hollweg to widen the Prussian franchise and openly to support peace without annexations. The chancellor made conciliatory noises regarding the franchise but was impotent to address the question of peace since the generals were insisting on retention of Belgium and other territorial gains. Bethmann at last resigned in July 1917 but his successor, Michaelis, was even more a puppet in the hands of the generals.

In France the Russian revolution had a direct effect in the summer of 1917 in an uprising of Russian troops fighting in the west. Most of the mutineers had simply had enough of the war and wanted to go home. Removed from the front where they might contaminate French units, they revolted again in their camp near Limoges and were eventually shipped to North Africa. The *Union Sacrée* was now dead and buried and, so long as Russia remained in the war, the pacifist wing of the French socialists felt free to campaign for a negotiated peace. Pétain inveighed against pacifists and agitators who encouraged defeatism in the Paris press, on the railways and in the factories. He demanded that French delegates be refused passports to attend the socialist peace conference at Stockholm. The prime minister, Ribot, complied. From July onwards Clemenceau redoubled his attacks on Malvy, Caillaux and all advocates of a compromise peace. 'The Tiger's' reputation as the scourge of the workers seemed to debar him from the premiership, but in November the unthinkable happened. Clemenceau symbolized the spirit of war *à outrance*. He imprisoned Caillaux and other advocates of peace and suppressed their newspapers. Even Clemenceau could not stamp out strikes and antiwar agitation, but once the draconian terms of Brest-Litovsk became known his demand for a clear-cut French victory received overwhelming support.[39]

By far the most serious repercussions of the Russian revolution occurred in Austria-Hungary. The Bolshevik demands for peace and social revolution fell on fertile ground among people now facing starvation. A cut in the Austrians' flour rations in January 1918 set off bread riots and strikes which spread rapidly to nearly all industrial areas and turned into antiwar demonstrations. This explosive situation was exacerbated by the return of thousands of prisoners released by the Russians. In Styria a Slovene regiment mutinied, shouting 'up the Bolsheviks, long live bread, down with the war'. Earlier, on 1 February, the Fifth Fleet had mutinied in the Gulf of Kotor, red flags were run up and the officers' mess band struck up the *Marseillaise*. This and the soldiers' mutinies in the Austrian and Hungarian sectors of the empire were quickly suppressed, but from the spring onwards the armed services themselves became so permeated with nationalist aspirations that they became unreliable as political instruments. Meanwhile, German diplomacy at Brest-Litovsk displayed a complete disregard for her ally's interests in Galicia and the Ukraine. Germany's dominance was confirmed in a meeting of the two emperors at Spa on 12 May when Karl accepted joint military forces and a customs and economic union. This was tantamount to a Hapsburg abdication since it offered the subject nationalities only the prospect of even stronger German hegemony. This document, and the knowledge that the Entente (urged on by America) favoured independence for the subject peoples, dealt shattering blows to the already tottering Hapsburg monarchy.[40]

At the end of 1917 Germany's home front looked more secure than in the terrible winter of 1916–17, but the staying power of all her allies was now in doubt. Encouraged by the victory in the east, the German army was inspired to make a final effort to break the morale of the Anglo-French armies in the west before American support made them unbeatable. After months of careful preparation and the perfection of new tactics, the offensive began on 21 March with a tremendous bombardment and overwhelming superiority of numbers concentrated on the sector opposite the British Fifth Army. Ludendorff achieved the greatest breakthrough since the German advance of 1914, and for a week it looked as though he might drive a wedge between the French and British armies and cause the latter to pull back to the Channel ports. The Entente rallied under the new coordination of Foch but the crisis continued throughout April. Then Ludendorff switched his main attack to the French front and by the end of May his vanguard was again on the Marne only fifty miles from Paris. The last major German offensive in mid-July actually crossed the Marne, but then Foch counterattacked. At the time it was not clear to the Entente that they had won the decisive battle, but by early autumn Ludendorff admitted that Germany could not win. Nevertheless the German armies in the west continued to put up stout resistance, and it was on the other fronts that military pressure first resulted in political capitulation. From mid-September the forgotten Anglo-French forces attacked in Macedonia which caused Bulgaria to ask for an armistice at the end of the month. Turkey, faced with defeats in Mesopotamia and Palestine, as well as the Arab rebellion, sued for peace on 14 October. The collapse of the Hapsburg empire, which merits examination in more detail, was complete by the end of October. A ceasefire began for their armies on 3 November, eight days before what proved to be the end of the war on the western front.[41]

In January 1918 both halves of the Hapsburg monarchy were briefly paralysed by mass strikes and mutinies provoked by starvation and war-weariness. The bulk of the armed forces, still loyal and disciplined, performed one of their last services to the monarchy by restoring order. Ironically, however, this restoration of order proved also to be a service to the radical nationalists in that it gave them a breathing space to gain control of an increasingly revolutionary situation.

From January onwards the Austro-Hungarian armed forces were increasingly committed to the maintenance of order on the home front. Hitherto the armies had been spared from the worst privations that lowered civilian morale, but now they too had to share the people's hardships. Front-line troops had to subsist on 200 grammes of meat per head per week and 120 grammes of maize per day, eked out with dried vegetables. There were frequent meatless days, and soldiers were actually advised that worms found in army rations were not injurious to health. Complete uniforms, even for officers, were a luxury. Men went into action in rags and were often short of boots. Revolutionary ideas were spread, particularly in the rear areas, by regiments reconstituted from released prisoners of war from Russia. What kept the army going, apart from its enduring loyalty to the monarchy, was the hope of a German victory in France. In June the army, mustering its last resources in support of Ludendorff, launched a double offensive on the Asiago and the Piave. Both failed dismally. Thereafter, though the armies amazingly retained some discipline and fighting spirit to the end,[42] they were powerless to prevent the internal collapse of the empire.

The Entente powers did not cause the break-up of the Hapsburg empire, though under President Wilson's leadership they encouraged it in 1918 by openly supporting the claims of the main subject peoples to national independence. Chief responsibility for the dissolution of the empire *before* the armistice lies with the monarchy itself due to incompetent government, subservience to Germany and military defeats. These failures allowed 'lesser peoples' to associate with the victors and proclaim themselves to be 'successor states'. A popular movement in Prague proclaimed the Czechoslovak Republic on 29 October, and almost simultaneously Count Karolyi announced the existence of an independent Hungary. The new state of Yugoslavia was proclaimed by the Slovenes, the German-Austrian national council favoured an independent state for the German-speaking peoples of the empire, and even the Ruthenes attempted to establish an autonomous state.[43] In the post-war peace conferences the victors could adjudicate on frontiers but there was no possibility of restoring the pre-war empire.

The German army possessed an inestimable advantage over the Austro-Hungarian army in its linguistic and cultural unity. It was also much tougher and more professional. Even so its leaders, notably Ludendorff, had to display skilful timing in jumping off the juggernaut so as to create an impression of political responsibility after the war had really been lost by the generals. Ludendorff did this at the end of September 1918. Prince Max of Baden formed a government which for the first time contained a substantial number of social democrats and was genuinely responsible to the Reichstag. These changes came too late however to prevent Germany's war effort terminating chaotically in naval and military disorder bordering on revolution. This happened at the end of October when the high seas fleet, largely though not completely inactive in harbour since the inconclusive battle of Jutland in 1916, was ordered to sea on a death and glory mission. Sailors at Kiel and Wilhelmshaven mutinied. Soldiers sent in to restore order fraternized, as had happened in Petrograd. Moderately though Prince Max handled these mutinies, the disorder spread. Workers' and soldiers' councils began to spring up everywhere without resistance, even in conservative, Catholic Munich where an antiwar socialist, Kurt Eisner, took control.

The social democrats realized that it was essential to stop the war before revolution engulfed Germany as it had Russia. For this denouement the kaiser's abdication was an essential preliminary. He accepted this unpalatable necessity on 9 November when it became clear that he could not rely on the army's support. A social democrat, Ebert, became chancellor notionally under the old constitution but in reality as the choice of the Berlin Workers' and Soldiers' Council. On 11 November Germany accepted the armistice on the western front which effectively ended the war.

In terms of military experience, the First World War had substantially borne out the pessimistic predictions of Ivan Bloch: no single decisive battle was obtainable on land or at sea; a tactical stalemate tended to set in on all fronts even where movement was possible; modern weapons such as poison gas, high explosives and bombing aircraft increased the horrors of front-line combat and extended the killing zone to the home front; naval blockade caused starvation among civilians and, finally, the conflict ended in the breakdown of order and even outright revolution through the interaction of military defeatism and civilian war-weariness. Unfortunately, though an economist himself, Bloch greatly underestimated the willingness and ability of the major belligerents, including Russia, to adapt their economies and people to the demands of total war.

Confronted with long siege operations where they had anticipated a short, mobile war, commanders and staff officers took a long time to adapt their thinking, acquire the requisite material and devise new tactics. In detail many of them are open to severe censure, particularly for persisting in offensives which were clearly bogged down and for overriding the first-hand knowledge of front-line commanders. But from the present perspective the historian must surely see these operations in terms of a tragedy long in the making through developments in technology, nationalist ideology and the structure of the European state system.

Given that the outbreak of war in 1914 turned out to be a tragedy for nearly everyone involved and that vain efforts were made to stop it from 1915 onwards, it is nevertheless empty rhetoric to say that it 'settled nothing'. The Russian, Hapsburg, Ottoman and German empires were destroyed, many new states created and the map of Europe drastically redrawn. The real power centre shifted from western Europe to Russia and North America. Twenty-eight sovereign states (or thirty if Albania and Persia are included) were ultimately involved as belligerents in a lopsided contest of twenty-four against four. One authority calculates that, eventually, out of a world population of 1,600,000 over 1,400,000 were formally at war.[44] Clearly the war affected the domestic developments, cultures and aspirations of all these countries in various ways: whether it was *worth it* at the cost of such material and human losses is a question that the historian simply cannot answer. Indeed he has his work cut out to distinguish specific effects of the war from what would have happened anyway, albeit more slowly.[45]

Related to this insoluble problem is the slightly more manageable one of distinguishing between what people thought about the war at the time and what they have come to believe about it since. As we have seen, there was very little of the euphoria and ecstasy of 1914 in evidence by 1918. Nevertheless war-weariness is not synonymous with disillusionment. Millions of soldiers and civilians were exhausted in 1918 but many probably still felt that they had served their countries well in a good cause and were hopeful that their efforts would be translated into a better world, domestically and internationally. Disillusionment (for the minority who had cherished illusions) and disenchantment flourished in post-war economic, social and political conditions and much of this was understandably projected back on to the war itself until that conflict has become a by-word for futility.[46] Perhaps the moralist may conclude that it was indeed so, but the historian has a prior need to *understand* and *describe* great events without necessarily feeling called upon to offer a moral judgement. On one specific point, however, the military events of 1914–18 did cause a fundamental change in popular attitudes to war. With the conspicuous exceptions of fascist Italy and Nazi Germany, war would never again be regarded coolly as a viable instrument of state policy, or embarked upon by a nation as a whole with the optimism or insouciance of 1914. Unfortunately this popular revulsion from the phenomenon of war was neither deep nor comprehensive enough to prevent another worldwide conflict from occurring within a generation.

5

THE TWENTY-YEAR TRUCE, 1919–39

To many contemporaries in 1914 the First World War seemed to have ended an era, and the passage of time has only served to underline the correctness of their perception. It shattered the nineteenth-century liberal idealist vision of increasing international cooperation in a peaceful and prosperous world led by the great European powers. Sir Edward Grey's premonition at the outbreak of war was well-founded: the 'lamps of European culture and civilization' were indeed being extinguished, some never to shine again. The Great War, soon to be termed pessimistically 'the First World War', quickly acquired the reputation as the most terrible of all modern conflicts and retains it despite all the horrors that have occurred since. Some 10 million men died as a direct consequence of combat and perhaps as many more from indirect effects. Whole nations had been subjected to the hardships associated with a prolonged siege. Capital resources had been used up more quickly than ever before. Three great dynasties had been overthrown (four if the Ottoman empire is included), destroying social and political certainties and laying central and eastern Europe open to revolution. Although superficially there was a rapid recovery from the material destruction and a ready adaptation to new political conditions, it would be a mistake to underestimate the less tangible repercussions. As James Joll has pointed out, casualties had long-term psychological effects which could not be measured in demographic statistics:

The sense of loss had a profound effect on political attitudes. To the feeling that 'this must never be allowed to happen again' was added the belief that the elite of Europe had perished, and that sometimes the burden was almost too heavy for their successors to bear.[1]

The First World War did not end tidily when the fighting stopped on the western front in November 1918. Revolutions had already convulsed parts of the Hapsburg empire in the autumn and by the following spring they had broken out in Germany, Austria and Hungary. Even the more stable political systems of the victorious countries, such as France and Britain, seemed to be on the brink of revolution. Both nations vainly attempted to destroy the threat at source by intervening in support of the White armies in the Russian civil war. The Bolsheviks had antagonized their former allies not only by unilaterally quitting the struggle against Germany, but also by repudiating their predecessors' debts. Moreover, in accord with Lenin's belief that revolution could not survive in isolation, the Bolsheviks attempted to foment it by means of propaganda throughout the capitalist world. The Comintern or Third International was founded in Moscow in March 1919 to serve as an instrument of Russian foreign policy, the Soviet Union being far too weak and preoccupied with domestic problems to attempt to extend its influence by military aggression. Though the nations of western Europe remained obsessed with the 'Bolshevik threat' throughout the interwar period, they had more to fear from Russian manipulation of their indigenous communist parties than from the Red Army. In France, by the later 1920s, the high command was even more concerned with the struggle against Bolshevism than with the potential threat from a revived Germany. The French high command associated the Bolshevik revolution in Russia with defeatism and treason at home. When the French communist party was founded it became, in their eyes, the incarnation of the enemy within. Military men received an enduring impression that a segment of French public opinion, predominantly working-class but with strong support in intellectual circles, was guilty of permanent treason. The army's response was practical: surveillance of all communist suspects, disciplinary manoeuvres, transfer to special units, uncovering of regimental cells and an attempt to root out the distributors of political pamphlets.[2]

Movements of the radical right, known after their Italian exemplar as 'fascists', proliferated like an ugly rash in the aftermath of the First World War. While undoubtedly in part a response to the Bolsheviks, these movements were also rooted in the experience of the war itself. As Michael Howard perceptively explains, these movements provided a haven for hundreds of thousands of ex-combatants who felt betrayed and disorientated in the post-war world. These new populist organizations offered the glamour and security of military hierarchies; they also offered a violent route to power. Fascists regarded war as a praiseworthy activity:

So far from reacting against the militaristic nationalism which had been endemic in Europe before the war, they took it to a yet higher pitch of intensity.

Fascism proclaimed the virtues of submission to the leader; of dominance and obedience; and of racial supremacy. There was thus only a weak middle ground for the democratic status quo powers between, on the one hand, the revolutionary forces of the left, who believed the millennium would be achieved only through armed struggle within and between nations, and the reactionary right who regarded warfare as the necessary destiny of man.[3]

The Free Corps and similar paramilitary organizations which flourished in Germany in the early 1920s derived from the same background as the Italian fascist *squadristi*: embittered demobilized soldiers with a nostalgic memory of front-line comradeship and a determination to continue a violent career in peacetime. In Hermann Göring's phrase, the men who set the spirit and tone of the movement were 'fighters who could not become de-brutalized'. The Free Corps were even more violent than their fascist counterparts. In January 1919, at the behest of the socialist minister of the interior Gustav Noske, they crushed the communist rising in Berlin and murdered its leaders Karl Liebknecht and Rosa Luxemburg. This was a significant episode in the sell-out by the Weimar Republic's socialist leaders to the profoundly conservative army and its paramilitary auxiliaries. Other victims of the Free Corps, whom they accused of betraying the German people, included Mathias Erzberger, the centre party leader who had signed the armistice, and Walter Rathenau, the foreign minister who signed the Treaty of Rapallo with the Soviet Union in 1922. Free Corps members who were tried for these and similar crimes received only mild sentences.[4]

It was in Bavaria, and particularly in Munich, that these counter-revolutionary movements flourished and established their base. There, after the ephemeral Soviet republic of 1919, they strove to foster the mystical, irrational *völkisch* atmosphere which so sharply contrasted with socialist Berlin and liberal Weimar. Adolf Hitler found this milieu with its rabid anti-Semitism congenial when he joined the 'national socialist' workers' party in April 1919. In addition to anti-Semitism, many of these paramilitary groups were also fanatically anti-communist. But, as the historian of the Free Corps stresses, many of the Free Corps factions were not opposed to communism on ideological grounds; it was simply that the 'Red Peril' gave them an excuse to fight. Indeed many of them admired communist extremism because it attacked what they most hated: liberalism, parliamentary democracy and 'the smug complacency of the *bürgerlich* mentality'. What they found repugnant in communism was its materialism (in contrast to their own Teutonic mysticism) and its internationalism which clashed with their faith in the future of Germany and a German domination of Europe. The Free Corps made an important negative contribution to the Nazis' eventual advent to power by doing even more than the extreme left to undermine the Weimar Republic; their positive contribution was their legacy of that pitiless exaltation of power and brutality of spirit which characterized the Third Reich.[5]

The Free Corps was only the most extreme and sinister manifestation of the ex-servicemen's organizations and associations which strove to preserve the comradeship and other virtues of the front-line combatants. Thus Old Comrades' Associations, *Ligues d'Anciens Combattants*, *Front Kämpferverbände* and their equivalents flourished in most of the former belligerent nations. For many individuals such as R. H. Tawney, Guy Chapman and Henri Barbusse, there was nothing sinister in their pride and nostalgia for the most intense experience in their lives; indeed genuine sympathy for *all* front-line combatants bred in such men an enduring internationalism. Again several organizations like the British Legion were founded for non-political social and charitable purposes. Elsewhere, the paramilitary forces of demobilization were followed by the more organized paramilitary of the depression years such as the German *Stahlhelm* and the French *Croix de Feu* which constituted powerful pressure groups of the antiparliamentary right. So as Alfred Vagts put it:

The road to power for the totalitarian movements was blazed by paramilitary formations, to which governments conceded their near-monopoly of uniform-wearing willingly enough. Fighting street and beer-hall battles, murdering opponents, applying

138

violence and threatening more, they lamed much of the opposition.[6]

Serving officers turned a blind eye, condoned and even actively encouraged these disruptive anticonstitutional organizations.

The higher leadership and staff work in the First World War provoked bitter criticism in the immediate aftermath of the conflict and increasingly as the years went by until it has become an unshakeable myth in the popular mind. But while there was certainly much cause for complaint, little of the criticism was based on a sympathetic or informed understanding of the commanders' problems. Retrospective anger and disenchantment was also exacerbated by the profoundly disappointing results – heavy unemployment, soaring inflation, strikes, political instability – which contrasted so sharply with the rash wartime promises of politicians. Nevertheless, just or unjust, the criticism heaped upon military leadership – as well as on war itself as an instrument of policy was an influential phenomenon of the 1920s.

Antimilitarism was most vividly and poignantly manifest in the flood of war literature – poetry, memoirs and fiction – most of it produced by junior officers who had first-hand experience of the tactical blunders and appalling suffering in the front line. Wilfred Owen, Siegfried Sassoon and other British war poets concentrated on the suffering of all front soldiers; Henri Barbusse's *Under Fire* (first published during the war) and Erich Maria Remarque's *All Quiet on the Western Front* broadened the scope of their attack to include the barbarization of ordinary life and values; and C. S. Forester's *The General* was merely the most brilliant of numerous savage indictments of the high command. Bernard Newman in *The Cavalry Went Through* encouraged the dubious popular belief that less 'hide-bound' leaders, such as the Australian Jewish engineer Monash, would have had the ingenuity and imagination to break the trench stalemate. Recently scholars have pointed out that some of the best-known 'antimilitary' memoirs, such as Robert Graves's *Goodbye to All That* and Edmund Blunden's *Undertones of War*, are by no means entirely critical of military *mores*, and it is interesting that several of the authors, including Owen, Graves and most notably Sassoon, were efficient, steadfast and zealous in performing their duties. Nevertheless these qualifications do not appear to have influenced the book-reading public who apparently believed the charges of 'what amounted to mass murder by professional stupidity'. In Professor D. C. Watt's phrase, for the middle-class intellectuals and consumers of this war literature, 'the losses of the war represented the last crime the military elites were to be allowed to perpetrate upon the ordinary people of Europe'.[7] There is scope for fascinating research on publishing fashions respecting war literature in the 1920s (Graves admitted that he had deliberately slanted his memoirs to appeal to the antimilitary mood of the day), sales of different types of books, and above all its influence in shaping as distinct from merely reflecting contemporary views. A special non-fiction case study might be that of Captain Basil Liddell Hart, a pioneering military theorist, respected journalist and early historian of the war and its military leaders. Liddell Hart's attitude traversed the whole spectrum from unqualified, ecstatic praise of the high command and staff *during* the war, through growing but still restrained criticism in the 1920s, to a bitter indictment in the 1930s. It is clear from reviews, and from his enormous correspondence files, that Liddell Hart's criticisms of Sir Douglas Haig and the military establishment met with widespread approval, but it is equally understandable that such writing (and others such as Major-General J. F. C. Fuller were far less restrained) would alienate a later generation of serving officers.[8]

Alienation is a term that might be applied more generally to the military hierarchies and general staffs in the interwar period; indeed it provides a major theme in D. C. Watt's stimulating study, *Too Serious a Business*. By one of the ironies of the post-war settlement, the defeated German army was limited to 100,000 long-service volunteers, thereby relieving it of many of the problems that beset the victorious but unpopular British and French armies. Both the latter, for example, found it difficult to secure sufficient volunteers for their regular cadres even in periods of high unemployment. Both armies permitted young officers promoted to high rank during the First World War to remain in service well into the 1930s, thus creating a promotion block which caused many able but frustrated juniors to retire prematurely. Poor pay, petty restrictions and falling grants for training and equipment also caused a profound malaise. In addition French middle-class officers were especially hard hit by the inflation of the early 1920s which caused profound uneasiness and discouragement. Even the war minister Painlevé admitted in 1926 that the position was serious. Many officers' wives took menial jobs to supplement their husbands' earnings, and officers themselves took to 'moonlighting'; one was reported to be wrapping parcels in a department store and another driving a taxi in the night hours. Whether we now feel much sympathy for such hardship and loss of status is not the point; it contributed to a turning inwards and an adoption of extreme political views which would have serious repercussions in the 1930s.[9]

The tendency for the military establishment to distance itself from civilian culture and values was much more pronounced in the Weimar Republic where the German army, under the guidance of generals Groener and von Seeckt created, in the well-worn phrase, 'a state within the state'. The German officer corps, denying the reality of defeat in 1918 and blaming the humiliation of the Versailles Treaty on the majority parties of the left, created the impression that its loyalty was owed to a mystical ideal of the German state, not to Weimar. Being above political parties (*Überparteilichkeit*) did not prevent von Seeckt and his successors, von Heye, von Hammerstein, and also Groener (as army minister) from intervening in politics to protect the army's interests from the antimilitarist left. In general the officer corps welcomed the rise of Nazism with its emphasis on over-throwing the Versailles *Diktat* and rebuilding the nation and the army. They were slow to realize that the Nazis might insidiously threaten the army's very existence to an extent that the overt opposition of the left never could. Many young officers sympathized with Nazi attacks on the disintegrating Weimar regime between 1930 and 1932, a few going so far as to spread Nazi propaganda. Finally, von Schleicher sought to make the Nazis into the political instrument of an army dictatorship but was cunningly outmanoeuvred by Hitler. Gradually, in the period 1933–8, the army's traditions and independence were progressively and subtly undermined until it became a more or less willing instrument of Hitler's megalomaniac ambitions.

In Italy the army proved far too weak to prevent the rise of fascism. Amidst the disappointments and defeats of the peace settlement the officer corps suffered a collapse of prestige and self-confidence. Rapid demobilization created a large pool of unemployed officers and even a substantial number of generals were impoverished. Not surprisingly the Italian military leadership became obsessed with status and appearances. Mussolini's fascist forces exploited this military discontent as part of their campaign to discredit parliamentary government. The officer corps proclaimed its loyalty to the crown rather than the state and Mussolini prudently avoided any direct challenge to the crown. General Diaz assured Victor Emmanuel that the army would defend Rome despite its great sympathy for fascism, but hinted that it would be better if the army's loyalty was not put to the test. In the event the fascist march on Rome was not opposed; indeed several prominent generals took part in it. When Mussolini gained power, generals like Diaz who had played their cards right were rewarded, while others who had opposed him, such as Badoglio, suffered professional eclipse or even exile.[10]

It is all too easy in retrospect to see that the forces making for internal and international disorder and disintegration presaging another world war were far more powerful than the flimsy structures erected after 1918 to secure peace, disarmament and a balance of power. Yet the brief period of optimism – even euphoria – in the mid- and later 1920s seemed at the time to herald a genuine return to peace. Even without the participation of the United States, the League of Nations, established by the Versailles Treaty, seemed to many idealists to be a reliable agency for maintaining peace. What few but cynical soldiers perceived was that the League was not necessarily an unsound idea, but that its promise of 'collective security' required the sword as well as words if it was to check aggression.

Germany's enforced disarmament, limiting her to the smallest forces necessary to maintain internal order and with no offensive capability, and the rapid disbandment of the huge victorious armies of 1918 for social and financial reasons, together fostered an unrealistic hope in universal and complete disarmament. Much of the passionate idealism devoted to this policy throughout the 1920s and well into the 1930s rested on the false assumption that armaments themselves (their enormous sales deliberately boosted by cynical 'merchants of death', the great armaments firms) had actually caused the First World War. Abolish offensive weapons such as tanks, guns and aeroplanes and you render a major war impossible. It all seemed so obvious and so reasonable.

Hopes for disarmament were boosted by the significant measure of arms control, involving the dismantling of numerous old warships, embodied in the Washington Naval Treaty of 1922. The leading naval powers agreed upon the following ratios for capital ships: the United States and Britain 5, to Japan's 3, to 1.6 for France and Italy. Subsequently at the London Conference of 1930 the American and

British ratio *vis-à-vis* Japan was adjusted in the latter's favour to read 10 to 7. France and Italy refused to accept this decision. While these treaties undoubtedly averted a renewed naval race like that of the 1900s, their limitations were obvious. Financial and economic pressures rather than disinterested concern for disarmament had been their chief inspiration, and even then the naval staffs concerned were unhappy at the outcome. Submarines – the deadliest naval instrument of the First World War – were excluded. Finally, Germany was not represented but would sooner rather than later have to be readmitted to the ranks of the naval powers.

In some respects the Locarno Treaty of 1925, which guaranteed the existing frontiers of western Europe on the part of all the states directly involved, seemed to offer more tangible hopes of peace and stability. Germany was readmitted to the club of civilized nations and French fears of her resurgence seemed to be allayed, particularly as Britain's participation provided the apparent reassurance of her military commitment which France had urgently needed since America's withdrawal in 1919. Aristide Briand, the French foreign minister, cultivated the 'spirit of Locarno' and three years later crowned his pacific endeavours with the Kellogg-Briand Pact whose signatories 'condemned recourse to war for the solution of international controversies and renounced it as an instrument of national policy in their relations with one another'. These impressive phrases proved valueless when put to the test. Unfortunately even the more specific Locarno Treaty was little more than 'a solemn Shibboleth', since the triggering concept of 'aggression' was left undefined and military terms of enforcement were never agreed. Britain's military commitment to the continent was more apparent than real; in practice Germany's inclusion gave Britain a pretext to evade any binding military arrangements with France.[11]

Although seemingly illogical, the nominal success in outlawing war did not prevent a continuing attempt through most of the interwar period to impose further restraints and limitations on its conduct. For the most part it was a matter of updating and extending the scope of the pre-1914 conventions. One notable success was achieved with the 1925 Geneva Protocol on gas warfare, for, contrary to general expectation, it was not in fact employed as a military weapon in the Second World War (though earlier it had been used by the Italians in Abyssinia).

As we saw in the previous chapter, considerable progress had been made before and during the First World War in mitigating the horrors of the battlefield for combatants and wounded and improving the status of prisoners of war. But a far greater problem lay in extending restraints to the civil population in conditions approaching 'total war'. As the British naval staff grimly indicated in 1921:

> Nothing can be clearer than the fact that modern war resolves itself into an attempt to throttle the national life. Waged by the whole power of the nation, its ultimate object is to bring pressure on the mass of the enemy people, distressing them by every possible means so as to compel the enemy's government to submit to terms.[12]

Britain had come close to defeat in 1917 from the economic effects of unrestricted submarine warfare, so it was only natural that in all the interwar arms limitation conferences from Washington onwards she should advocate the complete abolition of the submarine. This proposal was rejected by France and other weaker naval powers so Britain had to settle for the restrictions embodied in the London Submarine Protocol of 1936. By the outbreak of the Second World War the Protocol had been ratified by forty states including the Soviet Union and all the Axis powers. The effect of this Protocol was to impose on submarines the same limitations in their conduct towards merchant shipping as applied to surface warships: merchantmen must be stopped and visited; they must not be attacked without warning and only then if they refused to halt; they must not be sunk unless full provision had been made for their passengers and crew. In the event unrestricted submarine warfare occurred even more rapidly than in the First World War. This was due broadly to the fact that no belligerent would in practice deny itself the use of what appeared a vital instrument of war; but more specifically to technical developments which put the submarine at a hopeless disadvantage if it attempted to observe the rules.[13]

Even more determined and persistent efforts were made in the interwar period to codify the laws of air warfare in an attempt to protect the civilian population from the ordeal of air bombardment as foreshadowed in the limited experience of the First World War. Numerous proposals were advanced under three broad headings: a corpus of rules designed to define the legitimate objects of air attack; proposals for the restriction of bombing to such specified areas as 'the battle zone'; and the delineation of geographical areas which contained no legitimate military targets and were therefore to be immune from air attack. A commission of international jurists meeting at The Hague in 1923 did draft a code of aerial warfare but it was never ratified. The basic stumbling block proved to be article 24 of their code which specified that 'aerial bombardment is legitimate only when directed at a military objective'. In conditions of total war even the jurists failed to agree on what targets could possibly be excluded. Similar problems prevented any agreement on safety areas for civilians or definition of the battle zone. J. M. Spaight, the British representative on the panel of jurists which framed the 1923 code of regulations, was obliged to admit, against his own passionate commitment to securing limitations:

> In air warfare, more than in its elder brethren of the land and sea, the heart and the conscience of the combatant are the guarantee for fair fighting not any rule formulated in a treaty or in a manual.

The British government continued almost to the eve of the Second World War a vain quest for almost any agreement to restrict the horrors of the aerial bombardment of cities which greatly influenced its views on defence. But as its professional advisers pointed out a few months before the Munich crisis, an international agreement would produce an unjustified sense of relief and relaxation of effort, since the totalitarian states would surely ignore any restriction which proved a handicap to them.[14]

The broad lessons of the war as regards military organization and doctrine differed considerably from country to country. In Russia there was a particularly difficult problem of reconciling communist ideology with military efficiency in the midst of revolution and civil war. Professional armies with their supposedly reactionary outlook were anathema to left-wing theorists who advocated a militia system with a minimum period of military training for the mass of workers and peasants. Distinctions of rank were to be played down if not abolished and officers elected by the men. Leon Trotsky, an admirable pragmatist in military matters, achieved a short-term compromise by enlisting a large number of ex-tsarist officers to provide the leadership of the workers' and peasants' Red Army. Although this compromise was bitterly opposed, it enabled the Bolsheviks to win the civil war in 1919 and take the offensive against

Poland in 1920 before being checked at the gates of Warsaw. By this time Russia's army had swollen to some 5½ million men but it was poorly trained and deficient in nearly every respect. Doctrinal wrangles continued, with Frunze briefly establishing his notion of a specifically Marxist military science and style of warfare which was proletarian, revolutionary and designed for the offensive. Trotsky's criticisms resulted in another compromise in 1924 in the shape of a large (42-division) territorial army composed of two-year conscripts alongside a 29-division force composed of five-year regulars. In the absence of any immediate threat to her survival in the later 1920s, Russia could give a high priority to basic education and indoctrination with less attention given to training: commissars were attached to all officers except a handful of civil war heroes such as Timoshenko.[15]

Britain demobilized her huge, conscript armies with remarkable speed after 1918 and at the same time largely dismantled her defence industries. Swingeing reductions in the budget of all three services followed the Geddes report in December 1921 (the so-called 'Geddes Axe') and in the disturbed economic conditions of the next decade further cuts were made every year. Moreover, once the war was over, both the strategic reasons for Britain's part in it and the many lessons to be drawn from her greatest effort ever in a continental campaign, were forgotten or perhaps brushed aside as inconvenient and too disturbing. While it was perfectly sensible – indeed unavoidable – that first priority should again, as before 1914, be given to protecting and 'policing' her worldwide empire which now reached its greatest extent, the military dimension of Britain's European interests was badly neglected. Under the terms of the cabinet's 'Ten Year Rule', which prevailed from 1919 to 1933, the services were advised to expect no major war in the next ten years and not to prepare an expeditionary force for such a purpose. All the services suffered during these 'locust years', but the army was arguably the 'Cinderella'; the Royal Navy's traditional roles of home defence and global projection of maritime power were confirmed, while the Royal Air Force, in addition to its important contribution to imperial policing, was regarded as a 'deterrent' to potential European aggressors.[16]

France emerged from the First World War nominally victorious but burdened by strategic insecurity, war-weariness and heavy losses – nearly 1½ million dead (approximately twice as many as Britain) and three million wounded. After a brief and futile attempt to coerce Germany into keeping up her reparations payments in 1923, French military doctrine became mainly defensive: her military heroes opted for Pétain's slogan at Verdun 'they shall not pass' rather than the 'on to Berlin' spirit of 1914. Most experts agreed that the main lesson was to prepare for a war of material involving the mobilization of all national manpower and resources. Maximum use must be made of machines (such as artillery, tanks and fixed defences) to minimize casualties. This doctrine contrasted sharply with the pre-1914 emphasis on moral factors and reliance on *élan*. As regards military organization, political pressure to reduce the length of conscript service after 1918 was so strong that the only issue was whether recruits should serve for eighteen months or a year. The latter was adopted in 1926, but even this did not satisfy the socialists, who demanded a militia system like the Swiss with only eight months' service. By 1928, even before the great complex of frontier defences named after the war minister, André Maginot, began to be constructed, France had placed her trust in a defence-oriented conscript army based on only twelve months' service and the need to mobilize reserves even for limited operations. Many military critics in the 1920s pointed out that the army was sacrificing its offensive capability on the dangerous assumption that an adversary would lack initiative and move slowly. It was also argued that dynamism was being engulfed by the hazy idea of 'war potential'. But until Colonel de Gaulle developed his ideas concerning specialized armoured forces, these criticisms were depressingly negative.[17]

As we have seen, the *Reichswehr*'s organization and doctrine were largely determined by the restrictions imposed by the Versailles Treaty. With a maximum total of 100,000 troops composed of twelve-year volunteers, General Groener and his successors could select first-class soldiers and NCOs designed to form a pool of potential officers. Hence the remarkable position by 1922 when a mere 20,000 privates were under training by over 75,000 NCOs. The *Reichswehr* leadership, though formally denied a general staff or *Kriegsakademie*, revived the great tradition of military professionalism with the emphasis on coordination of the various arms, communications and mobility. The civil-military turmoil of the immediate post-war years caused the *Reichswehr* commanders to inculcate strict military obedience in the interests of corporate self-preservation. It must be stressed, however, that the *Reichswehr* remained weak throughout the life of the Weimar

Republic: it could certainly not have withstood a French attack, nor even have confronted a Polish invasion with any confidence. Making a virtue of necessity, von Seeckt and his colleagues stressed the need for mobile defence, and used the secret testing facilities in Russia to try out the equipment and tactics which would receive impetus and encouragement when Hitler came to power.[18]

Beyond the issues of military organization and doctrine what were the broader lessons of the First World War regarding national preparedness for a future conflict? In France the concept of the nation in arms received a broader interpretation by a senate committee, namely 'the nation on a war footing', i.e., workers in industry and agriculture would play an equally vital part in the war effort. As the official army doctrine of 1921 put it, 'It is now the people as a whole which wages war, which suffers from it . . .' A reorganization bill to establish the framework for a complete war economy and allocation of national resources was presented to the senate in 1927 but created so much party controversy that it did not become law for a further eleven years. Thus France in effect got the worst of both worlds: her forces became increasingly unprepared to mount a speedy offensive in a crisis, while reliance was placed on a theory of total mobilization for war which had not been translated into practice. The faults of the actual system adopted, i.e., reliance on fixed fortifications to allow time for the slow mobilization of reserves and the lack of a mechanized striking force, became plain from the Rhineland crisis of March 1936 onwards. But even had the national mobilization of 1939–40 fared better it would still have involved France in a long war of attrition resembling that of 1914–18.[19]

French socialists feared that an army based on anything but a militia system with minimal training would play into the hands of the militarists, while the communists went further in attacking the very concept of the nation in arms as a capitalist, chauvinist fraud.

There was much more cause for apprehension on this charge in Germany where the 'total war' notions of General Ludendorff and others really did smack of militarism. For example, Alfred Rosenberg, the mythologist of Nazism, wrote that:

It is a mark of the German style of life that no German wants nowadays to feel himself a private person . . . That is the secret explanation of why present-day Germany is uniformed and marching in columns.

Under Hitler's Four Year Plan of 1936 workers in key industries were subjected to almost military discipline and restrictions. Factories and barracks were to be run on similar lines. Desirable 'soldier products' had already been guaranteed through the militarization of education almost from the infant stage. Eventually, in the Third Reich, education and learning at all levels were subject to military interference or control.

In Italy there was an enormous gulf between fascist rhetoric and real preparedness for war. There was nothing resembling a combined chiefs of staff organization or a ministry of defence to mitigate the independence of the three services and their wasteful competitiveness. Mussolini monopolized the trappings of military authority but lacked both expertise and a proper staff. Even by 1939 virtually no plans had been made to create a war industry. Mussolini took little notice of the warnings of General Pariani, the chief of the Italian army staff, and Count Ciano the foreign minister, with the result that the Italian forces' deficiencies on the outbreak of war came as a total surprise. Mussolini was obliged to keep Italy on the sidelines until June 1940.[20]

Distinction must be made however between political schemes for total use of manpower resources in war, and the more professional inferences drawn from the experience of the First World War by the general staffs.

Revulsion against the huge casualty lists together with rapid technical innovation suggested that less emphasis should in future be placed on vast but ill-trained and unmanoeuvrable infantry masses ('bayonets' in the cold military term) and more on highly skilled military technicians operating in small groups, as already occurred in aeroplanes, tanks and submarines. Large conscript forces would still be needed but a much higher proportion would go into supply and maintenance; in repairing and maintaining vehicles, aircraft and communications systems, in keeping open lines of communication, in manning depots, hospitals and headquarters. Ensuring in short that 'the whole drab mass was administered, fed and paid'. By and large the Second World War in Europe was to follow this pattern, particularly in the early years while there were still reserves of manpower to select from, though in the Soviet Union the bulk of the infantry units with their small and primitive supply systems still resembled the 'mass armies' of 1914–18.[21]

Before examining the main strategic doctrines which evolved during the interwar period it is important to make it clear that a particular notion of future war dominated the public consciousness; namely that conflict would begin suddenly – perhaps even without a declaration of war – with an all-out air attack on defenceless cities. This was a legacy of the limited experience of so-called strategic bombing in the First World War magnified by fertile imaginations and by extrapolation from the 1914–18 statistics to future estimates based on increased numbers and bombloads of aircraft. Such fears were widely shared by politicians, air experts and writers of all kinds long before the creation of the *Luftwaffe* in the 1930s. In reality no air force was capable of sustained and effective long-range bombing against a major power in the 1920s, probably not even by 1939.[22]

The obsession with air attack was particularly intense in Britain because the advent of the bombing aeroplane and airship signified the end of centuries of insular security. Liddell Hart, in 1925 the newly appointed military correspondent of the *Daily Telegraph*, accurately reflected popular expectations and anxieties in his book, *Paris or the Future of War*. Assuming one side possessed a superior air force, he wrote, and provided the blow was swift and powerful:

there is no reason why within a few hours, or at most days . . . the nerve system of the country inferior in air power should not be paralysed . . .

Imagine for a moment London, Manchester, Birmingham, and half a dozen other great centres simultaneously attacked, the business localities and Fleet Street wrecked, Whitehall a heap of ruins, the slum districts maddened into the impulse to break loose and maraud, the railways cut, factories destroyed. Would not the general will to resist vanish, and what use would be the still determined fractions of the nation, without organization and central direction?

'Victory in the air', he added, 'will lie with whichever side first gains the moral objective.' He went so far as to suggest that ultimately the air would be the sole medium of future warfare.

But what if two or more warring nations possessed equal air power and resolution? Here again Liddell Hart was in tune with the thinking of the day in believing it would result in deterrence for fear of instant retaliation. Unlike most writers on the subject who envisaged gas as a probable and horrific ingredient in aerial bombing, Liddell Hart, who had been gassed himself on the Somme, saw gas as the 'salvation of civilization' because non-lethal forms could achieve paralysis without mass killing or destruction.[23] Stanley Baldwin also expected gas to be used, but his conclusion was wholly pessimistic. In a speech to the Classical Association in 1927 he said:

Who in Europe does not know that one more war in the west and the civilization of the ages will fall with as great a shock as that of Rome?

This predated by five years his gloomy prediction that 'the bomber will always get through' with the implication that ordinary people would simply have to endure while our bombers pounded enemy civilians. Similarly Lord Grey in the final reflections in his memoirs envisaged future war as 'the destruction by chemical agencies, of the crowded centres of population; it will mean physical, moral and economic ruin'. There is conclusive evidence from *Hansard* and other sources that these fears were widely shared in British political circles.[24]

The terrors of air warfare, with emphasis on gas and incendiary attacks on cities, also provided one of the main themes in interwar military fiction. As I. F. Clarke has pointed out, there was a marked shift of interest from the pre-1914 preoccupation with who will win the 'Great War' of some day in the near future; now the message was that war had become so terrible that there would be no winners. The rise of the Nazis caused a sudden increase in the flow of war fiction, the bulk of it focused on air attack and with titles such as *The Gas War of 1940, The Poison War, The Black Death, Menace, Empty Victory, Invasion From the Air, War Upon Women, Air Reprisal, The Shape of Things to Come* and *What Happened to the Corbetts*.[25] It would be impossible to prove that war fiction actually determined official policy, but there can be no doubt that some governments, notably those of Britain and France, were greatly influenced in their ordering of priorities in defence by their own and their public's obsession with air attack.

The central dilemma of strategic bombing theory has been implicit in the foregoing discussion. On the one hand the doctrine promised to avoid a repetition of a long static siege war of attrition by striking decisively at the enemy's nerve centre or, better still, to avoid war altogether through mutual deterrence. On the other hand, to the vast majority of civilians who expected to be defenceless victims, it threatened devastation and suffering unprecedented since the wars of religion.

The main tenets of the doctrine, associated with the Italian theorist Giulio Douhet but having strong independent roots in the Royal Air Force and with individual advocates elsewhere in the United States, France and Germany, can quickly be summarized. They comprised: belief in the superiority of autonomous air forces and their ability to deal a rapid knock-out blow; the importance of gaining command of the air and destroying the enemy's air forces – on the ground or in battle; the efficacy of the psychological blow against civilian morale as well as destruction of military targets; and the inherent superiority of the offensive. There were of course disagreements among the theorists on such aspects as the initial objective, how to gain command of the air and the feasibility of an all-purpose aircraft, but on the broad theme of strategic bombing as a war-winning instrument there was agreement – at least among most airmen and their supporters, though not in the older services. Critics from the latter indicated weaknesses at the time which were to be confirmed by later experience in war. First, many technical and tactical problems were underrated or simply ignored. Could bombers cover long distances and locate precise targets by day, let alone night? If so could they hit them and with what effect given the small bomb-loads available? Would fighter aircraft and ground defences improve and if so how was the unprotected bomber to survive? What would happen if both sides followed the same strategy and reached stalemate after a few weeks? What would be happening with the other forces and on other fronts?

Secondly the psychological assumptions which loomed so large in the doctrine – as in Liddell Hart's *Paris* – were never objectively analysed. Would city populations panic on a large scale or would they endure what was unavoidable? If their anger was aroused would it be directed at their own governments or at the enemy? If it *was* against the former, why assume that governments would be compelled to sue for peace?

Thirdly, on the political plane, strategic bombing was an extremely aggressive doctrine which depended on relentless and ruthless prosecution for success. Was it likely that democratic, status quo nations like Britain, France and the United States would be willing to implement such a strategy in a political crisis or on the outbreak of war? In fact it became very clear in the 1930s that the British (and French) governments would go to almost any lengths rather than become involved in an air slugging match. In contrast to air staff doctrine, Chamberlain declared in the House of Commons in 1938 that Britain would only bomb purely military objectives, and even then would take care to avoid civilian casualties. Ironically, Britain was herself deterred from pursuing the bombing strategy on which the RAF had set such store; whereas the *Luftwaffe*, which was assumed to be capable of destroying Paris or London, had in fact given priority to tactical cooperation with ground forces and was incapable of dealing a knock-out blow in 1939 – or even when operating from across the Channel in 1940. Yet the *Luftwaffe*, by reason of Nazi propaganda and allied fears, 'became one of the most effective weapons of persuasion in the arsenal of the Third Reich'.[26]

In land warfare military thinkers who sought to restore mobility to the battlefield, minimize casualties and give a decisive advantage to quality over quantity, found a solution in the tank and in armoured formations generally. Despite financial and other restrictions, steady progress was made in the 1920s in tank designs and in experimental exercises with other arms. But it was not until the early 1930s that wholly mechanized tank brigades were formed with all units able to communicate by wireless. Close cooperation with aircraft came even later. Britain, who had first introduced the tank into battle in September 1916, continued to blaze the trail through the 1920s thanks to the writings of Fuller, Liddell Hart, Broad and others, and with considerable support from the War Office. But other armies, including the French and Russian, displayed great interest in tanks and were roughly on par with Britain in experimental formations by 1930. In Germany, a few junior officers like Guderian eagerly studied the literature on mechanization, but up to 1933 the *Reichswehr* could only gain practical experience in Russia.

Even before the end of the First World War, and notably in his visionary 'Plan 1919', Colonel J. F. C. Fuller advocated the independent use of tanks (i.e., not constrained to supporting the infantry) and the eventual development of tank armies with wholly mechanized supporting arms. Even at this early stage (1918), Fuller devoted considerable space to the supporting duties of aircraft, including the imaginative notion of carrying tank brigade commanders above their sectors. Fuller's ideal was that small tank armies would be able to win decisive victories comparable to classical battles like Issus and Arbela; the secret would be to destroy the command structure, not after the enemy's personnel had been disorganized but before it had been attacked. His and Liddell Hart's idea of paralysing the enemy's command centre by surprise attack and deep penetration into the rear areas seemed far-fetched to more conservative soldiers but it was brilliantly exemplified by the Panzers' success in France in May 1940.[27]

Charles de Gaulle came late on the scene of armoured theory and his recommendations were more political and less technically specific than those of the British or German tank pioneers. Nevertheless he is the outstanding exponent of quality over quantity. His *armée de métier*, tragically rejected by French soldiers and politicians alike, by relying on professional training and employing elite armoured formations, was designed to relegate the nation in arms to oblivion and prevent France from engaging in a total war. With hindsight we can see that his proposal if adopted might well have saved France from humiliating defeat in 1940.[28]

In the second half of the 1930s several countries (Germany, Britain, France and Russia) were producing armoured divisions but everywhere within the framework of traditional establishments of infantry, artillery and cavalry. Germany led the way with six Panzer divisions ready in September 1939, but behind her spearhead formations the bulk of her transport was still horse-drawn. In fact Germany actually used more horses for military purposes in the Second World War than in the First. Britain alone went to war with all her units mechanized or motorized, but then hers was a comparatively small and mainly regular army. Also, although Hitler and influential senior German generals such as Blomberg and Reichenau supported Panzer fanatics like Guderian, there were also many conservatives who favoured the dilution of the armoured divisions. Recently there has been much controversy over the precise meaning of *blitzkrieg* both as a concept and in practice. This question will be examined later on in the chapter but, whatever term is used, no one disputes that Germany won the opening campaigns of the Second World War by the skilful use of armoured formations with close tactical air support.

While it is unjust to describe France's interwar defence policy as wholly defensive and passive, her strategic outlook certainly yielded the initiative to the enemy, while the construction of the Maginot

Line in the early 1930s did signify her heavy reliance on fixed fortifications in the first phase of a future war. The main sections of the defences stretched from Montmédy on the French-Luxembourg frontier to Teting west of the Saar gap, whence a light line of defences extended to Wittring. The Maginot Line proper resumed from Wittring to Lauterburg on the Rhine. In all some 200 miles of France's eastern frontiers had been fortified, perhaps one-third of the distance between Dunkirk and Lauterburg.

To a large extent the Maginot Line fulfilled its purpose and should not be held directly responsible for France's defeat. By protecting the most vulnerable sectors of the Franco-German frontier it provided a secure *couverture* behind which French reservists could assemble and become acclimatized. More important, it virtually forced the Germans to attack through the narrow Aachen gap and across Belgium where it should not have been too difficult to halt them. Indeed the German general staff and most senior commanders were pessimistic about the chances of a clear-cut victory, even after the defeat of Poland. Finally, the Maginot Line did prove impregnable to frontal attack though its garrison was eventually overrun from the rear. Having constructed a most impressive shield, the French high command failed to create 'a sword' in the form of a concentrated armoured force centrally placed for counterattack. The weakness of France's position was made painfully clear in 1936 when Germany reoccupied the Rhineland unopposed and Belgium declared her neutrality. Thereafter there was ample warning that the German forces were being prepared for mobile offensive operations, but no radical revision of French plans was ever seriously considered. British and French experts argued that the defensive was so inherently superior at this time that an aggressor would be taking unacceptable risks. This proved an expensive error as regards not only Germany but also Japan.[29]

One other strategic theory must be mentioned; namely the traditional employment of maritime forces to gain 'command of the sea' in order to control lines of communication. The benefits such control conferred included home defence against invasion, ability to conduct one's own forces overseas and, not least important, to impose a blockade. Since Anglo-French strategists calculated that Germany's dependence on imported raw materials was her Achilles heel, a naval blockade featured prominently in their war plans. Germany's naval forces were too small to pose a major threat in the

1930s, and in any case it was assumed that technical developments since 1918 had put a severe handicap on the effectiveness of submarines. The most serious area of controversy concerned the impact of shore-based and sea-based aircraft on wartime operations. Here Germany and Japan were soon to show that Britain and the United States had been complacent and negligent.[30]

The foregoing survey of the main strategic concepts should undermine the popular caricature of reactionary officer corps mindlessly opposed to technical and tactical innovation. In addition to the handful of well-known names such as Mountbatten, Slessor, Dowding, Montgomery, Fuller, Guderian and de Gaulle, a glance at the books and service journals of the period will show that a great many officers were thinking seriously about the future of their arms. True, some of the best-known innovators and prophets were not occupying responsible positions whereas many who were, such as Gamelin and Weygand, Deverell and Gort, Beck and Brauchitsch, were ambivalent in their advice to politicians and genuinely uncertain about the nature of future operations.

As Vagts perceived, with the exception of Japan, traditional militarism was everywhere on the wane as the Second World War approached. None of the general staffs were eager for war, as some had been before 1914; nor was there any of that 'ready to the last button' confidence of earlier periods. In some respects the professionals knew too much about the nature of war, in others not enough. The top commanders, even in the Axis countries, were hesitant and even pessimistic. Beyond all the operational unknowns, senior staff officers such as Beck were much more aware than their predecessors of 1914, such as Schlieffen, of the wider economic problems in sustaining total war.[31]

Civil-military relations are by their very nature – the attempt to reconcile strategic demands with what the economy and the electorate can support – subject to friction. In most countries in the interwar period the strain was apt to be intense for two obvious reasons: the legacy of the bitterness left by the conflict of soldiers and statesmen in the First World War; and the long economic depression which necessitated draconian cuts in the service budgets when purely strategic considerations demanded substantial increases.

Allowing for personality clashes and spells of bitter interservice rivalry, British civil-military relations were placed on a much more harmonious footing after 1918 due mainly to improvements in the institutional framework within which defence decisions were made. The Committee of Imperial Defence was revived and its scope greatly extended through a plethora of sub-committees, the most notable being the Chiefs of Staff, established in 1923. In the COS committee the service chiefs developed (some critics would say overdeveloped) the habit of compromise and consensus in providing advice for their political masters. At the CID itself, politicians and service spokesmen learned a great deal about each other's responsibilities as they strove to put national defence issues above party and separate service interests. Officers who served on the CID secretariat or graduated from the newly established Imperial Defence College, acquired wider experience which stood them in good stead in the Second World War. Closer association did not necessarily of course endear politicians to service leaders or vice versa. Mutual suspicion between 'frocks' and 'brasshats', if not unknown then or later, was at least based on more real knowledge than the prejudices and ignorance that prevailed before 1914.

Elsewhere relations were not so good. Vagts cites some amusing and some depressing examples. The Polish dictator Marshal Pilsudski made and unmade ministers without interrupting his game of solitaire. General Balbo returned from the war loathing politicians for betraying soldiers and reducing Italy to a shameful peace; he supported the fascist slogan of 'destroy everything' to begin again from the foundations. In Germany, General von Reichenau declared in 1935 that, under fascism, 'the size of the armed forces is independent of parliament or majority decision' – a great relief. In France there was close agreement at the top between successive governments and senior military advisers on the broad outline of national defence policy. Friction resulted, in the Rhineland and later crises, from each trying to 'pass the buck' to the other for their collective irresolution. As de la Gorce fairly concludes, the politicians were chiefly to blame for leaning so heavily on the soldiers for advice on political matters rather than giving them clear orders. Among the French officer corps generally there was increasing disquiet about governments' failure to deal with the communist 'enemy within' and a latent contempt for liberal democracy which was to surface in June 1940.[32]

With the disappearance of traditional militarists like Conrad, Schlieffen and Ludendorff, there emerged in several totalitarian countries the new phenomenon of the 'civilian militarist' or 'militarist in mufti'. These civilian rulers shared the soldiers' contempt for parliaments, political parties, trade unions, the free press and diplomacy. Mussolini, the archetypal civilian militarist, took over all three defence ministries himself but gave no long-term directives to his chiefs of staff. He remained in profound ignorance of Italy's unpreparedness for war, 'convinced by his own rhetoric that all was well with the forces of the inheritor of the mantle of Pompey and Caesar'.[33]

In the 1930s Mussolini was eclipsed by the supreme civilian militarist, Adolf Hitler. Hitler allowed the armed services to retain their professional independence until the later 1930s but then moved gradually and insidiously to undermine their authority until he eventually reduced the general staff and army headquarters to mere technical duties and usurped their responsibilities for decision and command in his own person. From the outset Hitler dominated every facet of German foreign and domestic policy; under his orders rearmament went ahead at a breakneck pace; and his aggressive, expansionist and racist ideology was given full rein. The majority of senior officers readily accepted these policies – though some failed to grasp their dangerous implications – and many of those who did protest or drag their feet were only really alarmed at the tempo of the build-up for war, not at the prospect of war itself.[34]

There is no need here to describe in detail the rapid deterioration in international relations and the prospects of lasting peace after the brief period of optimism at the end of the 1920s. The Wall Street Crash of 1929 followed by the European financial crisis in the next two years caused unemployment figures to soar, which in turn enhanced the appeal of extreme parties on the left and on the right. Japan's military intervention in Manchuria provided the first real test for the League of Nations and revealed its impotence. The Nazis' advent to power in January 1933, though technically legal, caused destabilization. In the autumn Germany walked out of the Geneva disarmament conference, effectively ending its usefulness, and was soon blatantly rearming in defiance of the Versailles Treaty. The Abyssinian crisis of 1935–6 further underlined the League of Nations' inability to stop aggression, but had several other serious consequences: it caused a rift in Anglo-French relations; ruined the short-lived Franco-Italian cooperation under the Stresa Pact; and drove a reluctant Mussolini towards alliance with Hitler. It was probably the last time that Britain and France, by a united show of strength, could have stopped aggression without a general war. But Prime Minister Stanley Baldwin's preoccupation throughout the crisis was to avoid war. He believed that French mobilization would have led to riots, the British Mediterranean fleet would have been in danger from air attack, and Italian bombers could get to London. He also had Germany in mind. As he told Thomas Jones, 'Had we gone to war our anti-aircraft munitions would have been exhausted in a week. We have hardly got any armaments firms left.'[35]

The international significance of the Spanish civil war (1936–9) seemed much greater at the time than it does to us because it was quickly overshadowed by the Second World War. It provided a testing ground for German and Italian air and ground forces on the fascist side, and to a lesser extent for Soviet military aid to the republicans. Many contemporary commentators viewed the war as a genuine conflict of ideologies and as tantamount to the start of the Second World War. It was widely but wrongly assumed that the victorious General Franco would combine with Mussolini and Hitler to shut Britain out of the Mediterranean and put a stranglehold on France. The war also showed that thousands of young men would volunteer to fight in a foreign country for what they believed to be a just cause.

The Spanish civil war also contributed to the hardening of mutually antagonistic alliances: the bellicose powers, Germany, Italy and Japan against the peace-at-almost-any-price powers, Britain and France. British and French political leaders displayed a very similar reluctance to establish a ministry of supply or an armaments ministry respectively – both test cases of serious organization for war. Indeed Daladier and Neville Chamberlain were at one in clinging to the idea that peace was the norm. The United States and the Soviet Union were also 'peace-loving' rather than bellicose powers although for very different reasons: the former because of geographical immunity from invasion, unwillingness to make sacrifices in Europe, and democratic belief in peaceful progress; the latter because it was in domestic turmoil and feared attack from east and west.

These different strategic positions, political traditions and current problems caused significant variations in the pattern of rearmament. Britain, for example, reluctantly began to rearm in a modest way in 1935 in response to its interpretation of Hitler's armaments policy. For understandable reasons treasury influence was prominent if not paramount. So far as possible budgets must be balanced and risk of renewed inflation avoided. Overseas credit must be jealously husbanded because it was held to be vital to a prolonged war effort. Economic and financial stability and access to essential war materials were thought to be Britain's winning card, the so-called 'fourth arm of defence'. Other tenets, such as the treasury's profound distaste for public borrowing, were of dubious validity. So also was a predominantly conservative government's reluctance to disturb big business interests on the one hand or take the trade union leaders into its confidence on the other.

In truth, Britain's central dilemma was strictly insoluble; she was a declining economic power with worldwide responsibilities faced by three potential enemies in Germany, Japan and Italy. She could not afford to rearm simultaneously against all three but nor was there any 'all purpose' rearmament programme which would be equally valid against all three or any permutation of them. A strong home-defence air force, for example, was useless against Japan or Italy, while a Far Eastern fleet would be vulnerable without powerful air cover. Britain's solution, making the best of a bad job, was essentially to give priority to the German threat relying on naval supremacy in home waters and a deterrent air force, while only a modest army was organized as the contribution to a continental alliance. It is only too easy to criticize Britain's 'appeasement' diplomacy and rearmament programme but once the latter got fully underway in 1938–9 it scored some remarkable successes in comparison with Germany, for example in aircraft production. It must be admitted however that the financial pessimists were also correct in that without Lend-Lease and subsequent American intervention Britain could not have sustained her war effort for over five years.[36]

By 1930 the Soviet armed forces seemed to have got over the confusion and ceaseless reorganization caused by ideological controversies. A compromise 'middle way' doctrine had evolved encompassing mass armies and preparation for total war; an offensive spirit was to be developed but through manoeuvre on a broad front rather than any notion of *blitzkrieg*. Manpower was not a major problem: Russia maintained a regular army of just over one million men, which could be increased tenfold by general mobilization. Infantry remained the basic arm with tanks largely assigned to its support. The main weaknesses were shortage of modern equipment and inadequate training. Handicapped by the party's insistence on working-class origins for all new officers (other than the ex-tsarists imported by Trotsky), the Soviet officer corps as a whole suffered from extremely low education and professional skills throughout the 1930s. Nevertheless by 1931 the Soviet army was poised for 'take off' and with every chance of emulating its main western rival, Germany, in technology, organization, and strategic doctrine. The inspiration behind an ambitious programme of military reform was the dynamic Marshal Tukhachevsky. Though of noble birth, he became a hero of the civil war and was still only thirty-eight in 1931 when he returned to favour with Stalin after a period in disgrace. Tukhachevsky had progressive ideas: he regarded cavalry as an obsolete arm to be superseded by mechanized formations; he also favoured a greatly expanded air force and the introduction of specialist airborne troops. Between 1933 and 1936 there was remarkable progress on several fronts. Many territorial divisions were converted and up-graded into regulars thereby increasing the standing army to over two million. Tank battalions (organized into brigades) increased from 20 to about 200. In 1934 three airborne divisions were created and in the following year during the manoeuvres at Kiev an infantry regiment and an artillery group practised a parachute drop. Foreign observers were deeply impressed. Most spectacular of all was the creation of a large air force with both strategic and tactical functions. Apart from the low quality of most officers, the only other defect seemed to be the supply system.

Just as Tukhachevsky's reforms were bearing fruit in the form of a large, modern and, above all, *national* army capable of offensive operations, he and seven other senior commanders were suddenly arrested and promptly executed for treason. Between this event, in May 1937, and autumn 1938, there took place the wholesale purging of the officer corps. When it ended only two out of five marshals survived, 75 of 80 members of the higher military council had disappeared and as many as 35,000 officers had been liquidated or deported. These losses included 90 per cent of general officers and 80 per cent of colonels. The high and middle commands were completely disorganized; general staffs of the future divisions, corps and armies were wiped out. This was a far more brutal and comprehensive slaughter than any other army had experienced in modern times, including the French army in the early years of the revolution. No war could have caused such indiscriminate devastation.[37]

Historians are still uncertain about the reason for the purges, if indeed there was an objective one other than Stalin's obsessive fear of competition from an emergent, elitist organization which had secured comparative immunity from the system of political commissars. The Red Army's 'crime' may have been that a few staff officers were tentatively trying to renew contacts with the German general staff which had been broken from the Russian side in 1933. There is also a strong possibility that an elaborately faked dossier was planted on Stalin by the SS.[38]

There can be little dispute about the short-term effects of the purges. In the process of rapid expansion the Red Army was completely disorganized. The majority of the elite, old or new, had disappeared. The survivors went in constant terror of denunciation by a malevolent comrade or subordinate. The troops could have little confidence in their leaders when so many had been found guilty of treason. The dual system of control – commissar and commander – was reintroduced but henceforth both were under surveillance from a third party, an agent from the newly established Special Section.

Doctrine was once again thrown into the melting pot. The new leadership had little faith in mechanized forces, airborne troops, a strategic air force or mobile operations. Not surprisingly the 1937 manoeuvres were a shambles and Russian troops performed badly against the Japanese in 1937 and 1938. The Red Army was much less prepared for war in 1939 than it had been early in 1937.[39]

As early as December 1933 the *Reichswehr* leaders put forward a plan for the rapid expansion of the army to 21 divisions in peacetime and 63 divisions on mobilization. The latter could only be achieved by the reintroduction of conscription and even so there would be a considerable gap between manpower and material resources. By 1936 Hitler and the service leaders faced the fact that the tremendous pace and expense of armaments production could not be maintained indefinitely: either the forces must be employed in offensive operations or the pace slackened by lowering the levels of combat readiness. At this time Hitler publicly declared his intention to gear the economy to rearmament. There was a similarly rapid expansion of the *Luftwaffe* and in this service there was by 1936 an even more critical shortage of raw materials than in the *Wehrmacht*. After Munich the planned monthly production rate of aircraft in Germany actually decreased while it was increasing in other countries such as Britain and France. The arms programme had reached the limits of economic capacity. Though its numerical expansion had been impressive, the

Luftwaffe was critically short of fuel, spare parts and airfield facilities. When, in 1938, its staff was ordered to consider operations against Britain the *Luftwaffe* was nowhere near ready to carry out this mission, though it proved to be excellent in tactical cooperation with ground forces.

The German navy did not rearm so soon or so expansively as the other services. Hitler was a severe critic of Tirpitz's naval strategy, nor did he wish to antagonize Britain; indeed he signed a naval treaty with her in 1935. However, Raeder and other admirals hostile to Britain eventually got their way and in the summer of 1938 planning for war against the latter began as part of an expansion programme which would have staggered even Tirpitz. Here the gap between long-term construction programmes and short-term political decisions was most glaring. At the outbreak of the Second World War the German navy was not expecting to have to face the Royal Navy before 1943. As Raeder gloomily reported: German sailors could only demonstrate their readiness to die honourably and thus pave the way for a new fleet.[40]

Germany's victories in 1939–41 gave the impression that rearmament had been well-planned, streamlined and coordinated but this was far from the case. Hitler was not interested in, or knowledgeable about, the economic underpinning of the rearmament programme, nor did he impose an overall scheme on the three services' extravagantly competing programmes or allow anyone else to do so. Instead each service was virtually allowed to go ahead independently in pursuit of grandiose goals without even consulting the other two. Bottlenecks and shortages soon checked production, but targets were seldom modified in accordance with economic realities such as shortage of steel. Instead, by the later 1930s Hitler was contemplating short offensive campaigns in order that the long-term rearmament programme could be resumed with the material benefits of conquest. This is not, however, to say that there was a guiding military doctrine or deliberate preparation for a particular kind of warfare soon to be popularly known as *blitzkrieg*.

The so-called *blitzkrieg* was thus not a coherent operative concept consciously evolved by the military leadership. On the contrary it was much more a reflection of Hitler's political demands and in fact a result of developments which had taken place in the domestic and in particular the armaments economies.[41]

Thus scholars now challenge the traditional view that Hitler and his military advisers deliberately organized their forces to wage short victorious wars which obviated the need for rearmament in depth. Not only the military concept of *blitzkrieg*, but also its economic rationale has recently come under attack. In particular Dr R. J. Overy has argued persuasively that Hitler's rearmament plans were grandiose not limited in scale and were intended to be completed in time for a major war of conquest which would be fought much later than 1939. So, far from organizing the economy for a particular form of warfare, Hitler ignored expert advice that the Allies were economically stronger and that Germany's preparations were inadequate. The theory of a carefully orchestrated economic programme does not accord with Hitler's personality and outlook. He did not think in narrow economic or social terms, but was obsessed with questions of race and foreign policy. 'Economic questions, when considered at all, were all subsumed into his great plans for the future; the plans for *Lebensraum* and the plan to wage a "life and death struggle" for the survival of the race.'[42]

Dr Overy concludes that Hitler's intention was to prepare for a long and total war, using all Germany's resources to achieve a final victory against Russia, France, Britain and even perhaps the United States. This perspective makes sense of the economic and rearmament programmes initiated in the mid-1930s which the *blitzkrieg* concept does not. Hitler expected this major confrontation to occur in the mid-1940s by which time the German position in central Europe would have been consolidated by a series of diplomatic coups such as those already achieved between March 1936 and August 1939. Unfortunately for Hitler this scheme broke down in September 1939 when Britain and France unexpectedly turned his Polish coup into a European war. That is why the German economy appeared to be geared to limited war; it was caught at a halfway stage with a military base capable only of mounting short and limited operations. That Germany fared so brilliantly in these campaigns had little to do with the economy, but stemmed rather from outstanding leadership, staff work and tactical skills against superficially impressive but in reality mediocre opposition. Hence, after the premature start of general war in 1939, Hitler was deluded by his successes into believing that he could launch his 'big war' in 1941 even though the huge economic preparations were still far from complete.[43]

In the background to our discussion of rearmament policies there has lurked the important but difficult issue of the influence of 'public opinion'. In Britain, after 1918, as Michael Howard has written, the ears of statesmen were increasingly attuned to 'the heavy and ominous breathing of a parsimonious and pacific electorate', but he also suggests that governments may have gone too far in tailoring defence policies to the supposed mood of public opinion. In any case the facts were ambivalent. Pacifist deductions drawn from the famous Oxford Union debate have been shown to be misleading. The relevance of the East Fulham by-election in October 1933 has also been challenged. True, a massive conservative majority was reversed by a young labour candidate who stressed disarmament and international cooperation through the League of Nations (a contradiction which has its equivalents in the 1980s), but it now seems likely that poor housing in the area and the government's unpopular domestic record were more important. Finally in the 'Peace Ballot' of 1935 eleven million of the 11½ million who voted favoured continued British membership of the League of Nations, and nearly seven million were prepared in principle to support military sanctions against an aggressor. At the time of Munich the government was certainly influenced by ministers' belief that there was no great public demand to declare war in support of Czechoslovakia. Yet, after the humiliation and shame of the Munich negotiations, and even more strikingly after the Nazi seizure of Prague, public opinion ran ahead of the government in demanding that a stand be made against Hitler. There was hard evidence for the change of mood in the upsurge of recruiting for the Territorial Army and in the absence of opposition to conscription, introduced for the first time in peacetime in April 1939.[44]

As war approached in 1939 the British public displayed none of the rejoicing or euphoria evident in 1914. There was rather a grim and fatalistic determination to 'see it through' and prevent a Nazi domination of Europe. This mood was doubtless greatly influenced by the correct assumption that in the coming war families left at home might be in even greater peril than the soldiers. It should not be assumed that the general public in totalitarian states – as distinct from party fanatics and politicized youth movements – was any keener to go to war. But of course public opinion was much easier to control and indoctrinate, as in Nazi Germany, through a thorough militarization of the press, films, radio and education. Victories in the early war years *did* cause nationalist rejoicing and strengthened genuine support for the Nazi regime, thereby making it harder for the Allies to distinguish between the German people and their Nazi leaders.

After the Munich crisis it became increasingly likely, despite Neville Chamberlain's hope of 'peace in our time', that Hitler's aggressive diplomacy and what would later be termed brinkmanship would result in a European war. But it was by no means clear that such a conflict need spread beyond central and western Europe or become 'total'. The United States appeared determined to stay out and the Soviet Union had overwhelming reasons for doing so. Italy was a partner in the Axis but was regarded as economically incapable of sustaining a major war effort and would probably, as in 1914, try to remain on the fence. The governments of France and Britain had repeatedly shown themselves unwilling to fight over Abyssinia, the Rhineland, the Spanish civil war, Munich and Prague, and seemed willing to climb down and compromise given the least encouragement. Hitler expected them to do so once again over Poland, which was anyway beyond their powers to protect. On the military plane, as we have seen, general staffs and independent pundits alike were fearfully uncertain about how operations would work out and many of them publicly doubted whether a decisive victory could be obtained. No one nailed his colours to the mast more boldly than the unhappily named General Chauvineau, a famous professor at the French *École de Guerre*, in his 1938 book *Une Invasion: est-elle encore possible?* which received the imprimatur of a laudatory preface by Marshal Pétain. Chauvineau was certain that a successful invasion of France was *not* possible. The war of movement had had its day.

Today, when progress has multiplied tenfold the strength of the defensive, the nation that prepares for a short war is heading for suicide...

As for the tanks, which were to bring a new epoch of short wars, their inadequacy is patent... It is the continuous front... which breaks the wings of offensive operations... The fear of the continuous front has become a factor for peace.

As de la Gorce comments, such extraordinary blindness was not confined to French military thinking; in fact before the experiences of 1939–40 very few armies had fully grasped the revolutionary potential of mechanization.[45]

Moreover, with the exception of a minority of 'civilian militarists' mentioned earlier, most statesmen and diplomatists (contrary to the slur cast by some writers of war fiction) were anything but reckless in believing that political crises could be solved by plunging into war. As we have seen, they were prepared to sacrifice principles and accept humiliation rather than resort to force, and in this stance, they were abetted and supported by their military advisers. If the worst came to the worst and war could not be avoided, they still hoped to keep it limited in extent, duration, intensity and the number of combatants; *vide* Britain's extreme reluctance to 'take the gloves off' with regard to strategic bombing.

It was a tragedy that the Allies' unpreparedness to wage a limited war in the short term meant that they could only hope for victory in a long and total war. There still seemed a more hopeful alternative in September 1939: if Hitler's ambitions were truly limited and reasonable – as surely they must be – then either the conflict would peter out without full-scale fighting, or Hitler would negotiate a compromise peace on the basis of a strategic stalemate. When both of these hopes were disappointed there was no alternative to an all-out war of both quality and quantity.

6

EUROPE AT WAR, 1939–45

One of the best books about the Second World War is titled *Total War*[1] but, strictly speaking, total war is just as much a myth as total victory or total peace. What is true, however, is that the fragile barriers separating war from peace and soldiers from civilians – already eroded in the First World War – virtually disappeared between 1939 and 1945. This poses special problems for the historian because military history and the history of warfare were now very different things. Military historians deal with war plans, strategy and the conflict of armed forces, but this is no longer sufficient. As we have seen, in the First World War a large proportion of the belligerents' populations were mobilized and indirectly suffered the effects of war, but it was still the armed forces which did most of the fighting and most of the dying. It is harder to make this distinction in the Second World War where 'home fronts' were as directly involved in the war as the 'military fronts' and indeed often suffered more. Moreover in the Second World War the movement of armies was often inextricably involved with the movement of populations on an enormous scale. Science and technology were much more intensively and widely exploited than in the First World War, permitting the early campaigns to be more mobile, mechanized and rapidly decisive. Nevertheless, despite the dramatic successes gained by *blitzkrieg*, the struggle lasted six years and became truly global whereas the First World War had remained essentially centred in Europe. Despite examples of brilliant generalship, supported by mechanized and highly trained armies, the Second World War was eventually decided by vastly superior industrial and commercial strength and sheer numbers – the Axis nations could not survive against the 150 millions of the American empire and 180 millions of the Soviet Union provided their governments preserved an alliance and the people were willing to fight.[2]

Though the combined strengths of the Soviet Union and the United States eventually overcame Germany, these two great powers were not formally at war with Germany until June and December 1941 respectively. For its first two years therefore, the struggle quite closely resembled that of 1914–18 with a ramshackle alliance of European nations (weaker than in 1914) again attempting to prevent German domination of the continent. This phase has been prophetically – and one hopes accurately – termed 'The Last European War'.[3] Though Germany's military power in the period 1939–41 was by no means so great as was believed at the time, she did possess decisive short-term advantages in Hitler's willingness to gamble (evident in successive crises since the Rhineland in 1936); the superior professional skills and very high morale of her armed forces; and the weakness and disunity of her opponents whose main aim was to postpone a decisive conflict for several years while they frantically rearmed. Thus the western Allies did nothing substantial to aid Poland in September 1939 when she was speedily overrun in the first impressive display of *blitzkrieg* and divided between Germany and the Soviet Union. Following the latter's eventual, undistinguished victory over Finland in the Winter war of 1939–40, Hitler occupied and conquered Norway despite the advantages enjoyed by the immensely stronger Royal Navy. Most sensational of all, in May and June 1940 the *Wehrmacht* defeated the Low Countries and France. British forces were expelled from the continent, and though her government remained defiant, it seemed only a matter of time before air and submarine attacks would oblige her to seek terms. Despite allied efforts to keep her neutral, Italy now entered the war as Germany's ally, and with Franco's Spain another prospective partner there was nothing to stop Axis expansion southward into the Mediterranean. Though Russo-German relations were tense, Stalin gave ample evidence of his wish to avoid war and maintain the pact with Hitler. Roosevelt was personally sympathetic towards Britain but was very reluctant to risk involvement in the European war, partly because 1940 was a presidential election year but more importantly because of the more direct Japanese threat to American interests in the Far East. He had declined Prime Minister Reynaud's last desperate appeals to intervene to save France in mid-June 1940. Thus between 1939 and mid-1941 Germany established an apparently impregnable position in central and western Europe, immune from attack on land and not seriously vulnerable either to aerial bombing or naval blockade.

What sort of war did the Nazis wage in this first, victorious phase? Hopes persisted among Hitler's opponents, notably in France and Britain, that this was a traditional, limited war for specific territorial gains. Germany's early conquests were even welcomed by substantial minorities, including right-wing parties in France and elsewhere favouring fascist policies of militarism, austerity and enforced discipline. For such groups Hitler appeared as Europe's champion against the real menace – Bolshevik Russia. Nazism also found wide support among the lower middle classes. From a later perspective it might be argued that Nazi behaviour in battle and in occupied territories was relatively civilized in comparison with the almost unimaginable barbarity that characterized their regime in eastern Europe from June 1941 onwards. This is a dubious assumption. True, Slavophobia and anti-Semitism only received their fullest expression after the invasion of Russia, but the gratuitous violence and sheer evil of Nazism was already evident in the occupation of Poland and the campaigns in the west. International treaties and the laws of war were treated with contempt; prisoners of war were executed in cold blood; and there were innumerable atrocities against civilians. Moreover, so far from being played down as regrettable necessities of war, Nazi brutality and mercilessness were deliberately extolled in propaganda broadcasts and war films. Though there were lingering hopes in Britain and the United States of a negotiated peace with Hitler's German opponents, if not with Hitler himself, Churchill struck the note of uncompromising determination which would characterize allied conduct of the war when he told the House of Commons in September 1939:

> This is not a question of fighting for Danzig or Poland. We are fighting to save the whole world from the pestilence of Nazi tyranny and in defence of all that is most sacred to man.[4]

This must have sounded exaggerated to many people in 1939 and 1940 but became ever more credible as the consequences of Nazi occupation became better known.

The general European war which Hitler had begun prematurely by miscalculation in 1939 was not a traditional conflict about national self-determination or better strategic frontiers; it was intended to fulfil an ideological, visionary Grand Design in which the main ingredients were *Lebensraum* for the Teutonic peoples in the east, and the self-sufficiency and racial purity of the Greater Germanic Estate stretching perhaps from the Atlantic to the Urals.

Mercifully the Grand Design was never realized, but in the brief time allowed them Hitler's lieutenants, notably Heinrich Himmler, went a long way towards creating a New Order for Europe. The first essential was the military conquest of land. Nazi values were to be exported from the homeland and the pattern of Nazi revolution and culture imposed. Ideology was more important than boundaries.

> Instead of finding where people lived and then drawing permanent or semi-permanent frontiers to fit the ethnic facts, the Nazis began by designating an area and then moved people around in order to make demography fit the facts of power.

It was not therefore a fixed area but rather 'a biological habitat like a nature reserve'.[5]

The Germans, though they were to be the masters and chief beneficiaries, would not be the only inhabitants of this Greater Germany. The Nordic races, albeit deprived of political and economic independence, would receive a status only a little inferior to the Germans, but non-Nordic peoples would be regrouped and assigned specific economic functions as virtual slaves of the master race. These peoples would be kept in permanent subjection by depriving them of education. As Hitler brutally put it, 'They were to know just enough to understand road signs, so as not to get themselves run over by our vehicles.' The Soviet Union would be Germanized and the population treated like Red Indians. Certain groups, too vicious and inferior even for a menial economic role, were to be eliminated. The Italians were assigned to a vague, peripheral role in Africa but their position in the racial hierarchy was left undefined.[6]

Despite the prior demands of military operations, the first phase of the war witnessed migrations of people on a vast scale. A minority of these were more or less voluntary including millions of Belgians and French who fled before the Germans in May 1940, many of them soon to return. But in the east fear of Soviet oppression was as powerful a motivator as German aggression. Thus nearly half a million Finns fled westward from Karelia; thousands of Lithuanians, Swedes and Germans escaped from the Baltic states in June 1940; and about 60,000 Bulgarians migrated from northern to southern

Dobrudja when the latter was annexed by Bulgaria in the autumn of 1940. But the enforced migrations were on an altogether greater scale. After the German conquest nearly one and a half million Poles were expelled from the Germanized western and southern provinces. Over a million Poles and more than 50,000 Ukrainians and White Russians were transported to the Soviet Union from Memel and Germanized Poland in 1940–1, and about 200,000 natives of the Baltic provinces were deported to the Soviet Union when the Germans invaded in 1941. At the same time 400,000 Volga Germans were deported to Siberia. Meanwhile hundreds of thousands of German and eastern European Jews were being forcibly concentrated in Polish ghettos. Altogether these cruel deportations of entire peoples with minimal provision for their resettlement elsewhere amounted to about four million.[7]

The economic dimension of the New Order was partially established during the phase of Nazi conquest but was then subjected to Germany's overriding needs for survival so that it never functioned as intended. Germany's interests were always meant to be paramount, but in theory the tributary nations' interests were not entirely neglected. The core of Greater Germany, including Luxembourg, Alsace-Lorraine, part of Belgium and Silesia, would contain most of Europe's heavy industries and all its arms factories. Outside this area the main purpose of specially permitted industry would be to provide a limited range of consumer goods for Germans. Each area's production would be strictly regulated to serve German needs. Thus all areas would become specialized producers with guaranteed and well-defined export markets, long-term agreements and fixed exchange rates. In theory this large economic entity offered several attractions, not least the abolition of unemployment but, as Calvocoressi notes, its purpose was still national: the real basis was German power and German requirements, not a genuine European cooperative. 'The benefits to everybody else would be the crusts from the rich man's table.'[8]

Most accounts of the German economy at war are vitiated by the assumption that until 1942 it was deliberately controlled and restrained as regards war production by a definite, well-understood doctrine of *blitzkrieg*. As we saw in the previous chapter, this assumption has recently been subjected to a powerful critique. Dr Richard Overy has shown that military spending rose at a consistent rate between 1938–9 and 1943–4; indeed the greatest percentage increases in military expenditure occurred in the years 1939 to 1941. Moreover, the *blitzkrieg* concept of switching production to and fro from consumer to military priorities in a matter of weeks demanded a degree of sophistication and overall control which were conspicuously lacking. In reality production for all the services expanded more or less continuously during the period 1939-41 because it was difficult to disrupt programmes at short notice, and anyway the services all jealously guarded their own economic empires. To be sure, Hitler explored the possibilities of running down arms production in 1940 and 1941 but this was due to short-lived euphoria over what his under-equipped but brilliantly organized forces had achieved rather than to any clear concept of a *blitzkrieg* economy. Even these explorations did not go far because even the Nazis appreciated that powerful enemies remained undefeated. Nor is it true that consumer goods were favoured at the expense of military expenditure. Car production was drastically reduced and the services took an increasingly large percentage of those available. The same trend is clear in the construction of houses. Textiles, leather goods, paper and, above all, food became ever scarcer for the civilian consumer as the war dragged on. It is true of course that Hitler was always concerned with the propaganda aspect of domestic living standards. Germany never suffered the acute food shortages of the First World War – though some of her satellites did – and female labour was notoriously under-exploited in the war effort until late in the day, compared to many other countries. Hitler insisted that the supply of certain goods such as stockings, cosmetics and cigarettes should be maintained to keep up home morale, but even so cigarettes were of poor quality and had to be rationed.[9]

There are several reasons why Germany did not get value for the enormous sums invested during the phase supposedly governed by the *blitzkrieg* concept. German insistence on high standards of workmanship and small-scale units of production entailed that she obtained fewer tanks and aircraft in 1940 than Britain in relation to expenditure. The problem was exacerbated by Hitler's ignorance of the true position or his wilful self-delusion which was encouraged by the incompetent Göring. Like Churchill, but with far more serious consequences, Hitler accepted new weapons uncritically; was impatient about the long time-scale in developing new weapons; and failed to distinguish between prototypes and battle-ready machines. There were also numerous problems in getting competitive and efficient civilian firms to adapt to armaments production. Most serious of all, however, was the lack of a competent central authority to oversee and regulate the entire war economy. On the contrary, as Speer's memoirs *Inside the Third Reich* demonstrate so graphically, the three armed forces and the SS carved out their own industrial empires and competed fiercely and with enormous waste for scarce raw materials, factory facilities and labour. Thus, as most commentators agree, the production 'miracle', begun by Todt and Milch in 1941 and developed more dramatically by Speer from 1942, did not entail any massive redirection of resources but simply the more efficient use of them.[10]

Fritz Todt had been appointed Reichsminister for armaments and munitions early in 1940, but at first he had only limited success in his efforts to transfer authority from *Wehrmacht* bureaucrats to industrial technicians. His ministry lacked power to enforce its will, notably in the crucial area of allocating raw materials, where factory managers and local Gauleiters continued to scramble for available stocks. Early in 1942 Hitler conferred greater authority on Todt *vis-à-vis* the *Wehrmacht*, but the latter was shortly afterwards killed in an air crash. His successor, Albert Speer, was a man of remarkable talents who achieved dramatic increases in war production between 1942 and 1944 despite the intensification of allied bombing and loss of initiative on the eastern front. At the outset Speer was given control only over production for the army; but with Hitler's backing he was able to stamp his ministry's authority over virtually the whole area of war production. Thus, for example, the *Wehrmacht*'s War Economy Branch was absorbed by Speer's ministry and Göring's Four Year Plan Office was deprived of any real power. Hitler allowed the establishment of a small central planning board with power to allocate raw materials, and Speer even gained some degree of control over naval and air force production. In general, industrialists' expertise was given much greater scope *vis-à-vis* the military bureaucrats in rationalizing the economy. But the degree of Hitler's support fluctuated and Speer was never omnipotent in economic matters: Himmler's SS went on developing its own private economic empire both within Germany and in the conquered eastern territories. Nor did Speer ever achieve complete control over allocation of manpower, a vital issue on which the divergence between business interests and Nazi ideology became ever more apparent.[11] We shall return to this topic later in discussing Germany's exploitation of her conquests.

Utterly different in so many ways, Britain and the Soviet Union were alike in one respect in the Second World War; both after a slow and fumbling start eventually organized their economies and manpower more comprehensively and effectively than did totalitarian Germany.

Britain and France had established the institutional and legal basis for a thorough war economy before 1939, but neither singly nor in combination did they make anywhere near full use of their respite in the 'Phoney War' period – for example by building up stocks of vital raw materials or experimenting to any degree with controls of imports, consumer goods and manpower. To be fair, Britain had already achieved conspicuous successes in one or two essential fields such as the production of fighter aircraft and the development of radar. But it took the shock of Dunkirk to inspire the nation, under Churchill's forceful leadership, to accept the need for all-out mobilization for what was likely to be a protracted struggle for survival. Even before the fall of France Churchill's war cabinet had moved to bring all large issues of economic policy under the supervision of a small ministerial group called the Lord President's Committee. By 1941 this body, headed by an extremely able civil servant, Sir John Anderson, had laid the foundations for the most thoroughly coordinated war economy among all the belligerents. It was a notable achievement to create a 'siege economy' in a democracy largely through popular consent. Complaining and 'grousing' were of course national pastimes, but the great majority of the electorate believed that the war effort was justified and necessary and readily accepted austerities provided they were seen to be evenly shared. After Dunkirk stringent controls were imposed on imports and exports and also on profits. Personal liberties were severely curtailed, as for example the prohibition on visiting areas threatened by invasion, and the enforced allocation of spare rooms to evacuees. Owners of large mansions and country houses – such as Evelyn Waugh's fictional 'Brideshead' – were obliged to surrender them to ministries or to the armed services, nominally for the duration but in some cases permanently.

Above all, Britain was faced by an acute shortage of manpower. Between Dunkirk and December 1941 a series of measures were introduced culminating in the National Service Act. Men aged from eighteen to fifty and women between twenty and thirty were made liable for either military or essential civilian war service. Subsequently the upper age limits were extended. The number of gainfully occupied persons increased by nearly 3 million during the war of whom over 2 million were women. No other warring nation, except the Soviet Union, imposed so great a burden on its women or so thoroughly diverted labour to essential war work. By mid-1944 a third of Britain's total labour force was engaged in civilian war employment. Acting on the advice of J. M. Keynes and other treasury officials, the government took vigorous steps to limit inflation: taxes were sharply increased, compulsory saving schemes were introduced and consumer rationing was extended to a great range of goods including, most obviously, foodstuffs and clothing. Financial disaster was staved off at the price of rigorous austerity. The Lend-Lease agreement with the United States from the spring of 1941 (and full economic collaboration as allies from December of that year) brought temporary relief and enabled Britain to endure until 1945. But Lend-Lease was a very mixed blessing: all Britain's dollar holdings and other assets in the United States had to be sold; the goods received did not outvalue payments for two years; and the conditions attached to the loans were stringent. Britain became heavily indebted to the United States (and to a lesser extent to Canada) and suffered badly when Lend-Lease was suddenly stopped in peculiarly damaging circumstances in August 1945.[12]

The impression must not be left that Britain's organization for war was flawless. Production often fell short of targets and *per capita* productivity remained low. Much of British industry remained archaic as regards plant and management techniques. Nor should the workers' effort be sentimentalized: the number of days lost due to strikes rose steadily between 1942 and 1944 and at the end of the war the total was still double what it had been in 1939. However, given these limitations and handicaps, it was an astonishing achievement to create a war economy which (in 1940–2) produced more tanks, aircraft and self-propelled guns than Germany, and in which, despite severe shortage of labour, British farmers increased the area under cultivation by a half.[13]

Although in strict economic terms Russia's uneasy alliance with Germany between 1939 and 1941 was considerably to the latter's benefit, Stalin put the breathing space to good use in developing a new eastern industrial base secure against enemy attack. By June 1941, for example, the Urals and western Siberia were already producing 39 per cent of Russia's steel, 35 per cent of its coal and 50 per cent of its tractors. Only in the vital commodity of oil were Russian sources seriously exposed to German attack. Moreover, under the third Five Year Plan stockpiling of strategic materials had begun, and both aircraft and tanks were being turned out by production-line methods. On the other hand Stalin was certainly guilty of trusting Hitler up to the last moment with the result that massive supplies of grain, oil, timber, iron and non-ferrous ores were supplied to Germany. Also Russia's western industrial regions were developed only to be overrun and captured in 1941.

Russia certainly owed her narrow escape from defeat in that year mainly to the existence of her new industrial base in the east but even so it was a close-run thing. Quite apart from the enormous losses in trained soldiers and thousands of tanks and aircraft, industrial output by the end of 1941 was down by more than half. Aircraft production, for example, fell by two-thirds. Allied military aid was as yet a mere trickle.

The surmounting of this crisis understandably became part of the heroic legend of the 'Great Patriotic War' which in some respects bore a close resemblance to the struggle against Napoleon. The dismantling and transfer of factories from the path of the rapidly advancing Panzer columns was a truly staggering feat. Between June and December 1941 some 1500 enterprises were dismantled, hauled eastward to the Urals or beyond by rail and reassembled in new buildings. It has been calculated that one plant required as many as eight thousand railroad wagons to transport it. In addition to these unprecedented migrations of workers with their factories, thousands of new plants were built in the eastern regions between 1942 and 1944. Though oil and coal remained in short supply Russia made a rapid and enormous recovery in and after 1942 so that she was able to provide the bulk of the armaments needed by her huge armies.

Russia made a similarly rapid recovery from the loss of about 40 per cent of its labour force in 1941. Unhampered by the need for consent, the government in February 1942 ordered the mobilization of men between sixteen and fifty-five and women between sixteen and forty-five. Women already supplied 38 per cent of the labour force in 1940, by 1942 the figure had risen to over half. In contrast to Britain *per capita* productivity rose each year from 1942. A similar heroic effort was made in agriculture where nearly half the cultivated land had been lost. Here again women played a conspicuous part but recovery was slower than in industry. The barbarian at the gates inspired a superhuman patriotic effort which probably owed more to historic tradition than to the communist regime, though party membership was greatly extended and 'a new unity in national patriotic feeling seemed to be opening between party and country'.[14]

There is no need to examine all the belligerents' economies, but a few words must be written about the United States. Like the Soviet Union the United States kept out of the conflict until 1941, but unlike the former her homeland was virtually immune from attack. Another advantage was that there was considerable slack in her economy which could easily be taken up; there were for example as many as 9½ million unemployed on the eve of war in 1939. The European war therefore provided a great stimulus to American industry. Lastly, she had no need to improvise under the immediate threat or actuality of war but could organize deliberately as regards reallocation of resources and the redirection of industry to meet the needs of the war. At the top this was fairly successfully managed (in comparison for example with Speer's problems) by the creation of a large number of agencies such as the War Production Board, the Manpower Commission and the Office of War Mobilization. In economic terms these arrangements, which relied as much as possible on voluntary submission to central direction and a minimum of government interference, proved an astounding success. By the end of 1942 America was producing more war material than all the enemy powers combined. By the same date America had produced 8 million tons of merchant shipping and by 1945 over 50 million tons. In the course of 1942 alone aircraft production jumped from 3000 to a staggering 48,000. As much new plant was built in the first three war years as in the previous fifteen, and total production nearly doubled between 1939 and 1942. Although there was a dilemma in 1942 as to what proportion of war materials to send to hard-pressed allies at the expense of her own rapidly expanding forces, and continuing tension between the requirements of the European and Pacific theatres, the American economy when in full operation was powerful enough to assure the Allies of victory in both theatres. Indeed it should be stressed that despite continuous and sometimes bitter disputes about strategic priorities, Anglo-American planning and cooperation in the use of scarce resources and war materials reached a far higher degree of efficiency than anything achieved by Germany, despite her apparent advantage of being a unitary, authoritarian state.[15]

As was noted earlier, there was a grand economic design behind the Nazis' policy of territorial expansion; namely a manufacturing heartland in Greater Germany supplied with raw materials and foodstuffs by peripheral areas inhabited by inferior peoples. There was an inherent contradiction in this theory in that a large measure of support for the Nazis in Germany derived from a section of the people whose sympathies were antipathetic to the world of big business. Not only was a good deal of Nazi rhetoric anticapitalist; there was also legislation which aimed to establish inalienable, hereditary peasant tenures, to restrict the size of retail firms and to limit the movement of labour out of agriculture. In broader terms the Nazis' racial ideology was driving towards irrational goals utterly at odds with business interests. As Professor Milward put it:

> National Socialism was as much a yearning for a stable utopia of the past as a close alliance between major capital interests and an authoritarian government.[16]

The clash between economic exploitation of conquered territories with the cooperation of the people and Nazi barbarism was most glaring in the Soviet Union. As a Nazi official in the Ukraine enquired plaintively:

> If we shoot the Jews, liquidate war prisoners, starve the major part of the big cities' population and . . . reduce the peasants through famine there will arise a question: who is going to produce the economic goods?[17]

The types of government imposed by Germany on the conquered territories and the manner in which their economies and manpower were exploited for Germany's benefit varied enormously from the lenient and indirect administration of Denmark as a Nazi showcase at one extreme, to the ruthless treatment of Poland and other eastern countries at the other.[18] Everywhere, however, the aim was to make conquest pay by supporting German occupation forces and enhancing her war-making capacity. France was a particularly valuable source of raw materials for Germany even when the latter was dealing with the nominally independent Vichy regime up to 1942. By 1943, for example, Germany was taking three-quarters of French iron-ore output, over half of her bauxite and 15 per cent of her coal. France's contribution to the German war effort was still increasing in 1944; in January of that year 85 per cent of the total train movements in France were for German purposes.

In contrast, the contribution of a poor country like Norway to Germany's war effort was marginal though her own economy was disrupted and she had to pay for a large army of occupation. The countries of western Europe also made an important contribution to the German war effort by supplying hundreds of thousands of labourers, a high proportion of them voluntary migrants in the early years when Germany appeared to be winning, but increasingly by compulsion from 1943. By mid-1941 there were about 2 million foreign workers in Germany most of them nominally volunteers, but out of the 5 million foreign workers there in 1944 only about 200,000 were voluntary. [19]

Professor Milward points out the confusion and contradiction in the German policy of exploitation. Between 1940 and 1942 German policy regarding France and the Low Countries was characterized by short-term exploitation, yet these developed economies made the dominant contribution to the German war effort and it would have paid to have interfered with them less, notably by removing fewer workers and encouraging their profit motive. In this phase the eastern European contribution to Germany was marginal despite its pre-eminent role in Nazi theory. For example, during the whole war France contributed as much to Germany's food supply as all the eastern territories together. After 1943 Germany's increasingly desperate military position caused her to step up the policy of ruthless exploitation in the east, for example, of Caucasian oil. As regards the west there was some inclination to reduce depredations of plant, raw materials and labour in order that factories would produce more and could be milked more profitably. [20]

It was indeed over the optimum method of exploiting foreign labour that a sharp dispute occurred between Speer and his potential rival, Fritz Sauckel. The former believed that foreign labour could be more valuable if left at home to operate factories producing mainly for Germany's benefit, whereas the latter insisted on rounding up as many workers as possible and transporting them to Germany. On purely utilitarian grounds Speer was surely correct because transport problems, appalling living and working conditions and the ever-intensifying air bombardment all combined to make the foreign workers in Germany far less cooperative and productive than they had been in 1940–1. Sauckel retained the control and procurement of foreign labour to the end (and paid the full penalty for it of execution after the Nuremberg trials, whereas Speer lived to tell the tale), but even with limited powers Speer managed to double war production by mid-1942 and more than trebled it by mid-1944. In the final months of the war Germany still possessed ample stocks of weapons but she was fast running out of fuel and military manpower.[21]

Although we have argued that the Nazi philosophy of conquest was arrogant, racialist and cruel from the start, there can be no dispute that the invasion of Russia in June 1941 marked a plunge into new depths of barbarism. This indeed was the racial and ideological crusade which had always featured so prominently in Nazi writings and rantings. Shortly before the invasion Hitler told his military chiefs that it was to be a war of extermination. Himmler instructed his SS officials that the destruction of 30 million Slavs was a prerequisite of German plans for the east. The word *Untermenschen* now entered the German language of propaganda; soldiers and civil officials had to be convinced that the eastern enemy was subhuman. In his diary Goebbels recorded the view that the Russians were not a people but rather 'a conglomeration of animals'. Hitler also referred to the enemy soldiers as 'beasts'. Specially selected photographs and propaganda were used to ram home the message. The Nazi leaders and all too many of their military and civilian associates became convinced of the truth of this utterly inhumane and callous philosophy. There were a few brave protests but, alas, no widespread revulsion or refusal to serve. Himmler epitomized Nazi barbarity, as this statement to a group of SS generals in 1943 shows:

> Whether nations live in prosperity or starve to death interests me only in so far as we need them as slaves for our Kultur: otherwise, it is of no interest to me. Whether 10,000 Russian females fall down from exhaustion while digging an anti-tank ditch interests me only in so far as the anti-tank ditch for Germany is finished . . . [22]

This policy was at once translated into action, for example in Hitler's notorious 'Commissar Decree' ordering the immediate execution of captured Soviet party officials. In addition Himmler's special 'action teams' (*Einsatzgruppen*), already used on a small scale in Poland, were expanded to act as extermination squads on the heels of the advancing armies. One of the four unit commanders testified that his group alone had accounted for 90,000 victims during the first year of fighting. In addition to these massacres – often perpetrated in public – a combination of neglect, ill-treatment and slave labour accounted for the lives of the great majority of the five million Russian prisoners of war captured by Germany.[23]

This policy of deliberate cruelty, total oppression and ruthless exploitation in the east was short-sighted as well as wicked. It quickly disillusioned many Nazi sympathizers and would-be collaborators in other countries (and there were many in 1941) about the reality of the New Order in Europe. As the war dragged on Nazi-occupied western Europe was increasingly exploited to keep the eastern campaign going thus encouraging resistance – especially among young men earmarked for forced labour in Germany. Most notoriously the Nazis failed to make use, as Goebbels wished to, of the genuine welcome which German forces received, as supposed liberators, in the Baltic provinces, the Ukraine and other border areas. Hitler brusquely rejected any ideas of setting up puppet states or of anti-Soviet measures to win over the peasants. Instead Himmler's racialism strengthened Russian resistance and increased the ferocity of partisan warfare in the Germans' rear. Not until too late did Himmler realize the counterproductive effect of his policies on the supply of slave labour to Germany.[24]

Despite Hitler's specific orders, some half a million Russian prisoners and civilian volunteers were allowed to work for Germany in return for food and protection. Many of these *Hilfswillige* (or 'Hiwis') donned German uniforms to perform menial tasks or fight against the partisans. There was some talk of organizing a Russian liberation army and in July 1942 a potential Russian 'de Gaulle' appeared in the person of General Andrei Vlasov, a prisoner from Leningrad, who advocated the removal of Stalin and a separate peace in the east. Hitler and most of the Nazi leaders remained adamantly opposed to a Russian liberation army or any form of puppet state. Vlasov remained in virtual confinement until 1944 and was not given a military command until it was too late to go into action. This typified Hitler's failure to exploit propaganda opportunities in the east in sharp contrast to his finesse in manipulating successive crises between 1936 and 1939.[25]

Anti-Semitism was always prominent in Nazi ideology and the German Jews were discriminated against and persecuted throughout the 1930s. Hitler's obsession was to prevent contamination of the Aryan race by interbreeding, but this was held to require the prevention of all human contact: this might have been achieved by mass migration but the Nazis placed prohibitions on the export of wealth and property, while the British severely restricted emigration to the obvious haven – Palestine. The Nazi occupation of Poland, where some three million Jews were already living, saw a stepping up of anti-Semitic persecution and brutality and also provided a convenient 'dumping ground' for German and west European Jews. But even in the early war years Hitler and the Nazi leadership seemed to have favoured expulsion rather than extermination; indeed there was much talk of establishing a Jewish homeland in Madagascar but the island was not accessible. It is schemes like this which remind us of the stark madness of Nazi thinking. Hitler's conquests between September 1939 and June 1941 put the majority of central and west European Jews at his mercy but killing of Jews and other 'unsociables' like the gypsies and homosexuals only began on a vast scale with the invasion of the Soviet Union. Reference has already been made to the terrible deeds of the *Einsatzgruppen*. In the largest single operation 33,000 Jews were killed in Kiev in two days in September 1941 as a reprisal for the blowing up of an hotel. On another occasion 16,000 Jews were killed in a day at Pinsk with pistols, grenades, clubs, axes and dogs. These mass murders were witnessed by thousands of civilians and German soldiers; some of the executioners had to be bribed or befuddled with drink and a few brave individuals refused orders and protested. The Nazi leaders' attitude was ambivalent. Their speeches openly called for the elimination of the Jews and bestial deeds were filmed for propaganda purposes. On the other hand Hitler never signed execution orders or publicly acknowledged what was being done. It looks as though the Nazis felt no compunction about exterminating the Jews but preferred not to know – or tell the German people – how it was actually carried out. To the end the fiction was maintained that the mass extermination centres were 'work camps'. Himmler, the chief executant of the 'final solution', was sickened by the only massacre he witnessed. He ordered less shooting and more gassing.[26]

There was a much deeper reason for the introduction of the policy of systematic execution of the Jews by gassing from January 1942. By the end of 1941 Russia's survival and America's entry into the war suggested to Hitler that he might not win. The Jews of Europe could no longer be expelled to America and, given Nazi ideology, there was virtually no other way out for them. Far-fetched though it may sound the 'final solution' of the Jewish problem became one of Hitler's major war aims – indeed it may have been his overriding aim – from 1942 onwards. Near the end of the war Hitler boasted to his private circle that though he may have lost the war he had cleansed Germany and central Europe of its Jews. Despite the murder of between four and six million Jews in Auschwitz (where at the peak period of operation 12,000 victims were gassed every day) and the other extermination camps, Hitler's boast was untrue. Perhaps as many as three million Jews had survived, though – with a few privileged exceptions – in conditions that beggar description. Hitler's achievement had been to make anti-Semitism unspeakable nearly everywhere in the civilized world.[27] This was by no means the first or last example of genocide but the cold-blooded bureaucratic way in which it was carried out in the midst of a great war makes it particularly horrific.

The Soviet record as regards genocide was less appalling than the German because it was less systematic and less ideologically inspired and took place on a smaller scale. But the Russians deported over a million Poles and half a million Black Sea Germans to Siberia from which very few returned. Moreover, it now seems clear that the Russians were responsible for the murder of several thousand captured Polish officers whose mass grave was discovered by the Germans in the Katyn Forest. The wave of wartime sympathy in the west for 'Uncle Joe' and the gallant Russians made it difficult to understand that in some respects they were almost as brutal and callous as the Nazis. Allied sins were rather of omission than commission though some critics, mostly from hindsight, have condemned strategic bombing as a war crime. What recent studies[28] have shown beyond doubt is that ample evidence of the Nazis' 'final solution' of the Jewish problem by mass gassing in specially constructed camps was received by western governments as early as 1942. For a variety of reasons, including individuals' anti-Semitism, but more importantly because Nazi treatment of the Jews held a very low priority in comparison with great strategic problems such as opening a second front, very little was done. It should be added that utter non-cooperation by the Soviet Union was a further drawback, particularly as regards allied bombing missions in eastern Europe. Attention has recently been focused on Jewish pleas in the summer of 1944 for the Allies to bomb the railway connections and gas installations at Auschwitz. Group Captain Leonard Cheshire, VC has testified that this was operationally feasible but the political directive was never given by either the British or American governments.[29] How many Jewish lives might have been saved and how severely the Allies should be censured remain controversial issues.

Another aspect of the war on which there has been a good deal of revisionist writing is collaboration, and the other side of the same coin, resistance. Allied propaganda fostered a powerful myth of Nazi-occupied nations seething with discontent over lost liberties and eager to rise up, whatever the cost in loss of life and destruction, to overthrow the hated oppressor. Even a little sober reflection suggests that such a picture exaggerates the heroic element in the general population of some 180 million Europeans obliged to live under German rule. True, only small minority pro-Nazi or fascist parties positively welcomed the Germans and were eager to govern under their auspices and fight alongside them against Bolshevism. But, so long as the enemy appeared to be winning, it would be realistic to expect the great majority of people to collaborate in various degrees, simply by passive acquiescence with a premium on survival, or more positively in pursuit of business profits or enhanced status. The 'qualified collaboration' practised by Pétain's Vichy regime in the hope of a lucrative partnership in Hitler's great empire was particularly valuable to Germany. As we have seen France made a bigger industrial contribution to the German war effort than any other conquered country, yet it did not save France from brutal treatment, including thousands of men deported and many publicly executed. A recent authority on collaboration suggests that other countries 'may be said to have plied Germany with more goods than were demanded or expected of them'. Without voluntary cooperation on a vast scale Germany could not have continued to expand her war production until well into 1944.[30] It is only fair to add that several countries, notably Denmark and Holland, displayed a form of tactical collaboration as a facade behind which non-collaboration and resistance could be secretly fostered. One can sum up by saying that while the large mass of the population were anti-German by instinct and experience, few could risk open rebellion and had no choice other than to live and work for German-controlled political and economic systems.

It is noteworthy that even in countries racially congenial to the

Nazis such as Norway and the Netherlands, the invaders never found enough local fascist support to permit genuinely independent collaborationist governments to function. This is conspicuously true in Norway where Vidkun Quisling's name became a synonym for 'traitor'. Similarly Anton Mussert's fascist party in the Netherlands was cold-shouldered by the great majority of his compatriots.

In the sphere of military collaboration the Nazi crusade against Bolshevism won a substantial amount of voluntary government support in Spain and Rumania and rather less from France, Hungary and Italy. As regards individual volunteers, Himmler's elite *Waffen SS* attracted numerous Scandinavians, Dutch, Belgians and Frenchmen. Later the privilege of membership was extended to Ukrainians, men from the Baltic states and even a few Moslems. By the end of the war foreigners formed a major proportion of the troops fighting with the SS divisions at the front. This form of collaboration was, however, more symbolical than the essential administrative support provided by businessmen, local officials and police.[31]

The word 'resistance' probably for most readers conjures up the intrepid saboteur, but this activity was only one extreme of a gamut which began with non-cooperation and a 'wall of silence'. Active resistance depends upon hope and the sad fact is that for millions of people in the early war years Germany's triumph must have appeared total and final. What kept the spark of hope alive, apart from the supreme confidence of individuals like de Gaulle, was continuous access to information from the outside world. The main sources of accurate news were the radio networks of neutral countries such as Switzerland and Sweden and, most important of all, the BBC whose bulletins were eagerly listened to by millions of people often at the risk of their lives. The clandestine press also flourished in all the occupied countries. In Belgium some 12,000 people were engaged in publishing about 300 papers; in France the underground press became a huge industry publishing more than 1000 papers and pamphlets; and in the Netherlands the confiscation of radios in 1943 only stimulated the circulation of papers some of which appeared three times a week. Many active resisters began their apprenticeship in this risky work.

German behaviour was the greatest stimulator of resistance. The rounding up of Jews and other groups for forced labour; random seizure of hostages; wholesale looting, pillage and wanton destruction; and vastly excessive reprisals – such as the utter destruction of the Czech village of Lidice and all its inhabitants after the assassination of Heydrich – all combined to stir up real hatred of the Germans. The various forms of opposition included networks for aiding the escape of stranded aircrews or other servicemen who had escaped from prison camps; the collection and transmission of military intelligence; industrial strikes and sabotage of factories and communications; and ultimately organized resistance groups especially in rugged terrain like that of Greece, Yugoslavia and southern France.[32]

One must be careful not to be over-romantic about the resistance groups. Many bands of young men, in central France in 1944 for example, were more concerned about avoiding forced labour service than in killing Germans. By July 1944 there were nearly 400,000 active resisters in France but less than 30 per cent possessed firearms. There were also internecine struggles between various (mostly left-wing) partisan groups who increasingly looked beyond the defeat of Germany to the post-war seizure of power. A recent survey of the voluminous literature on resistance is extremely sceptical about its strategic contribution to the defeat of the Axis powers. No one disputes the value of certain intelligence passed on by the resistance, for example, the location of German direction-finding sites near the Channel coast, or the destruction of select industrial or military targets, but the ability of the partisans to divert, let alone destroy, German divisions seems to have been exaggerated. Partisan operations rarely became more than a nuisance unless they were coordinated with, or coincided with, the operations of regular forces that absorbed the enemy's main attention. Even then, all the European resistance movements suffered from lax organization, poor discipline and training and erratic, volatile behaviour. This is in no way to denigrate the courage and self-sacrifice of many thousands of anonymous men and women whose defiance harassed the enemy, assisted the Allies and held out a moral example to occupied Europe. 'Resistance', concludes Werner Rings, 'may have been far less a military phenomenon than a manifestation of political and human impulses.'[33] This does not mean, however, that resistance in all its forms did not make a substantial contribution to the defeat of the Axis powers.

In the phase of the Axis triumphs, 1939–42, the Allies certainly placed too much faith in national resistance movements which, they hoped, with outside encouragement and assistance, might actually escalate into such widespread open rebellion that a mere 'mopping up' operation would be left to the invading armies. It proved extremely difficult to control national resistance groups, as the Allies found for example in Yugoslavia, and impossible to coordinate the movements in different countries. Excessive faith was also placed in propaganda as a positive strategic instrument.

This is not to underestimate the importance of propaganda, for the Second World War more than any previous conflict since perhaps the seventeenth century, was a battle for men's minds. Entire peoples had to be convinced that the war was worth fighting and that ultimate victory was assured. Previously radio was mentioned in connection with clandestine opposition, but it was also of course a prime means of open propaganda between warring governments and, no less important, in competition for the sympathy or allegiance of neutrals. High-quality foreign broadcasts could be seductive quite apart from their political content. For instance, as many as six million people in England may have listened to the traitor William Joyce ('Lord Haw-Haw'), but probably more for entertainment than information. Soviet broadcasts were so monotonous that even communists preferred to tune in to London rather than Moscow.[34] The capacity of ordinary citizens to be entertained but not persuaded to change their views, was something that propagandists everywhere were slow to grasp.

In Germany Joseph Goebbels's great achievement in the use of propaganda was to keep the home front united and determined virtually to the end. The German people had been 'brainwashed' by a ceaseless barrage of propaganda in the 1930s through the means of radio, entertainments like the Berlin Olympics, and the brilliantly stage-managed party rallies. The majority of the people fervently supported Hitler but they were never enthusiastic about war. During the years of victory Goebbels's task was comparatively simple particularly as internal dissent and freedom of expression had been suppressed. Victories were fully exploited to reinforce the image of Hitler as the infallible leader of intuitive genius. German aggression was repeatedly rationalized in terms of justified pre-emptive self-defence, and when the invasion of Russia did not bring a quick victory Goebbels plugged the theme that a ruthless effort was needed to crush the brutal, subhuman Slav.

Unlike some of his colleagues and rivals, such as Otto Dietrich, head of the press division in propaganda, Goebbels generally skilfully avoided over-optimistic forecasts or predictions which could be disproved by events (such as the Allies never being able to bomb Berlin or set foot in occupied Europe), but even he found it increasingly difficult to combat the turn of the tide on the eastern front and the increasing intensity of strategic bombing. Goebbels faced up far more courageously than Hitler to adversity and impending defeat. He publicly admitted the disaster of Stalingrad to an accompaniment of muffled drums and a three-minute silence. Thereafter he pledged the nation to total war and – to counter the reality of the silent Hitler skulking underground in his bunker – launched the new image of the Führer as the supreme sufferer, stoically enduring adversity like Frederick the Great. Goebbels, who frequently visited devastated cities, could not deny the increasing destructiveness of allied bombing so instead he used it to stir up hatred against the enemy. By several drastic measures in 1944, including the conscription of women up to the age of fifty, Goebbels persuaded the people that they must all endure hardship together. Morale undoubtedly declined but it was not allowed to turn into opposition to the regime. By telling the people frankly that the future was grim he kept them from concluding that it was hopeless.[35]

Historians have said that the allied policy of 'Unconditional Surrender' was also a propaganda gift to Goebbels, but recently it has been convincingly argued that he was not in fact able to exploit this to any extent since the terms of the formula were too mild for the bloodcurdling images Goebbels wished to conjure up in the event of defeat. On the other hand, attacks on the formula for vagueness might have provoked the Allies into spelling out their intentions which would not have suited him either.[36]

Compared to Germany, Britain and France were raw beginners in the arts of propaganda and psychological warfare in 1939. The very notion of government-controlled information and subversion was obnoxious to many democratic leaders. It is inconceivable that an equivalent of Goebbels could have held high office in either country (or in the United States) in the 1930s. Consequently the early efforts of both Britain and France in the 'Phoney War' months were fumbling and ineffective. Their ministries of information and similar agencies had overlapping fields of interest and ill-defined aims; they overemphasized the written word at the expense of radio; and adopted too much of a lofty and mandarin tone to impress a mass audience.

France never had an opportunity to correct her errors and, despite the shocks of Dunkirk and the Battle of Britain, British propaganda continued to be badly organized and confused in its aims for another year.[37] From the moment of taking office, however, Churchill struck the right note in his speeches; namely that of 'blood, toil, sweat and tears' rather than anodyne optimism. Once they had survived the darkest days in 1940 and 1941 the British people, in contrast to the Germans, could be increasingly confident about eventual victory. This made the task of allied propagandists inherently easier, but institutional reforms also helped. In 1941 the internecine struggles of three overlapping agencies were largely – though never entirely – resolved by the creation of the Political Warfare Executive, which controlled policy regarding all broadcasts and pamphlet propaganda directed at enemy and occupied countries.

The fundamental belief on which the PWE's operations were based was that in a long war a reputation for accuracy and consistency would pay greater dividends than Germany's mixture of bombast, bullying and the 'big lie'. The BBC in particular risked being dull in order to provide solid information and as much truth as was feasible in wartime. These assumptions proved correct. As the credibility of German broadcasts diminished, the BBC attracted millions of clandestine listeners all over Europe. Neither straight reporting (or 'white' propaganda) nor subversive (or 'black' propaganda) seem to have been very effective in lowering German morale or driving a wedge between the people and the Nazis. But the BBC *did* play an important role in encouraging and organizing resistance movements in countries such as France and Denmark. Quite apart from active resisters, the BBC kept up morale in occupied countries by the daily reminders that Germany had not won the war. An anonymous genius at the BBC hit upon the single most effective propaganda symbol of the whole war in the V-for-Victory morse signal and its accompanying motif – the opening notes of Beethoven's Fifth Symphony.

When the Soviet Union was invaded in June 1941 her rulers predictably rebuffed allied attempts to coordinate their psychological warfare campaigns. Equally predictably, the early Soviet propaganda aim in broadcasts and pamphlets to drive a wedge between the ordinary German soldier and the Nazis failed completely. From 1942 onwards Soviet propaganda placed less emphasis on Marxist-Leninist concepts of the class war and more on the Germans' instinct for self-preservation in a war which they were bound to lose. The Russians failed also in their effort to secure German desertions on any significant scale; nor did they have much success in 'turning' German prisoners of war to change sides. However, Russian 'black' propaganda designed to lower German morale was insidious enough to worry the enemy.

On the domestic front the rapid advance of the Nazi invaders caused confusion in the Russian propaganda sphere as in other ways. The government had so little confidence in the people that all private radios were confiscated by the police to prevent citizens listening to enemy broadcasts. Defeats in the field and the fall of great cities were not publicly admitted for weeks. Once the crisis was surmounted the Kremlin changed its main theme from communist ideology to an appeal to Russian patriotism to withstand and expel the barbarian invader. The heroes of 1812 and earlier epics of resistance were extolled in pamphlets, broadcasts and above all in films. Nevertheless Stalin took care that no single military hero should emerge in the present struggle to threaten his own dictatorial authority.[38]

In the interwar years great hope had been placed in strategic bombing, first as a deterrent and, should that fail, as a war-winning instrument. In the event, the bombing of densely populated areas brought the realities of war home to more civilians than any other conflict for several centuries, but its economic, psychological and political effects all fell far short of expectations. In other words, bombing attacks everywhere failed to cripple economic resources, break civilian morale or force governments to seek peace. The main reasons for this shortfall were that politicians did not understand the limitations of air power (they grossly exaggerated its likely impact on their own societies as well as the enemy's) while many professional airmen underestimated the enormous practical difficulties of locating, hitting and destroying targets in wartime conditions. In any case, the types of aircraft and their 'payloads' were inadequate for their strategic role in the first three years of the war. The *Luftwaffe* was the first to discover this in its failure to bomb London and other British cities into submission in 1940 and 1941, and later in the war the German unmanned aircraft and rockets (V1s and V2s) were also to prove indecisive. It should be noted however that the *Luftwaffe* had not been prepared primarily for this role and the tonnage dropped on Britain was only a tiny fraction of that received by Germany.[39] As for the V2s, their terror effect promised to be considerable but the launching sites were quickly overrun. By the end of 1941 RAF Bomber Command was forced to face the fact that its raids up to this point on precise targets had been ineffectual and its losses excessively high. Thereafter Bomber Command concentrated mainly on night attacks designed to obliterate industrial areas and disrupt production by 'de-housing' workers. American bombers in turn suffered unacceptable casualties when they attempted day attacks but they eventually found a partial solution in long-range fighter escorts. Both the Russians and the Germans gave priority to the tactical employment of air power and the Allies also gradually learnt both the techniques and the need for interservice cooperation. In the last three years of the war Germany rarely enjoyed tactical air superiority abroad, and in the last year or so of the European war they lost it even over their home territory.

Strategic bombing was a controversial subject during the war and it has become even more so in recent years. It is now fashionable to assert that these great operations were misguided, immoral and futile, but such judgements tend to ignore the complexity of the issues involved. As stated above, British air power was inadequate to implement an offensive strategy in the early years but, after Dunkirk, it was the only way to strike directly at Germany. Ideally it would have been morally desirable to confine destruction to military targets but for most of the war this was simply not feasible. The substantial charge against Bomber Command is that its leaders persisted with 'area bombing' in 1944 and 1945 after the possibilities of tactical cooperation (as in the build-up to D-Day and in the weeks following the landings) and relatively precise targeting had been demonstrated. On the psychological plane no people's will to fight was completely broken, but it would be a mistake to conclude that say, in the Ruhr, civilian morale was not seriously lowered, or that in no circumstances could bombing have achieved this objective. Its economic effects are even less suitable for glib generalizations. German war production increased dramatically between 1942 and 1944 but the rate of increase would have been even greater had it not been for the disruptive effect of the air raids. Indirectly Anglo-American bombing diverted skilled labour and scarce resources into repair work and home defence, most importantly by tying down air resources which might otherwise have been employed on the eastern front. Lastly, in the final months of the European war (from May 1944) the Allies did at last find the enemy's Achilles heel in the form of oil installations, and hit it so decisively that Germany was barely able to maintain air defences or army mobility through the final winter. Poor intelligence, vacillation in target priorities, interservice disputes and bad weather all militated against the earlier success of strategic bombing in achieving its ambitious economic goals, but a careful examination of the German home front in 1944 and 1945 refutes sweeping condemnations of the effort as a failure.[40]

Too much hope was also placed in Germany's dependence on imported raw materials and her assumed vulnerability to naval blockade. This dependence was real enough, as witnessed by the frantic quest for new sources of supply in the 1930s, but was greatly lessened by Hitler's conquests and (until June 1941) by the enormous flow of food and raw materials such as manganese from the Soviet Union. Even so the British (and later the allied) blockade would have severely handicapped Germany's war production but for the traditional problems posed by neutrals. Only Spain, Portugal, Ireland, Switzerland and Sweden remained neutral throughout the war but the latter two, plus Turkey who was neutral for most of the war, proved useful 'windpipes' for Germany. Lists of goods deemed to be of military value to the Axis powers were published and proclaimed as contraband, which enabled the Royal Navy to prevent their import into enemy harbours and, if necessary, to seize them on the high seas. The list of contraband was by now nearly all-inclusive and, in principle, the combined power of the British and American Atlantic fleets was sufficient to cut off all Axis and non-European merchant shipping from enemy ports. In practice, however, some respect had to be paid to neutrals' trading rights. The United States Board of Economic Warfare urged the British to join them in a ruthless blockade policy, but the British government demurred, mainly because it was acutely conscious of its own precarious commercial position and rightly feared that lasting damage might be done to international trade relations. The Allies consequently compromised by attempting to restrict or prohibit only vital items of the neutrals' export trade to Italy and Germany, such as Swedish iron ore and ball bearings, machinery and weapons from Switzerland, chrome ore from Turkey and other ores such as wolfram, from Spain and Portugal.

Quite apart from deficiencies in industrial intelligence (and an underestimation of pre-war stockpiling) and lack of consistency in attacking key economic targets, it proved impossible, except for brief periods, to deprive Germany of adequate raw materials for most of her war industry. For example, the Allies persuaded Turkey to export all her chrome ore to them until January 1943, but although no less than 88 per cent of Germany's entire chrome imports had derived from Turkey and the Balkans in 1941, she still managed to get by thanks to her ruthless exploitation of remaining Balkan sources. Again, Germany drew about 63 per cent of her wolfram imports from Spain and Portugal, but despite tremendous allied efforts to stop this trade, Germany still had enough stockpiles for two more years at the end of 1944.[41]

The allied blockade policy made a mockery of existing international law on the maritime rights of neutrals, but still failed to do substantial damage to the German economy, though Italy and Japan were more seriously affected. The European neutrals suffered in some respects, such as a fall in the volume of their trade, a sharp decline in real wages, and shortages of some consumer goods. But countries such as Sweden and Switzerland which had strong and sophisticated industrial structures in 1939, both benefited from their close wartime economic links with Germany. Machinery and armaments, for example, accounted for half the value of Swiss exports to Axis countries in 1943. These states enjoyed rapid economic growth in the early post-war years, thanks mainly to their freedom from the destruction and dislocation suffered by the combatant and occupied states. All this is not necessarily to conclude that economic warfare is not a potentially crucial branch of strategy. Indeed German weaknesses might have been exploited earlier and more effectively, while Japan and Italy were completely unsuited to wage a long war against a great industrial and naval power like the United States. However, deficient industrial intelligence and, more broadly, the lack of precise knowledge of how a complex economic system functioned, proved formidable handicaps to the operation of such a strategy in the Second World War.[42]

The final strand in allied strategy towards Germany to be examined is the relationship with the anti-Nazi opposition in Germany and the alleged sacrifice of possible gains from this cooperation by the allied adoption of a policy of 'Unconditional Surrender'. During the 'Phoney War' months the British Foreign Office took considerable risks in making contacts with and offering indirect encouragement to various anti-Nazi groups in Germany, most importantly those with key members in the Army Command

Headquarters (OKH) and the *Abwehr* (German Service Intelligence).[43] Exposure of these clandestine contacts, made through the Vatican and neutral countries and by individual agents, would of course have undermined Britain's apparently resolute stance both at home and in the eyes of neutrals. These risks were underlined by the capture at Venlo in November 1939 of two British agents who were in fact unwittingly dealing with the SS. The German opposition also lost credibility by its frequent (and in fact accurate) warnings of the impending attack in the west which was repeatedly postponed due to bad weather. But the real obstacles to cooperation lay deeper. The British government was extremely reluctant to deal with 'traitors' and particularly with traitors who could not deliver the goods by carrying out a *coup d'état*. Finally there was the awkward question of what terms the conspirators would demand if they did overthrow the Nazi leadership; it was suspected, and not without some foundation, that the opposition really wanted Hitler's territorial gains without the Führer himself. For their part the anti-Nazi groups, who vainly attempted to kill Hitler on several occasions before 20 July 1944, protested that they needed outside (i.e., British) support if they were to stand a chance of seizing power and opening peace talks.

Beyond these tactical and political problems lay a wider issue. With whom was Britain at war and what were her war aims? Until the outbreak of war, perhaps even until May 1940, it was possible to believe that the opponent was the German state and its temporary Nazi rulers who were seeking excessive territorial gains in the traditional way. If it was not a 'total' ideological conflict and a firm distinction could be drawn between the Nazis and the German people, then a compromise peace was possible. Britain declared war in September 1939 more for traditional reasons than in the spirit of a crusade against Nazism; indeed it is conceivable that had Hitler been willing to withdraw from Poland and discuss terms in a reasonable way Chamberlain and Halifax would have been willing to negotiate.

These faint hopes dwindled as Hitler's victories in the east and the west consolidated his authority in Germany and greatly weakened Britain's bargaining position, deprived as she was of her main ally and threatened by invasion. Churchill both personified and championed a resolute and even ruthless spirit of all-out war to impose total defeat on Germany and exterminate Nazism. In pursuit of this grand strategy, which the United States endorsed in December

1941, there was no room for distinctions between good and evil Germans, or at least not until the war had been decisively won. Thus a policy of unconditional surrender was implicit in allied attitudes long before it was openly announced in January 1943. Its main purpose then was to reassure the understandably suspicious Stalin that Britain and the United States would never contemplate a separate peace with Germany. This declaration is frequently criticized by historians on the grounds that it robbed the German people of hope and consolidated resistance behind the Nazis. But, as we noticed earlier, Goebbels did not in fact make much use of the term in his propaganda; the German people were more terrified of the advancing Russians than of western intentions after capitulation. Finally, as Michael Balfour stresses, unless the Allies were to avoid any public reference at all to war aims, any precise terms were likely to be far harsher not more lenient than those enunciated in the policy of unconditional surrender.[44]

Thus, for all the theorizing of the interwar period, there proved to be no short cut or single path to victory. The belligerents were very successful in keeping up their own people's morale but failed to exert any significant influence on the enemy people. The war was therefore decided mainly by the classic principles of defeating the enemy's armed forces and occupying his territory. Only against Japan did the latter prove unnecessary, thanks to employment of the atomic bomb which had been developed for possible use against Germany. After the war it was discovered that German scientists had been attempting to produce an atomic bomb but were a long way behind the United States and Britain. If Hitler had possessed atomic weapons in 1945 he would surely have used them.

Statistics by themselves can convey only a faint notion of the destruction and suffering caused by the war. In the European war Russia suffered most seriously with perhaps 20 million deaths and even more people made homeless. By their scorched earth policy in the final months of the war, the Germans devastated occupied territories, especially in the east, and extinguished as much as two-thirds of their wealth. In the east, 'There was one cow where there had been ten, one sheep or goat where there had been four, one pig in place of two. Crops had to be sown by hand.'[45] Most of Russia's rolling stock and about 40,000 miles of track had been destroyed. The rigours of war continued there for at least a decade. Poland lost 15 per cent of her population and her deaths (including a majority of

Jews) approached 6 million. Germany also suffered heavily. She lost at least four and a half million, including about a million civilians. Her military casualties were far heavier than in the First World War. Most of her cities had been reduced to wastelands of rubble and were to remain so for many years despite the remarkable economic recovery in the western sector. In contrast Britain, France and Italy all suffered fewer deaths than in the First World War. Britain's case was the most remarkable since she fought throughout and in all the main theatres: her fatal casualties including civilians, totalled 450,000 with another 120,000 from the empire. Italy's losses were slightly fewer than Britain's but as many as one-fifth of them were civilians. Belgium's military casualties were approximately equal to those of the First World War but in the Second she lost more civilians than servicemen. The Dutch people suffered acute food shortages in the later stages of the war and this partly accounts for Holland's extremely heavy civilian losses; at least 200,000, from a small population. In central and eastern Europe civilian casualties as a direct result of the war were high but they were swollen by the mass extermination of some 6 million Jews, another 4 million non-Jews and perhaps as many as a million Yugoslav resisters – the terrible price paid for a 'successful' partisan struggle. Greece's 250,000 deaths also included a majority of civilians due to anti-Nazi and internecine guerrilla conflicts. Western historians tend to overlook the Balkan regular forces in the Second World War, but they too suffered heavily: Yugoslavia and Hungary lost about 400,000 men each; Poland, Rumania and Austria about 300,000 each. Total losses in the whole war add up to something like 50 million but the precise figures will never be known. Never before had civilians so widely shared with soldiers the effects of war: almost half of Europe's dead were civilians compared to one-twentieth in the First World War.[46]

Earlier we noted the vast disturbances and forced migrations of peoples in the first year of the war. Between 1939 and 1947 16 million Europeans were permanently uprooted and transplanted. In 1945 in central and eastern Europe there was a gigantic demographic upheaval resulting in approximately 11 million refugees or 'displaced persons' mostly huddled in primitive refugee camps in Germany. Resettling them constituted a major problem for the occupying powers for many years. Several thousand remained as rootless and bitterly resentful aliens in West Germany. This was an ironic reversal of the *Drang nach Osten* which featured so prominently in Nazi doctrine. From another viewpoint Hitler had won a macabre and devilish victory by transforming central Europe into 'a vast dilapidated slum and poorhouse'.[47] The allied liberation of Belsen, Dachau and the Polish death camps belatedly brought home to a wider public the full horror of Nazism. In retrospect this seemed to justify allied ruthlessness in the bombing campaign.[48] Fortunately, at least in West Germany and western Europe, the recovery from psychological wounds[49] and economic dislocation was much more rapid than could have been imagined: it is to Russia, eastern Europe, parts of the Balkans and to the survivors of the 'final solution' that we must look for lasting material deprivation or mental suffering.

Considering the duration and intensity of the conflict, the map of Europe changed astonishingly little in 1945. There was no great peace conference like Paris in 1919; indeed, except those concluded in 1946 with Italy, Finland and the ex-enemy Balkan states, there were no formal peace treaties. Most of the boundary changes that did occur were in central and eastern Europe. Estonia, Latvia and Lithuania were absorbed into the Soviet Union, which also annexed parts of Finland, Czechoslovakia and Rumania. Poland never regained real independence and her boundaries were shifted westward. Stalin was an expansionist but formally annexed less than he could have done because he expected that new Soviet republics would spontaneously emerge.[50] When this did not happen communist takeovers were engineered and the Soviet Union came to exercise real control in Poland, East Germany, Bulgaria, Hungary, Czechoslovakia and Rumania. Yugoslavia, though communist, soon left the fold, and Austria was permitted neutral (and genuinely independent) status in 1955. Churchill and even more Roosevelt have frequently been reviled for their 'sell-out' to Stalin at Yalta, but it is hard to see how they could have restricted Soviet expansion by formal agreement. The brutal facts of military power were dominant: the Soviet armies had borne the brunt of the land war against Germany and power passed to them by conquest and military occupation.[51] It was also widely expected that communist parties would seize control in some western European countries, Italy and France in particular, but this never happened.

In other respects the war's aftermath was better than the pessimists had predicted. The democracies in most cases recovered their full constitutional rights and restored individual liberties. Wartime conscription did not prove to be 'the cancer of democracy' as Major-

General J. F. C. Fuller had called it. On the contrary, national service was retained in nearly every west European state after the war and, with a few exceptions like Britain and the United States, remains in operation to this day. Nor were states like Britain and France permanently 'militarized' by their experience in the Second World War; millions of young men now appreciated the realities of military power and military life but this, if anything, enhanced their love of civilian status and values. The establishment of the Welfare State in Britain in the later 1940s may be seen as a direct benefit in return for the general sacrifice and deprivation of the war years. Though the post-war rooting out of Nazis in West Germany fell far short of the ideal, that country seems to have abandoned Nazi-style militarism, a generalization which could not be applied so confidently to East Germany. Sobered by her total military defeat, culminating in the only experience to date of atomic bombing, Japan has moved furthest of all from her pre-1939 brand of militarism.[52]

A. J. P. Taylor concludes a study of the war fully illustrated with the manifold forms of suffering with the following remarkable sentences:

> Those who experienced it know that it was a war justified in its aims and successful in accomplishing them. Despite all the killing and destruction that accompanied it, the Second World War was a good war.[53]

This opinion may to some savour of hindsight and regionalism, i.e., more acceptable to a citizen of London or New York than a Cold War victim in Warsaw or Budapest. Given, though, that the war began as an attempt to prevent German hegemony, it was nonetheless a great and noble achievement to overthrow Nazism and its dependent despotisms. These regimes constituted 'the worst challenge ever presented to liberal civilization and its conception of the humane society'.[54] This challenge was the great, albeit retrospective, justification of the war. Most readers will surely now agree with Mr Taylor's judgement that the war was just and its outcome a cause for rejoicing, but what about the enormous suffering inflicted along the way, much of it on the completely innocent? Though hard for many to accept, the Second World War drives home the lesson that there *are* causes worthy of such sacrifices. Recently television has done much to revive memories and educate younger generations in the sheer horror of the Nazis and the vile things they did to individual human beings of both sexes and all ages. As time passes and memories fade of what happened in Nazi-dominated Europe we need to be reminded regularly of

The battered, but living skeletons found in the stinking degradation of the torture camps in 1945 [which] are Hitler's truest memorial.[55]

It is either cynical or careless to say that wars settle nothing. The Nazis and their fascist allies were beaten; the history of Europe, and indeed of the world, would have been vastly different (and worse) had they not been. The particular brand of antirational, antidemocratic authoritarianism of the Hitler-Mussolini era was probably defeated and vanquished for ever from Europe in 1945. Though the political outcome was far from ideal, western Europe and the free world beyond had gained a reprieve[56] – a reprieve which they are still enjoying nearly forty years later.

7

POST-WAR EUROPE,
1945–70

There have been no major interstate wars in Europe since 1945 and very few minor conflicts apart from civil war in Greece, Soviet repression of rebellions within her sphere of influence and the protracted intercommunal strife in Northern Ireland. For nearly forty years Europe has existed under the shadow of nuclear weapons whose employment would probably bring about the general catastrophe mistakenly expected from previous generations of 'horror weapons'. No atomic or nuclear weapons have ever been employed in Europe and none has ever been used against a power capable of retaliation in kind. This remarkable period of relative stability and peace in central and west Europe is partly due to the appearance after 1945 of two 'super powers', the United States and the Soviet Union, whose rivalry would have affected the traditional balance of power adjustments even without the advent of nuclear weapons. But nevertheless it does seem a reasonable inference that it is *mainly* due to the deterrent effect of nuclear weapons that hardly a shot has been fired in anger in Europe for so long and that the major powers have conducted their global ideological conflict with so much circumspection.[1]

In the late 1940s and early 1950s successive crises provided realistic political grounds for fear in an atmosphere of east-west suspicions, mutual misunderstandings and, above all, uncertainty about the military balance. Writing in 1966, the late Alastair Buchan remarked that the era of the Berlin blockade and the Korean war provided:

little indication of the restraints on large-scale international conflict in the familiar cockpits of the world, or of the fragmentation of violence into other forms in other areas, that has been so evident in the past fifteen years.

In 1950 Liddell Hart thought that the countries of western Europe regarded another war as almost inevitable, and that next time there would be no recovery. He thought the Soviet imposition of an 'Iron Curtain' would foment so much friction that an unpremeditated outbreak of war was quite possible. The atmosphere was 'perilously inflammable'. He believed that if one side had an overwhelming advantage in atomic weapons it would probably use it.

> But if both sides possess the same weapon – or even imagine that the other has it ready – there is a fair chance that both may hesitate to unloose it, from mutual fear of the common consequences . . . Mankind, and even its governments, can show uncommon sense and restraint when they see clearly enough that it is a matter of mutual preservation.[2]

Since Liddell Hart wrote these words the 'balance of terror' has become a fact of international relations, indeed even a cliché, but it is important to describe briefly how it was achieved in both political and strategic terms.

What in restrospect seems to be the unavoidable development of the 'Cold War' in the years 1945–50, and the resultant permanent division of Europe into two enormous armed camps on either side of a clearly drawn frontier, were by no means the intentions of the victorious Allies who met at Potsdam in the summer of 1945. True, the course of the war on the eastern front since Stalingrad left little room for doubt that the Soviet Union would occupy a large buffer zone in eastern Europe between the Baltic and the Balkans, and indeed this had been tacitly accepted by Roosevelt and Churchill at the Yalta Conference. Nevertheless the extent of the Soviet advance and the ruthlessness with which communist rule was imposed throughout the area controlled by the Red Army, came as a shock to Britain and the United States who had expected wartime collaboration to continue after the defeat of Germany. The extension of Russian power into central Europe and as far west as the river Elbe has been called without hyperbole 'the main theme of the post-war era and probably of the second half of the twentieth century'.[3]

The future of Poland was a test case in relations between Russia and the west because Britain had gone to war ostensibly to defend Poland, and subsequently made it clear that she did not recognize any territorial changes effected there during the war. Russia's callous failure to make even a gesture to aid the Warsaw rising in 1944 and her contempt for the non-communist resistance foreshadowed her hostility to the exiled Polish government. Although the latter was represented in the post-war 'Provisional Government of National Unity', communists held the key posts and controlled the subsequent elections. By 1948 all opposition parties had been crushed and Poland had become a communist state.[4]

The breakdown of wartime allied agreements was nowhere more unpremeditated, embittered and serious in its consequences than in the case of Germany. Roosevelt, Churchill and Stalin all agreed, from 1941 onwards, that Germany must be disarmed and demilitarized and the Nazis removed. Stalin was understandably obsessed with the fear of yet another German revival and convinced the Allies without much difficulty that Germany should be permanently dismembered. There was also agreement that an allied control commission would administer the defeated country and that reparations would be exacted in kind rather than in cash. In 1944 Britain and the United States briefly flirted with the Morgenthau Plan for 'pastoralizing' a truncated rump of Germany, but it was quickly realized that converting the most highly industrialized area of Europe into a 'rural slum' would have disastrous economic effects. At Yalta three occupation zones were agreed (France was later allotted an area) and the city of Berlin was to be similarly parcelled out, though the details were left vague. These were intended to be temporary military arrangements, pending the dismemberment of Germany. The French were even keener on this idea than the other three powers and clung to it longest. However, by the time of Germany's surrender the major powers were all changing their minds about dismemberment; Britain and the United States because they were worried by the expansion of Soviet influence, and Stalin because he hoped to exact reparations from the Ruhr and eventually to gain control over a united Germany. At Potsdam therefore it was argued that the unity of Germany should be preserved, albeit a considerably reduced Germany since Russia had annexed part of the former East Prussia, and the new Polish frontiers had been pushed westward to the Oder-Neisse river line.

Two developments soon made the goal of unity unattainable. On the political plane, local elections in 1946 foreshadowed the emergence of dominant socialist-communist parties in the Russian zone and a democratic multiparty system in the western zones. It was on the economic plane, however, that an impasse was quickly reached.

Germany was supposed to be treated as a single economic unit but the Russians, while ruthlessly seizing industrial equipment in the western zones up to the 15 per cent permitted, refused to allow the transfer of any raw materials and food from the east. In 1946 the Americans abruptly forbade any further dismantling for reparation purposes in their zone. The Russians, justifiably from their viewpoint, accused the Allies of being more concerned with German than Russian recovery, whereas the Allies felt that the Russians were preoccupied with strengthening their own position to the neglect of a general European settlement. The crisis was reached early in 1947 when the British and Americans (followed by the French) tacitly accepted the failure of the Potsdam agreement by combining their zones into a single economic unit. They had grown tired of supplying the basic imports to maintain a minimum standard of living in western Germany, without any return, while the Russians refused any support to western Germany and continued to remove industrial equipment from their own zone. This action led to mutual recrimination and the German question became the main issue in what was now openly called the 'Cold War'. By October 1949 two separate German states had been formally set up.[5]

In eastern Europe it was the presence of the Red Army rather than the revolutionary power of the local communist parties which ensured that political, social and economic systems were made to conform with Russian interests. Though most of these countries displayed individual nationalistic traits and elected coalition rather than purely communist governments, by the end of 1948 Poland, Hungary, Rumania, Bulgaria and East Germany were all under communist control. A communist coup in Czechoslovakia in that year followed the Russians' refusal to allow the coalition government to accept Marshall aid. The exclusion of all non-communists, and Jan Masaryk's mysterious death shortly afterwards, shocked the west which had seen Czechoslovakia as an outpost of democratic government within the Soviet sphere. In only two countries in this area did Stalin refrain from pressing home his military and psychological advantages in the immediate aftermath of war. Surprising though it seems, most commentators agree that Stalin allowed the communists to be defeated in the Greek civil war rather than break his 1944 agreement with Churchill. Yugoslavia was unique among German-occupied nations in that Tito's partisans, with British and American assistance, had virtually liberated the country before the Red Army could intervene. Tito's independent line in both domestic and foreign policies antagonized Moscow to the extent that Yugoslavia was expelled from the recently created 'Cominform' (the Russian-dominated international communist information bureau) in 1948. Tito's personal popularity and party support were so strong that he was able to defy Russian political pressure and economic sanctions, and in this case a Russian invasion was probably ruled out from fear of British and American reactions.

Only three months after the communist takeover in Czechoslovakia occurred the first open trial of strength in the Cold War. In 1948 the Soviet government exploited the imprecision of the allied powers' rights of access to Berlin by attempting to impose its own East German currency in the allied sectors. When the Allies resisted, the Russians first cut off power supplies to the western sectors and then stopped all road, rail and canal traffic from the west. Stalin evidently expected an allied capitulation, but instead they responded with a massive airlift which lasted a whole year and kept the city supplied with food, fuel and raw materials through a particularly severe winter. Rather than provoke the east-west war, which at times seemed almost certain, the Russians eventually lifted the blockade. This dramatic confrontation helped to confirm the emergence of two separate German states which were also to be mirrored by two separate municipal administrations in Berlin. In the west, Bonn was soon to be accepted as the permanent capital city since Berlin would obviously remain divided. Within Berlin, contacts between east and west remained comparatively easy until 1961 when the East Germans erected a massive, heavily guarded wall to stop the flow of refugees from their zone.[6]

In June 1950 troops from North Korea, probably with Russian encouragement, invaded South Korea and were resisted by a predominantly American force acting under the auspices of the United Nations. At this distance in time it is hard to understand why this onslaught was thought to herald a Soviet attack on western Europe, but at the time the analogies between Korea and Germany seemed obvious. Both were countries which the western powers had hoped to see unified; both were divided with a communist and non-communist half; and both included a Russian satellite. Although the North Atlantic Treaty Organization (NATO) had been set up in April 1949, there had as yet been no real effort to provide a defence force in western Europe; indeed it was estimated that the British,

French and Americans together could only raise 4 divisions in Germany against as many as 175 Russian divisions. Worse still, the Russians had recently tested their first atomic weapons so the American monopoly was already broken and with it much of the credibility of a nuclear response to a Russian conventional attack. The Korean war exerted a critical influence on American attitudes to the defence of western Europe. The United States had entered NATO on a limited liability basis, hoping that a small commitment of military forces would encourage greater defence spending and mutual cooperation by the European members. It was far from certain initially that the United States would make a large and permanent military effort in Europe. This the Korean crisis brought about and so for the first time the United States became a *fixed* part of the continental balance of power.[7]

Although we do not know for sure whether Russia actually contemplated further westward expansion during this period of crisis, it seems reasonable to assume that 'to Stalin western Europe was the prize, and that it was the formation of NATO, that is the American commitment to the defence of what remained of free Europe, which denied it to him'. Within a decade of the outbreak of the Korean war, the diversification of Soviet military power into long-range bombers, intercontinental missiles and a large submarine force as well as the mighty Red Army, had made an organization such as NATO absolutely essential to coordinate defences over the largest possible geographical area.[8]

NATO has been described as 'the largest and most ambitious alliance structure in history'. In the early years America was the unquestioned leader and she remains far more than a *primus inter pares*. The supreme commander, from General Eisenhower onwards, has always been an American with Britain usually providing a deputy. Until 1963, when Britain committed RAF Bomber Command to NATO, the nuclear deterrent was entirely American and fully under American control. In 1966 General de Gaulle withdrew France from the military command structure of NATO while remaining a party to the Treaty. This unilateral French action, not to mention the enormous difficulties in coordinating so many sovereign states in event of war, makes it easy to understand why NATO has always placed great emphasis on deterrence.

NATO's strategic planning in the early years can be summarized briefly. For its first five years, until the introduction of hydrogen bombs, NATO's staff thought in terms of matching Russian ground forces in what was expected to be a lengthy conventional war. Thus NATO set a fantastic target of 96 divisions, of which about 40 would be immediately available and the remainder mobilized within a month of the declaration of war. This old-fashioned concept was dropped in 1954, by which time only 15 divisions were in existence. For the next three years much reliance was placed on the threat of 'massive retaliation', even in response to a limited Soviet attack, by American hydrogen bombs delivered by long-range bombers. So long as this doctrine seemed valid, little attention was given to ground defence: NATO's weak conventional forces were regarded merely as a 'tripwire' in the jargon of the day, intended to set off the last trump of massive retaliation. Further reflection brought home the truth of what critics like Liddell Hart had been saying all along; namely that a tripwire which would trigger off the thermonuclear holocaust might be an appropriate response to an 'all-out' Soviet threat, but it left NATO (and other troubled areas to which John Foster Dulles's threat of 'massive retaliation' had been applied) helpless against a wide spectrum of threats and challenges below the nuclear level. Instead of a tripwire it was decided that NATO needed a 'shield' in the form of some 20 to 30 mobile divisions which could hold up a conventional attack and provide a breathing space in which negotiations could take place, thus obviating the need for a spasm-response which could well result in mutual destruction.[9]

It cannot be overstressed that for many years NATO's conventional forces were utterly inadequate to resist a Soviet attack. Starting from 'little more than nothing', the original American, British and French forces were organized as armies of occupation and were quite unsuitable to fight against the Red Army. All the member countries had to be persuaded to reverse the post-war trend towards decreasing expenditure on defence and to rearm along lines agreed by the whole alliance (in practice from the American example) and with a fair sharing of the burden. This was never easy to achieve and defence experts have never been satisfied with the result, especially in ground forces. Writing in 1960, for example, Liddell Hart concluded gloomily that 'there is still no adequate defence against any major attack on the main front in central Europe'. There were barely 20 divisions available (including 7 from West Germany) and these varied in size, mobility, equipment and weapon power. The time required for mobilization in the different national armies varied from three to forty-five days. It was hard to imagine such a mixed force putting up a prolonged resistance, particularly if it was heavily outnumbered. Liddell Hart argued that throughout the 1950s free Europe's safety had really depended on the *deterrent* effect of the US strategic air force – its power to counter any Russian aggression on the ground by retaliating with nuclear bombs against the Russian homeland. He was scathing about the effectiveness of NATO's costly forces as a contribution to the deterrent:

> The most that can be claimed for it [the huge outlay] is that the feeling of doing something towards their own protection may have helped to maintain the morale of the European peoples, in face of Soviet menace – even though this feeling rested on an illusion, as regards the protective value of their own military shield.

Liddell Hart believed that NATO could provide an effective conventional shield provided its main members would follow Britain's example of spending more than 8 per cent of her gross national product on defence.[10]

Only four days before the outbreak of the Korean war the western powers were still insisting on the demilitarization of Germany, but Churchill found a ready response when he argued that the Federal Republic must share in the defence of western Europe. Hopes were at first placed in the integration of a German military contingent in a European Defence Community to be modelled on the successful European Coal and Steel Community, but after protracted discussion the EDC was vetoed by the French National Assembly. In fact German rearmament went ahead with the approval of the western powers and this process hastened recognition of the sovereign status of the German Federal Republic. In 1954 a rearmed Germany was admitted to the Western European Union and West Germany also became a member of NATO. Certain restrictions were voluntarily accepted by the Bonn government. Her forces would be employed solely in the NATO area and they would never be equipped with nuclear, bacteriological or chemical weapons. Moreover in its uniforms, drill and organization care was taken that the *Bundeswehr* should be very different from the Nazi *Wehrmacht*. Great stress was placed on the soldier's moral responsibility (*Innere Führung*) and on his role as a citizen in arms.[11] The problems involved in creating an army of highly technical citizen soldiers in a materialistic antimilitary society will be discussed later.

In response to the rearmament of West Germany and her incorporation in NATO, the Soviet Union formalized her dominance of eastern Europe by creating the Warsaw Pact in 1955. Though certain of the satellites, such as Bulgaria and Rumania, would later show some signs of independence from Moscow, notably in their domestic economies, none of them are substantial powers in their own right. Russia called the tune on ideological and strategic issues. She was greatly helped in this by the satellites' profound anxiety about the revival of German militarism. The Warsaw Pact is smaller than NATO but more tightly organized and more blatantly dominated by Soviet military might than is NATO by the Americans. The Pact has had one minor defector, Albania, which for a time enjoyed special ties with China, but it is impossible to imagine Russia allowing any members of the Pact to pursue a semi-independent policy like France.[12]

As we noted earlier, from 1954 NATO's strategy was heavily dependent on the American doctrine of massive retaliation, namely the threat that all aggression would be countered with nuclear weapons regardless of magnitude. This doctrine was translated into practice to the extent that the US Air Force virtually deprived itself of the capacity to carry conventional bombs, but its impracticability was revealed in several minor crises such as that over the Chinese communist threat to the offshore islands of Quemoy and Matsu in 1958. Meanwhile in 1957 the Soviet Union astonished and profoundly alarmed the west by being the first successfully to launch a satellite into space (the Sputnik), and first to project a long-range missile of remarkable accuracy. These events suddenly converted western complacency and confidence in its superiority in military science and technology to feelings of near panic in the belief that Russia had taken a decisive lead. For three or four years western strategic thinking was influenced by the notion of the 'missile gap' which suggested that Russia enjoyed both a qualitative and a quantitative lead in missiles which would make a pre-emptive strike on the United States a feasible option for her. The European Allies became alarmed about the validity of the American guarantee to Europe, suspecting she would only resort to nuclear weapons in response to a direct attack on her homeland; and Soviet diplomacy became more truculent, especially as regards Berlin. Khrushchev's speech to the Supreme Soviet in 1960 boasting of Russia's prowess in rocketry has been described as 'a kind of sabre-rattling unheard since the days of Hitler'. By the early 1960s, however, it became clear that the 'balance of prudence' had not been seriously disturbed; indeed so far from there being a missile gap favouring Russia, it was discovered that the United States had a qualitative and quantitative superiority in missiles.[13]

An unfortunate legacy of these years is that NATO became heavily dependent on battlefield nuclear weapons. This stemmed partly from the deliberate rundown of conventional forces from 1957 on the grounds that they were too costly, unpopular with the electorate and anyway could never match the 5 million or so troops available to the Soviet Union; but also from a loss of confidence in the feasibility of conventional defence in the new missile era. In principle, tactical nuclear weapons could be used against specific military targets and attacking forces through the means of aircraft or short-range rockets. American strategic analysts have devoted immense effort to developing a concept of limited nuclear war as part of a localized defensive war, but it seems extremely doubtful if they could be used without causing escalation to an all-out nuclear exchange. Tactical nuclear weapons were stockpiled in thousands, all manufactured in the United States and directly controlled by American servicemen, though other NATO members also operated delivery systems. Close political control was established and there was virtually no danger that they would be used by accident or through over-hasty reaction by a subordinate commander. Their most serious consequence was to introduce great uncertainty as to whether or when they would be used. This has made planning for conventional defence extremely difficult.[14]

Despite this problem of tactical nuclear weapons, and other factors which militated against an effective conventional defence in western Europe, elaborate doctrines were designed to secure mutual deterrence at nuclear and non-nuclear levels and the means to permit a graduated response in proportion to the challenge should Soviet aggression occur. By 1970 it seemed clear that the 'arms race', including the successive stages of submarine launchers, antiballistic missile defences and multiple warheads, was being run (on both sides so far as could be judged) with a view to maintaining deterrence through a combination of fear and uncertainty, rather than trying to gain a 'decisive' advantage which could be militarily exploited. Writing in 1966 Leonard Beaton concluded:

after years of trying each other's will and capacity, the two sides seem to have found a military balance which they prefer not to tamper with. There is no sign – in spite of the 2,000,000 troops, the thousands of tactical nuclear weapons and the strategic armouries – that either side of Europe now thinks itself insecure.[15]

In the political sphere this 'balance of terror' or, more accurately, 'balance of prudence', has had the effect of establishing mutually recognized spheres of influence and the exercise of considerable restraint compared with, say, the behaviour of the great powers before 1914. Restraint operated in two ways: allies or dependants of the super powers dared not risk going to war with other non-nuclear powers from fear of the use of nuclear weapons by their enemy's protector; while the super powers not only restrained each other but also kept a watchful eye on their allies or clients lest they be drawn into their conflicts.

We noted that in the immediate post-war years the west reluctantly accepted that too high a price would be paid for intervention in eastern Europe to save Poland and Czechoslovakia from authoritarian communist rule. Since then the west's impotence in that area has been demonstrated on several occasions when the Red Army, with or without Warsaw Pact forces, has repressed anti-Moscow rebellions with more or less brutality. In June 1953, for example, there were full-scale riots in East Berlin and several other East German cities in protest against economic reforms instigated by the Russians. Government buildings were attacked and Russian flags torn down. Moscow at first rejected the East German communists' request for armed intervention, but when the East German police and troops failed to control the crowds Soviet tanks moved in and the riots collapsed. Three years later, in October 1956, the Polish communists were more successful in standing out for some measure of autonomy. The sudden visit of leading Soviet ministers to Warsaw – usually an ominous sign in troubled times – and the movement of Soviet troops in eastern Poland, only served to unite the Polish communists behind Gomulka and Khrushchev accepted that armed intervention was unnecessary. Gomulka began to construct a 'Polish way to socialism', including the abandonment of collectivization, while taking care to show respect and deference for his powerful neighbour.

These events in Poland were eclipsed by the more spirited and ultimately tragic rising in Hungary, which also of course coincided with the Anglo-French-Israeli war with Egypt over the Suez Canal. The Hungarian rising began on 23 October 1956 in classic nineteenth-century style with students demanding university reform and factory workers demanding higher wages. The Hungarian army proved unwilling to fire on the demonstrators and a few units actually joined them. Many more soldiers simply took unauthorized leave. Soviet tanks and troops began to arrive in the capital the next day but at first improvised resistance seemed successful and the Russian conscripts were clearly unhappy about their role. Revolution rapidly spread throughout the country causing the Russian forces to beat a tactical retreat while bringing up fresh troops in the east of the country. There was briefly an atmosphere like that of 1917 with formerly proscribed political parties reappearing and spontaneous popular councils taking over local government. On 4 November Soviet troops and armour renewed their ruthless and this time carefully planned attack on Budapest. They were met with heroic but futile resistance, the rebellion was crushed and a hard-line, pro-Moscow government established under Janos Kadar. Serious damage had been done to the morale of the Hungarian army which probably took a decade to recover in terms of political reliability and training. Its role in the suppression of the Czechoslovak rising in 1968 revealed many professional shortcomings.[16]

In the 'Prague Spring' of 1968 there was an exhilarating atmosphere of hope and enthusiasm associated with Alexander Dubcek's attempt to pursue a Czechoslovakian route to socialism which rejected Soviet insistence on continued class struggle. In mid-May there was the inevitable military mission under the Soviet minister of defence, Marshal Grechko, but a full-scale invasion by Warsaw Pact forces did not occur until 20 August. There was no armed resistance on the Hungarian model but instead a good deal of passive resistance which resulted in a number of casualties. Dubcek and other 'liberal communists' were arrested and most of their reforms were rescinded. This act of repression was felt to be particularly nauseating in the west ('like the renewed symptoms of a vile and dangerous disease' in the words of one commentator), because of Czechoslovakia's comparatively civilized and democratic recent history. Moreover this act of repression shattered growing hopes that the Soviet Union was becoming less paranoiac and more willing to contemplate a genuine detente. It also showed once again the advantages to Russia of her complete control of her own news media. While television screens throughout the world revealed allied disunity and embarrassment over Suez, but also showed the Czechs' hostile reaction to Soviet tanks in Prague, the Russian people were persuaded that their troops had liberated Czechoslovakia at the request of the people.[17]

Paradoxical though it may seem to talk of Soviet restraint in pursuing its interests as a super power and its ideological crusade in various parts of the world, especially in the Middle East, Africa and Central America, its leaders generally displayed sound judgement in avoiding a direct confrontation with the United States, as could easily have occurred during the Vietnam war. More generally, as in its 'monitoring' of NATO naval manoeuvres, the Soviet Union steered a fine course between irritating its potential enemies and provoking them to a military response. There was of course one notable exception when in 1962 Khrushchev badly underestimated the effects on the United States of his attempting to install missile bases in Cuba. Even in this notorious breach of the rules of the game from the western viewpoint, it should be remembered that from Moscow American missiles in Turkey looked equally provocative. They were removed shortly after President Kennedy's successful defusion of the Cuban crisis.[18]

In addition to exercising restraint in their foreign policies and keeping a watchful eye on potentially adventurous allies or satellites, the super powers displayed a positive interest in maintaining a reciprocal deterrent capability and in ensuring that minor clashes did not accidentally escalate through misreading each other's intentions. As long ago as 1956 a commentator referred to the 'Russo-American alliance against total war', and subsequently Russia's interest in preserving a limited understanding with the United States was underlined by her quarrel with communist China. In 1963 a 'hot line' in the form of a constantly manned teleprinter link, was established between Moscow and Washington, and in the same year the super powers signed a treaty banning atmospheric tests of nuclear weapons which, besides guarding against radioactive fallout, also inhibited the development of larger weapons. In sum, both governments showed an awareness that a balance of mutual deterrence had to be carefully and continuously managed. Though not of course impossible, by 1970 it appeared unlikely that a nuclear war would begin by a physical accident which defeated the rigorous 'fail-safe' procedures, or from an act of wilful disobedience or misunderstanding by a local commander.[19]

Returning to our theme of armed forces and society, the years 1945–70 witnessed a general trend away from semi-trained, primitively equipped, mass conscript armies towards more streamlined, highly professional forces relying increasingly on sophisticated technology and weapon power rather than sheer numbers for their effectiveness. Among the more obvious consequences of this trend were spiralling defence costs which caused increasing public unease, and tough competition for skilled men whose services were in demand from other sectors of the economy. These developments may be illustrated by a brief look at the recruiting systems and career patterns of some of the leading states.

The Soviet Union is in some respects an exception to the general trend in other industrialized countries in that she retained very large forces raised essentially by two-year conscription. She also differed in that her defence budget was not at the mercy of the usual democratic pressures. The keynote of the Soviet military system, as in Soviet society generally, was fear. Even the senior ranks must always be wary of the secret police and party spies. In the lower ranks especially there was hardly any scope for men in uniform to lead a private life or express their individuality. The troops were kept hard at work for long hours under a system of incessant political indoctrination and police surveillance. These conditions would be intolerable in an open society, but individual initiative had traditionally been suppressed and all Russians were indoctrinated early on with the belief that the country was surrounded by enemies who were pledged to destroy communism. The events of 1941, ceaselessly rammed home by propaganda, greatly aided such indoctrination. The obligation to military service was universal between the ages of sixteen and fifty, conscientious objection was unheard of, and little notice was taken of individual preferences, though there were certain compassionate grounds for exemption. By the mid-1950s the Red Army had completed its post-war reorganization and was stabilized at about 4 million men, which enabled the authorities to raise standards by implementing a selective call-up. Military training was strenuous and realistic, the daily diet monotonous. In the satellite countries, especially East Germany, restrictions to prevent off-duty soldiers moving freely among the local population were only slowly relaxed after the death of Stalin. Rates of pay for the other ranks were very low, barrack accommodation usually spartan, and leave very sparingly allowed. Discipline was extremely strict at all levels, the Code of 1940, for example, laid down harsh punishments for officers who failed to discipline offences, however slight.

What was more surprising in an authoritarian and theoretically egalitarian society was the extent to which the officer corps became a privileged and sharply stratified caste. The officer corps was one of the segments of Soviet life set aside for special consideration. Officers enjoyed the priceless advantage of receiving free apartments and could buy scarce goods at special stores at reduced prices. Field officers (majors and above) were assigned a soldier as a servant, and higher officers had a considerable domestic staff. Socially the Red Army officer was encouraged and required to consider himself removed from and superior to enlisted men and civilians. Within the hierarchy there were distinct castes demarcated by separate messes and remarkable pay differentials. In 1961 the caste barriers and pay differentials were more marked even than in the British services. The highest ranks in Russia then received 115 times the pay of the lowest in contrast to the British pay differential of 20½ and the American of 15. Officers were treated with great respect in the Soviet press and in public – an understandable mark of gratitude for their efforts in the Second World War. But the Soviet officer was also

> bedizened in his dress uniform, with the gold on his epaulets to show he is the heir of the aristocratically officered Imperial Russian forces.

This is not to suggest that these privileges were unmerited: professional skills and political reliability were under constant scrutiny, and with about 10,000 new commissions awarded each year there was no room for slacking or complacency. Though the Soviet armed forces remained formidable on virtually all counts they too were not completely immune from the recruitment and career-structure difficulties which beset most western countries.[20]

There is no need to describe the military organizations of Russia's satellites in the Warsaw Pact in detail. Their early post-war development under Soviet control was largely determined by their varied wartime roles: Bulgaria neutral but pro-Soviet; Rumania and Hungary allies of Germany; Poland divided but with a large part of its old army under Russian control; and Czechoslovakia under

German domination but with no distinctive role. The East German army was founded in 1948 largely from volunteers among German prisoners of war in Russia, and was built up under close Russian supervision with Soviet advisers attached to all headquarters. Wherever possible Russia relied on Russian-born or Russian-trained officers for senior appointments in all the satellite armies and ruthlessly purged officers with dubious personal histories or uncertain political views. The Polish army remained the largest and best equipped of the satellite forces but has been carefully watched by a network of senior Russian officers. The satellite armies have been standardized on the Russian model – in organizational terms right down to the platoon. Uniforms, with minor variations, were copied from the Red Army, as also were drill, training and military textbooks. In order of efficiency an expert assessment in the mid-1950s put Poland first, followed by Bulgaria, Czechoslovakia, Rumania and Hungary. The East German army was well-equipped but would be difficult to use alongside the Poles or Czechs because of recent bitter memories. The reliability of these armies as a whole in a war in which the Soviet Union was involved was extremely hard to assess because so much would depend on domestic conditions in each satellite at the time and the nature of the war.[21]

At the end of the war France's armed forces lacked either a clear organization or role. The army and military institutions of 1940 had been discredited by the humiliating defeat, and a large part of the forces (particularly the navy) was further tarnished by close association with the Vichy regime. It took several years to create a new army from the diverse (and often antagonistic) elements of de Gaulle's Free French Forces, the ex-African Vichy army which had joined the Allies in 1942, and the communist-dominated resistance groups. In 1945 many officers and men who wished to serve on were summarily dismissed, and about 4000 ex-Vichy officers were purged. The officers' rates of pay remained low and many married officers had to endure a 'nomadic' existence without parallel in the army's history. Several years after the war the French army offered:

a rather lamentable spectacle. It was dislocated by the trials of the war and the occupation, morally cut off from a regime whose origins were alien to the Army, and materially reduced – almost to vanishing point – by the harsh limits imposed on its resources and on the credits voted.

A new sense of mission was found when France joined NATO in 1949. Ex-Vichy officers in particular welcomed the idea of a general crusade against communism, not only in the Soviet Union but also at home and in Indo-China. Many officers, however, felt that this crusade was a betrayal of the army's traditional role as a bastion of French nationalism. Their indignation found an outlet in bitter opposition to German rearmament, not so much out of fear or hatred of the Germans as from a desire to maintain an independent and predominant role for the French army.

Between 1946 and 1954 the French army made its main effort in the revolutionary war in Indo-China, losing many of its best officers and eventually accepting a bitter defeat. Thereafter Algeria became an ulcer, draining most of France's military strength away from NATO. In the early 1960s France had the longest period of conscript service – 28 months – and some two-thirds of her front-line strength of about one million was concentrated in Algeria. The eventual target for France's contribution to NATO was 20 divisions but in 1961 she had less than two fully constituted divisions in Germany – a total of 15,000 troops including a large number of staff, storekeepers or partly trained recruits. France's decision to build her own independent nuclear deterrent epitomized her determination to prove herself still a great power. The French army was extremely active in internal politics between 1958 and 1962. These years saw the culmination of the army's semi-independent colonial role which encouraged some of the generals in Algeria to believe that they, not Paris, embodied the greatness of France. In May 1958 the army was instrumental in ending the Fourth Republic through its acquiescence in, and tacit support of, the disturbances in Algeria, Corsica and in metropolitan France. Certain (mainly paratroop) units also took a leading role in the anti-Gaullist revolt in Algiers in January 1960 ('the week of the barricades') but this proved abortive because the bulk of the army, and notably the conscripts, refused to join the rebels. An attempted 'putsch' by discontented generals on 22 April 1961 also failed to win sufficient military support. By 1968, the last time when its constitutional loyalty was openly tested, the army fulfilled its traditional role as *la grande muette* and took no part in the demonstrations designed to oust de Gaulle.[22]

There has been a continuous British military presence in Europe since the Second World War, initially as an army of occupation and since 1949 as a founder-member of NATO. When the war ended, the strength of the British army was approximately 2,262,700 but, quite apart from war-weariness, the country could not afford to maintain such a huge force in peacetime and by 1949 it had been reduced to 394,000. Defence expenditure rose sharply during the Korean war (1950–3) and this period also witnessed an increase in extra-European and mainly imperial 'policing' duties (notably in Kenya, Malaya and the Canal Zone) which would stretch the armed forces to the limit over the next fifteen years. Nevertheless in 1954 Britain made the critical decision to maintain in Europe for fifty years a force of four divisions (a target of 55,000 troops) and a tactical air force. At the same time, with a view to securing manpower reductions, Britain decided to create a strategic nuclear force to serve as an independent deterrent.

A series of National Service Acts between 1947 and 1955 set up a system under which all young men registered at the age of eighteen and, unless exempted, served for two years (with occasional variations) in one of the armed forces, the great majority in the army. The prolongation of national service in peacetime was understandably unpopular with the regulars because a large proportion of them were diverted to the basic training of fortnightly batches of conscripts at the expense of professional training for war. By the later 1950s the army's equipment was markedly inferior to the other services': it was reported to be common practice to send two cars on a journey to ensure that at least one reached the destination; and in Germany units borrowed equipment from other armies in order to make a passable show in combined exercises.[23]

The event which more than any other forced Britain to adjust to her reduced status in the world was the Suez war of 1956. Quite apart from its adverse political consequences (American opposition and a vote of censure by the United Nations) this week of 'armed conflict' seemed to demonstrate that Britain no longer had the logistic capacity to mount an efficient amphibious operation in the Middle East. Meanwhile the development and greater sophistication of nuclear weapons and their delivery systems encouraged the pessimistic view that in Europe there was no realistic alternative between complete deterrence and a nuclear holocaust – large, ill-equipped conscript armies seemed redundant. Duncan Sandys grasped this nettle in his defence white paper of April 1957. He announced that national service would end in 1960 and by 1962 the all-regular forces would be stabilized at a strength of about 375,000. For many years there were recurrent recruiting crises, particularly for the army, and the number of men leaving the service early exacerbated the problem. The rapid liquidation of imperial commitments in the 1960s, particularly the withdrawal of nearly all the forces from east of Suez, eased the situation and the reintroduction of national service has never been seriously contemplated – at least on military grounds. By 1970 British defence policy was giving first priority to NATO, but even before that the Northern Ireland emergency had begun and this would remain the army's most onerous active duty.[24]

As regards West Germany, at any rate, the Allies succeeded in the Second World War where they had failed in the First; that is, in stamping out militarism. This was achieved by the moral, physical and political devastation caused by the Nazi regime culminating in its utter defeat in total war, and was reinforced by the allied policies of de-Nazification and re-education in liberal, democratic values. All this had such a profound and widespread effect that in the later 1940s most West Germans seemed to express revulsion, not merely against aggressive war but against all things military. Franz-Josef Strauss, a few years later to be a successful minister of defence at Bonn, proclaimed in 1947, 'May every German hand wither that touches a gun again.' Consequently, when the threat of Soviet aggression compelled the NATO powers, more or less reluctantly, to invite West Germany to rearm the response was much cooler than expected. The permanent ban on Germany's acquisition of nuclear weapons aroused little domestic controversy, but the new and rigorously functional organization adopted by the *Bundeswehr* entailed a sharp and painful break with tradition. In particular infantry, cavalry and armoured units associated with appropriate districts were keen to incorporate the identities and honours of vanished imperial regiments, but this was officially discouraged. Though the navy retained some of its glamour, army and air force officers suffered a marked reduction in social status.

The more or less clean break with the past also had its advantages. Not having to worry about regimental tradition and with a fixed ceiling of 12 divisions, the West Germans were able from the outset to draw on their admirable technical education to stress the need for technical skills and to keep 'simple cannon fodder' to a minimum. By 1960 the initial problems of combining an older generation of ex-

Wehrmacht soldiers with teenage conscripts had been overcome and the *Bundeswehr* had established a successful 'mixed' recruiting system, i.e., long-term enlistments (13 per cent), short-term enlistments (48.5 per cent) and conscripts (38.5 per cent). As regards conscription, the *Bundeswehr* was highly selective: all male citizens between the ages of nineteen and forty-six were liable for armed service (women could only serve as volunteers) but only about one man in four was actually conscripted in 1960 though the ratio increased during the next decade. Between 1960 and 1970 the numbers successfully appealing against conscription on grounds of conscience rose from about 3400 to nearly 34,000. Conscripts normally served for only one year until 1963 when the term increased to eighteen months, but a few years later it was reduced to fifteen months. A continuing problem for the *Bundeswehr* was to maintain a high standard of officers because so many of the ablest men resigned after a short-service engagement. The services could not afford to match the high financial rewards of the business world, but at least for long-service officers (twelve years or more) a great improvement was made in the early 1970s with the establishment of two *Bundeswehr* universities (at Hamburg and Munich) awarding mainly science-based degrees after four years' study, largely free from military distractions. Despite an occasional Nazi or neo-Nazi demonstration (usually occasioned by the funeral of a once prominent Nazi such as Admiral Doenitz), West Germany showed no substantial signs of wishing to revive its military past. Quite the contrary, the antimilitary, pacifist and antinuclear trend seemed to be growing year by year especially among the young.[25]

Brief mention must also be made of two small and proudly neutral countries which created efficient defence forces based upon citizen militias: Switzerland and Sweden. The Swiss system demanded universal male citizen service between the ages of twenty and sixty. Only Swiss citizens were permitted to serve and very few professions were exempted. Though recent Swiss history has been far less warlike than the Israelis' they were similar in that the idea of military service pervaded the nation's life and was taken for granted by everybody. Again like the Israelis, Swiss officers were selected largely on military merit and without undue regard for their social status. In 1960 there were less than a thousand full-time career soldiers, including about one hundred on the general staff, but the Swiss compensated by exploiting the pupil-teacher system. In 1970 there were still a few traditional military families, supplying successive generations of officers, and in some parts of the country local units enjoyed considerable prestige. So fully accepted by the public was the Swiss militia system that all soldiers kept their personal weapons at home, as well as their uniforms and three days' rations. Although such a small part-time force would have obvious limitations in a major war, the Swiss militia's formidable defensive capabilities earned general respect, notably from Germany in 1940 and 1944 who dropped its invasion plans on account of the likely cost – a fine example of deterrence.[26]

Sweden had the unenviable problem of defending an area about twice the size of Great Britain with a population of 8¼ million. In 1970 the regular cadre of her armed forces comprised approximately 50,000 men. The Swedes did not pursue the citizen army system quite so thoroughly as the Swiss – their reserve training arrangements, for example, were considerably less demanding – but the two had much in common. Both abjured nuclear weapons, though Sweden probably had the capacity to produce her own nuclear warheads. Like the Swiss and the Israelis, the Swedes relied heavily on their comprehensive mobilization scheme which permitted them in effect to maintain a standing army on indefinite leave. Sweden possessed an excellent home guard system which was concerned with welfare organizations and civil defence as well as the ultimate role of guerrilla-style resistance. Again like the Swiss, personal weapons, including even machine guns and hand grenades, were kept at home. Sweden was long famous as a producer of first-class military weapons. Unlike some other European countries, morale within the services remained high and the general public gave strong support. The Swedish forces have been said to constitute the most impressive example of the militia system outside Israel.[27]

Following these brief sketches of a small selection of European military systems, let us explore in a little more detail the attitude of the public to its defence forces and their place in a changing society. It is hardly surprising that countries relying entirely on voluntary recruitment experienced difficulties in attracting (and, equally important, retaining) sufficient young men with the necessary ability and commitment to service, and even conscript systems encounter legal objections, hostility and passive resistance. Most western European nations, and especially the generations born since 1945, became accustomed to regular pay rises, high living standards, a great variety of leisure activities and, above all, minimal restriction on personal freedom as regards dress, behaviour and travel. In sharp contrast armed services demanded a comparatively disciplined life with much emphasis on strict observance of regulations and routine. Self-interest must be subordinated to the needs of the unit, the service and the nation. Many of the services' traditions date from the eighteenth century or even earlier, and in the 1960s seemed anachronistic to young people 'whose natural characteristic is indiscipline, [and] who are being brought up moreover in a rapidly changing world where all established rules and doctrines are open to question'.[28] When the draft was in force in the United States the social reputation of service in the other ranks was so low that thousands of young men volunteered to serve for four years as sailors, airmen or marines in preference to two years as private soldiers.

There are numerous problems in reaching even reasonably precise information about the attitudes of 'society' to its armed services. So much depends on the exact phrasing of the questionnaire, its timing and location. Anyone who has performed any kind of military service will know that it is normal to hold ambivalent and even contradictory views. Researchers into public opinion report that most groups of people know remarkably little about each other, and their beliefs are all too often derived from stereotypes often completely false or outdated. In the case of the armed services, many civilians are influenced by the attitudes of friends or relatives who are serving or have served. Thus, for example, generations of disillusioned and occasionally bitter ex-national servicemen disseminated a highly unflattering view of the British army which was far less applicable after it became an all-regular volunteer force again. It may seem surprising in retrospect that national service enjoyed steady support from a majority of the public as long as it remained in operation. In January 1949, for example, 57 per cent of those interviewed agreed that conscription should be continued in peacetime, while 33 per cent were opposed. By September 1956 44 per cent favoured abolishing national service and 38 per cent wanted it to be retained. In the period 1949–56 public support reflected the firm commitment of both major parties to conscription. There was a similar public reaction to questions about the level of total defence expenditure. In February 1952, for example, 58 per cent said they supported the increases for the following year. Colonel John Baynes, who carried out a research project on these lines on a defence fellowship in 1968–9, concluded that:

during the later 1960s at least, support for the armed forces as a useful organization has been quite considerable, and that the taxpayer has in general terms [felt] himself to be getting value for money.

Colonel Baynes was surprised by the bitterness towards the services shown by certain 'communicators' who seemed under a compulsion to insult and slander the army. He cites a review of a book on the prison service which gratuitously concluded: 'In the end there is not much difference between the old regular and the old lag.'[29] By 1970 it seemed unlikely, on both political and military grounds, that national service would be reintroduced in the foreseeable future.[30]

One issue on which a section of the British public became very aroused in the late 1950s was the matter of the independent nuclear deterrent, carried until the mid-1960s by heavy 'V' bombers and since then in Polaris submarines. Public concern was aroused by the testing of the first British hydrogen bomb in 1955 and in the late 1950s opinion polls suggested that between one-quarter and one-third of the public favoured unilateral discarding of nuclear weapons. The Campaign for Nuclear Disarmament was founded in 1958 as a public pressure group whose main activity was the annual Aldermaston march. The campaign reached a peak in 1960 when the annual labour party conference adopted a resolution in favour of unilateral disarmament, but the decision was reversed the following year and in its long tenure of office the labour party after 1964 supported Britain's retention of a semi-independent deterrent.[31]

Concluding reflections on the period covered in this final chapter must begin by reiterating that Europe enjoyed an exceptional period of peace between 1945 and 1970 which was largely the product of mutual deterrence operating between east and west. Permanent peace through nuclear deterrence could not of course be taken for granted: a full-scale rebellion in Poland, America's sudden withdrawal of its forces from Europe or an attempt by the Arab oil producers to hold the west to ransom were just a few nightmare scenarios which could bring disastrous consequences. By 1970 nuclear war seemed unlikely to begin by accident, and it was perhaps too alarmist to assume that if there was an accident it would cause escalation to general war. If, however, war began with the use of conventional weapons, for example by NATO resistance to a Soviet attack somewhere in Europe, then the dividing line between conventional and *any* nuclear weapons whatever remained the only sure and easily recognizable 'firebreak'. The soaring costs of modern weapons systems, which could take ten years or more to develop and deploy, put a considerable strain on the economies of even the most advanced industrialized nations, and were beyond the means (except perhaps when purchased in token numbers) of poorer Third World nations which, paradoxically, were more likely to need them for armed conflict with their neighbours. By 1970 there was growing appreciation in Europe that conventional forces were a vital component of deterrence and needed to be strengthened. Over-reliance on nuclear weapons in the 1960s had created a dangerous imbalance in NATO. Unfortunately the existence of huge stocks of nuclear weapons had by no means ruled out wars and armed conflict *outside* Europe.

The ingredients of the terms 'war' and 'society' and their inter-relationships have changed drastically in the century covered by this volume. The two World Wars not only approached the 'total' form sketched by Clausewitz as regards the size, geographical extension and intensity of operations, but also in drawing in more and more elements of what had previously been recognized as civil society, until in the Second World War, the distinction could scarcely be maintained. Indeed, in as much as 'war *and* society' suggests two distinct and separate identities it has been increasingly inappropriate in the twentieth century. But for the suggestion of civil war, 'war *in* European society' would be closer to reality.

In the era of the Prussian wars which achieved the unification of Germany, Europe was still the hub or power centre of international affairs, but its dominant position was thrown into question by the shifts of financial, economic and political power during the First World War and had clearly been lost by 1945 when the United States and the Soviet Union emerged as undeniable super powers with Japan defeated, Germany divided and the former European imperial powers all in the process of contraction and decline. Fortunately the super powers avoided a showdown in the highly unstable period (*c.* 1945–53) when their relative armed strength was asymmetric and their intentions of using it uncertain. By 1970, through taking under their protection nearly all the European states in NATO and the Warsaw Pact, they had created a balance of power which had become reasonably stable. The rapid development of nuclear weapons, though not the initial cause of the division of Europe into two armed camps, played a vital role in underlining the need to avoid any kind of provocation or adventurism that might spark off a general conflict. Thus for strategic as well as, one hopes, economic, social and cultural reasons, interstate wars had become outmoded in central and western Europe. Historians anticipate future events at their peril, but it would certainly be tragic should a sequel be needed to this volume. Unfortunately, as Liddell Hart and a few other perceptive theorists realized in the 1940s, the deterrent effect of nuclear weapons has been extremely limited. In Europe it prompted the transfer of ideological and great power rivalry into other spheres (economics, commerce, propaganda and subversion), but certain other areas such as Central and South America, parts of Africa and above all the Middle East now seemed to be experiencing their era of national conflicts. Even in Europe the blurring and softening of national sovereignty in military alliances and economic communities should not conceal from us the harsh truth that:

Nothing has occurred since 1945 to indicate that war, or the threat of it, could not still be an effective instrument of state policy. Against peoples who were not prepared to defend themselves it might be very effective indeed.[32]

NOTES

1

1. Robert C. Binkley, *Realism and Nationalism 1852–1871* (Harper Torchbooks, NY, 1963), p. 293.
2. Ibid., pp. 295–6. Theodore Ropp, *War in the Modern World* (revised edition, Collier Books, NY, 1962), pp. 171–5.
3. Carlton J. H. Hayes, *A Generation of Materialism 1871–1900* (Harper Torchbooks, NY, 1963), p. 2.
4. Alfred Vagts, *A History of Militarism* (revised edition, Hollis and Carter, 1959), p. 213.
5. Martin Van Creveld, *Supplying War: Logistics from Wallenstein to Patton* (CUP, 1977), pp. 84–5.
6. E. A. Pratt, *The Rise of Rail Power in War and Conquest, 1833–1914* (P. S. King, 1915), p. 142.
7. Van Creveld, pp. 90–108.
8. G. A. Craig, 'Command and Staff Problems in the Austrian Army, 1740–1866' in Michael Howard (ed.), *The Theory and Practice of War* (Cassell, 1965), p. 64.
9. Ropp, p. 173.
10. G. A. Craig, *The Politics of the Prussian Army 1640–1945* (OUP Galaxy paperback ed., 1964), p. 222.
11. John Gooch, *Armies in Europe* (Routledge and Kegan Paul, 1980), pp. 96–7, 123–4.
12. M. Howard, *The Franco-Prussian War* (Collins, Fontana, 1967), pp. 242–4. R. D. Challener, *The French Theory of the Nation in Arms* (Columbia University Press, 1955), pp. 30–1.
13. Binkley, pp. 299, 306. Hayes, p. 4.
14. Howard, *The Franco-Prussian War*, p. 449.
15. Vagts, pp. 164–6.
16. G. Best, *Humanity in Warfare* (Weidenfeld and Nicolson, 1980), p. 145.
17. Hayes, p. 18.
18. Howard, *The Franco-Prussian War*, p. 373.
19. Ibid., pp. 361–2, 376. Best, *Humanity in Warfare*, pp. 202–3.
20. Best, pp. 189–99.
21. Howard, *The Franco-Prussian War*, pp. 250–2.

22. Best, pp. 142, 150–2.
23. Ibid., pp. 199–200.
24. Ibid., pp. 175–7. F. S. L. Lyons, *Internationalism in Europe 1815–1914* (Leyden, 1963), part V *passim*.
25. Craig, p. 217. Vagts, p. 203. R. Girardet, *La Société militaire dans la France contemporaine, 1815–1939* (Paris, 1953), pp. 164, 169.
26. Vagts, pp. 213–14, 220–1. Gooch, pp. 96–7.
27. Girardet, pp. 175–81. Challener, pp. 33–40, 47.
28. John Whittam, *The Politics of the Italian Army* (Croom Helm, 1977), pp. 107–16. Gooch, pp. 86, 95, 117–19.
29. Gerhard Ritter, *The Sword and the Scepter*, vol. 2 (Florida, University of Miami Press, 1970), pp. 77–9. Gooch, pp. 121–2.
30. For a good survey of recent research on British military history in this period, see Edward M. Spiers, *The Army and Society 1815–1914* (Longman, 1980).

2

1. Vagts, *A History of Militarism*, p. 300.
2. A. J. P. Taylor, *The Struggle for Mastery in Europe* (OUP, 1957), p. xxv.
3. Ibid., p. xxiv. Carlton J. H. Hayes, *A Generation of Materialism 1871–1900*, pp. 102, 299.
4. M. Howard, 'The Armed Forces' in *The New Cambridge Modern History*, vol. XI (CUP, 1962), p. 208. B. and F. Brodie, *From Crossbow to H-Bomb* (Indiana University Press, paperback ed., 1973), p. 152.
5. Brodie, p. 161.
6. Hayes, p. 101. See also Maurice Pearton, *The Knowledgeable State: Diplomacy, War and Technology Since 1830* (Burnett Books, 1982).
7. Vagts, pp. 367–70.
8. Ibid., p. 371. William H. McNeill's *The Pursuit of Power* (Basil Blackwell, 1983) takes a far more favourable view of the armed services' response to technological change. See especially chapters 7 and 8.
9. Donald M. Schurman, *Julian S. Corbett 1854–1922* (Royal Historical Society, Studies in History Series, 1981).
10. J. Colin, *The Transformations of War* (Hugh Rees, 1912), pp. 41–6. Ropp, *War in the Modern World*, p. 215.
11. Colin, pp. 69–72.
12. F. Maurice, *War* (Macmillan, 1891), pp. 73–84. C. von der Goltz, *The Nation in Arms* (Hugh Rees, 1903), pp. 128–32, 380–1.
13. Ropp, pp. 218–19. Colin, pp. 192, 331–5.
14. Goltz, pp. 389–91.
15. Brodie, p. 166. Taylor, p. xxvii. McNeill, pp. 285–99, disputes this orthodox view of the Royal Navy's policy regarding technical change.

16. G. Best and A. Wheatcroft (eds.), *War, Economy and the Military Mind* (Croom Helm, 1976), pp. 45–57.

17. See Howard (ed.), *The Theory and Practice of War*, pp. 97–125.

18. Maurice, pp. 63–7.

19. On *The Battle of Dorking* and war fiction in general, see I. F. Clarke, *Voices Prophesying War, 1763–1984* (OUP 1966).

20. See S. P. Huntington's essay in C. J. Friedrich and S. E. Harris (eds.), *Public Policy* (Harvard University Press, 1958).

21. Ropp, p. 202n.

22. Paul M. Kennedy, *The Rise of the Anglo-German Antagonism, 1860–1914* (Allen and Unwin, 1980). Holger H. Herwig, *'Luxury' Fleet: the Imperial German Navy, 1888–1918* (Allen and Unwin, 1980).

23. V. R. Berghahn, *Germany and the Approach of War in 1914* (Macmillan, paperback ed., 1973).

24. Taylor, pp. xxvi–xxix.

25. Whittam, *The Politics of the Italian Army*, pp. 124–7.

26. Gooch, *Armies in Europe*, pp. 142–3. Hayes, pp. 324–5.

27. James Joll, *Europe Since 1870* (Penguin Books, 1976), pp. 58–9.

28. Ibid., pp. 60–1. See also V. G. Kiernan's essay in M. R. D. Foot (ed.), *War and Society* (Elek, 1973), pp. 141–58.

29. See V. R. Berghahn, *Militarism: the History of an International Debate, 1861–1979* (Berg Publishers, 1982).

30. Craig, *The Politics of the Prussian Army*, pp. 239, 242n, 250.

31. Ibid., pp. 275–7. Howard, 'The Armed Forces', pp. 223–4.

32. Girardet, *La Société militaire*, pp. 194–9, 253–6. David B. Ralston, *The Army of the Republic* (MIT Press, 1967), pp. 172, 199ff.

33. Girardet, pp. 258–61, 290–3. Douglas Porch, *The March to the Marne: the French Army 1877–1914* (CUP, 1981).

34. Whittam, pp. 124–7, 134–7. Pearton, p. 116 mentions that at Adowa the Italians were destroyed by French-instructed Ethiopian troops equipped with French weapons.

35. Ritter, *The Sword and the Scepter*, vol. 2, pp. 80–8. Ritter points out (p. 283n) that only 21 per cent of Russia's working population were trained soldiers compared with 36 per cent in Germany and 41 per cent in France. As Berghahn stresses, however (see note 29), Ritter's definition of 'militarism' was very restricted.

36. Vagts, p. 322. In the Curragh incident 58 cavalry officers opted for dismissal but 280 from other arms resolved to do their duty. 'The army was neither rent apart internally nor the object of profound distrust by the rest of the society.' Spiers, *The Army and Society*, p. 283.

37. Ritter, pp. 93–104. Craig, pp. 235–8, 252n.

38. Martin Kitchen, *The German Officer Corps, 1890–1914* (Clarendon Press, Oxford, 1968), pp. 30, 37–9. N. Stone, 'Army and Society in the Habsburg Monarchy, 1900–1914' in *Past and Present*, no. 33 (1966). Although practising Jews were excluded from the German officer corps,

converts from Judaism were usually treated like everyone else: see Ulrich
Trumpener, 'Junkers and Others: the Rise of Commoners in the Prussian
Army, 1871–1914' in *Canadian Journal of History*, vol. XIV, no. 1 (April
1979), p. 36.

39. Kitchen, pp. 151–4, 180–1.
40. Kennedy, pp. 369–72. Herwig, pp. 40–1.
41. Kiernan, pp. 141–7, 155–7.
42. Girardet, pp. 279–95. Porch in his revisionist study, *The March to the
Marne* (chs. 9 and 10 *passim*), challenges the views of previous historians
such as Girardet and Ralston that there was a revival in the French
army's spirits and training between 1911 and 1914. He also disputes the
orthodox view that the French reserves performed well in 1914.
43. Goltz, p. 4. F. von Papen, *Memoirs* (Deutsch, 1952), p. 10. Kiernan, p.
148.
44. Kiernan, pp. 152–4.
45. Stone, 'Army and Society in the Habsburg Monarchy' (see note 38).
46. Gooch, pp. 124–7.

3

1. Philip Larkin, *The Whitsun Weddings* (Faber and Faber, 1979), p. 28. John
   Gooch, 'Attitudes to War in Late Victorian and Edwardian England' in
   B. Bond and I. Roy (eds.), *War and Society*, vol. 1 (Croom Helm, 1975),
   p. 99.
2. G. Ritter, *The Sword and the Scepter*, vol. 2, pp. 109–10. P. Kennedy, *The
   Rise of the Anglo-German Antagonism*, pp. 370–2.
3. Kennedy, pp. 373–5.
4. T. H. E. Travers, 'Technology, Tactics, and Morale: Jean de Bloch, the
   Boer War and British Military Theory, 1900–1914' in *Journal of Modern
   History*, vol. 51 (June 1979), pp. 264–86.
5. Ibid., pp. 279–80.
6. Kitchen, *The German Officer Corps, 1890–1914*, pp. 139–41.
7. Kennedy, pp. 362, 366–9.
8. David French, 'Spy Fever in Britain, 1900–1915' in *The Historical Journal*,
   vol. 21, no. 2 (1978), pp. 355–70.
9. Ibid.
10. Ritter, vol. 2, pp. 113–16.
11. Girardet, *La Société militaire*, pp. 241–7. D. B. Ralston, *The Army of the
    Republic*, pp. 369–71. John C. Cairns, 'International Politics and the
    Military Mind: the Case of the French Republic, 1911–1914' in *Journal
    of Modern History* (September 1953), pp. 273–85.
12. N. Stone, 'Army and Society in the Habsburg Monarchy, 1900–1914' in
    Past and Present, no. 33 (1966), pp. 95–111.

13. Berghahn, *Germany and the Approach of War in 1914*, pp. 70–84. Herwig, '*Luxury Fleet*': *the Imperial German Navy, 1888–1918*, pp. 57, 71–92.

14. Clive Trebilcock, 'The British Armaments Industry 1890–1914: False Legend and True Utility' in Best and Wheatcroft (eds.), *War, Economy and the Military Mind*, pp. 89–107. See also M. Pearton, *The Knowledgeable State*, part III *passim*.

15. R. D. Challener, *The French Theory of the Nation in Arms*, pp. 109–14.

16. Vagts, *A History of Militarism*, pp. 352–3. D. Porch, 'The French Army and the Spirit of the Offensive, 1900–1914' in Bond and Roy (eds.), *War and Society*, vol. I, pp. 117–43. T. H. E. Travers, 'The Offensive and the Problem of Innovation in British Military Thought, 1870–1915' in *Journal of Contemporary History*, vol. 13 (1978), pp. 531–53.

17. Travers, 'Technology, Tactics, and Morale', pp. 285–6 and 'The Offensive', pp. 533–5.

18. For critical comments on the staff conversations and their political implications see N. d'Ombrain, *War Machinery and High Policy* (OUP, 1973) and Schurman, *Julian S. Corbett 1854–1922*, pp. 65–6. For a contrary view that in fact no commitment was made (a view with which the present author agrees), see Trevor Wilson, 'Britain's "Moral Commitment" to France in August 1914' in *History*, vol. 64 (October 1979), pp. 380–90.

19. Cairns, 'Internal Politics and the Military Mind', pp. 274–5, 284. J. Whittam, *The Italian Army in Politics*, pp. 161–8, 182–3.

20. N. Stone, 'Conrad' in *History Today* (July 1963), pp. 480–9.

21. Cairns, pp. 276–8; T. Wilson, op. cit. On 2 August 1914 Asquith wrote 'a good three-quarters of our own party in the H. of Commons are for absolute non-interference at any price' and he added, 'we have no obligation of any kind either to France or Russia to give them military or naval help'. He was even prepared to turn a blind eye to a minor infringement of Belgian neutrality by Germany but could not ignore the all-out invasion that actually occurred. See M. and E. Brock (eds.), *H. H. Asquith: Letters to Venetia Stanley* (OUP, 1982), pp. 146–7.

22. N. Stone, 'Moltke and Conrad: Relations between the Austro-Hungarian and German General Staffs, 1909–1914' in P. Kennedy (ed.), *The War Plans of the Great Powers, 1880–1914* (Allen and Unwin, 1979), pp. 222–51.

23. Van Creveld, *Supplying War*, pp. 119–24, 138–41.

24. Ritter, vol. 2, p. 205 and *The Schlieffen Plan* (Wolff, 1958), pp. 89, 96.

25. Taylor, *The Struggle for Mastery in Europe*, p. 529.

26. David French, *British Economic and Strategic Planning, 1905–1915* (Allen and Unwin, 1982).

27. Challener, pp. 95–8, 128–9.

28. Travers, 'The Offensive', pp. 539–43 and 'Technology, Tactics and Morale', pp. 273, 285.

29. Vagts, p. 353. Travers, 'The Offensive', p. 546. Bond, 'Doctrine and

Training in the British Cavalry' in Howard (ed.), *The Theory and Practice of War*.

30. Taylor, p. 528. Kennedy (ed.), *The War Plans of the Great Powers*.
31. Taylor, pp. 529–30.
32. C. E. Playne, *The Neuroses of Nations* (Allen and Unwin, 1925), p. 463.
33. Paul Fussell, *The Great War and Modern Memory* (OUP, 1975). Eric J. Leed, *No Man's Land: Combat and Identity in World War I* (CUP, 1979), chapter 2 *passim*.
34. Fussell, p. 231. Leed, p. 64.
35. Fussell, pp. 21–2.
36. Leed, pp. 30–1. Travers, 'The Offensive', p. 543.

4

1. A Marwick, *War and Social Change in the Twentieth Century* (Macmillan, 1974), p. 2.
2. M. Howard, *War in European History* (OUP, 1976), pp. 110–11.
3. Quoted in A. Marwick, *The Deluge: British Society and the First World War* (Penguin ed., 1967), p. 41.
4. J. M. Roberts, *Europe 1880–1945* (Longman, paperback ed., 1976), pp. 266–7.
5. The best account of tactical developments on the western front is probably still G. C. Wynne, *If Germany Attacks* (Faber, 1940). See also E. K. G. Sixsmith, *British Generalship in the Twentieth Century* (Arms and Armour Press, 1970), and S. Bidwell, *Gunners at War* (Arms and Armour Press, 1970). An important new study is S. Bidwell and D. Graham, *Fire Power: British Army Weapons and Theories of War 1904–1945* (Allen and Unwin, 1982).
6. Roberts, pp. 267–8. M. T. Florinsky, *The End of the Russian Empire* (Collier Books, NY, 1961), pp. 209–10.
7. Marwick, *The Deluge*, p. 40. M. Ferro, *The Great War 1914–1918* (Routledge and Kegan Paul, 1973), pp. 157–8.
8. Marwick, *War and Social Change*, p. 34. Florinsky, p. 156. F. P. Chambers, *The War Behind the War* (Faber, 1939), p. 183.
9. Chambers, p. 326. Whittam, *The Politics of the Italian Army*, p. 195.
10. Marwick, *War and Social Change*, p. 53. Chambers, p. 180. Florinsky, pp. 59–63.
11. Marwick, *The Deluge*, pp. 37, 51–2, 58–9. Florinsky, p. 74.
12. Quoted in Marwick, *The Deluge*, p. 52.
13. Marwick, *War and Social Change*, pp. 28–9. Chambers, pp. 184–5.
14. Marwick, *War and Social Change*, pp. 34–5. Florinsky, pp. 44–52.
15. Marwick, *The Deluge*, pp. 39–40, 53–4, 163–4, 168–82.

16. See Brian Bond, 'The First World War' in C. L. Mowat (ed.), *The New Cambridge Modern History*, vol. XII (second edition, CUP, 1968), pp. 197–9.

17. N. Stone, *The Eastern Front, 1914–1917* (Hodder and Stoughton, 1975), pp. 159–63.

18. Stone, pp. 165–71. Florinsky, pp. 127, 198–9. Florinsky (p. 210) cites a case of 500 prisoners assaulting Cossacks who had rescued them and upbraiding them: 'Who asked you to do this you sons-of-dogs? We don't want to suffer again from hunger and cold.'

19. Stone, pp. 249–55. Z. A. B. Zeman, *The Break-up of the Habsburg Empire 1914–1918* (OUP, 1961), p. 96.

20. B. H. Liddell Hart, *The Revolution in Warfare* (London, 1946; New Haven, Yale University Press, 1947), p. 75. G. Best, *Humanity in Warfare* (Weidenfeld and Nicolson, 1980), pp. 217–24.

21. Best, pp. 225–7, 236–7. Ritter, *The Sword and the Scepter*, vol. 3 (Florida, University of Miami Press, 1972), p. 369. All references in this chapter are to volume 3.

22. Best, pp. 249–50. See also B. Ranft's essay in M. Howard (ed.), *Restraints on War* (OUP, 1979).

23. Best, pp. 50–8. T. A. Bailey and P. B. Ryan, *The Lusitania Disaster* (The Free Press, NY, 1975).

24. Best, pp. 266–9. Liddell Hart, *The Revolution in Warfare*, pp. 35–7.

25. Roberts, pp. 270–1. Chambers, pp. 222–3. Ferro, p. 121.

26. Stone, pp. 208–11. Florinsky, pp. 117–20, 165.

27. Chambers, pp. 338–9, 345–6. Roberts, pp. 285–6. Ritter, p. 220. Marwick, *War and Social Change*, p. 30.

28. Florinsky, pp. 214–15.

29. Ibid., pp. 191, 213–15. Ferro, p. 145. For vivid personal accounts of the 'front mentality' see R. Graves, *Goodbye to All That* (Cassell, 1957) and G. Chapman, *A Kind of Survivor* (Gollancz, 1975).

30. Ritter, pp. 68–71.

31. Ibid., pp. 290–1. Zeman, pp. 111–13.

32. Marwick, *The Deluge*, p. 205.

33. Roberts, pp. 287–8. Chambers, pp. 340–4. Ritter, pp. 307–27. Herwig, *'Luxury' Fleet: the Imperial German Navy, 1888–1918*, pp. 194–8.

34. Ferro, pp. 181–4. G. Pedroncini, *Les Mutineries de 1917* (Presses Universitaires de France, Paris, 1967).

35. Whittam, *The Politics of the Italian Army*, p. 197.

36. Ibid., pp. 203–6. Ferro, pp. 201–3.

37. Stone, p. 283. Chambers, p. 450. Florinsky, pp. 228–9, 238–40. See also Ferro's important article 'Le Soldat Russe en 1917' in *Annales* (January 1971), pp. 14–39.

38. Chambers, p. 452. Roberts, pp. 292–4.

39. Ferro, pp. 195–200.

40. Roberts, pp. 296–7. Zeman, pp. 130–46.

41. Roberts, pp. 299–303. Chambers, pp. 483–5. Ferro, pp. 217–18.

42. Zeman, pp. 251–6. Chambers, p. 506. 'At the time of the collapse of the empire, the Austro-Hungarian army was certainly unvanquished. Yet it was clear, by October 1918, that the ultimate catastrophe was unavoidable.' N. Stone, 'Army and Society in the Habsburg Monarchy, 1900–1914' in *Past and Present*, no. 33 (1966), pp. 95–6.

43. Ferro, p. 219. For a recent analysis of the historiography of this controversy see A. Sked, 'Historians, the Nationality Question, and the Downfall of the Habsburg Empire' in *Transactions of the Royal Historical Society*, 5th series, vol. 31 (1981), pp. 175–93.

44. Chambers, pp. 240–1.

45. Arthur Marwick has made a bold though not entirely satisfactory attempt to tackle this problem in *War and Social Change*.

46. Marwick's summing up on this issue in *The Deluge*, pp. 233–40, seems to me admirably perceptive and balanced.

5

1. Joll, *Europe Since 1970*, p. 301. J. M. Roberts, *Europe 1880–1945*, pp. 304–6.

2. Howard, *War in European History*, p. 119. P.-M. de la Gorce, *The French Army* (Weidenfeld and Nicolson, 1963), pp. 197, 208–9.

3. Howard, pp. 118–19.

4. Joll, pp. 245, 269. R. G. L. Waite, *Vanguard of Nazism: the Free Corps Movement in Post-war Germany, 1918–1923* (Norton library ed., NY, 1969), p. 29.

5. Joll, p. 269. Waite, pp. 29, 271–2, 281.

6. Joll, p. 301. D. C. Watt, *Too Serious a Business: European Armed Forces and the Approach to the Second World War* (Temple Smith, 1975), p. 28. Vagts, *A History of Militarism*, pp. 444, 458–9. In 1936 the British parliament prohibited the wearing of uniforms by political organizations – a shrewd move to deprive Sir Oswald Mosley's Blackshirts of their glamour.

7. Watt, pp. 32–3. For thoughtful analyses of war literature see Paul Fussell, *The Great War and Modern Memory* (OUP, 1975) and Andrew Rutherford, *The Literature of War* (Macmillan, 1978).

8. Brian Bond, *Liddell Hart: a Study of His Military Thought* (Cassell, 1977).

9. de la Gorce, pp. 191–4.

10. Watt, pp. 34, 40–3.

11. de la Gorce, p. 190. Watt, p. 97. Arthur Marwick, *Britain in the Century of Total War* (Pelican ed., 1970), pp. 142–3.

12. Cited in Howard (ed.), *Restraints on War*, p. 10.

13. Ibid., pp. 53–4.

14. Uri Bialer, *The Shadow of the Bomber: the Fear of Air Attack and British Politics, 1932–1939* (Royal Historical Society, 1980), pp. 109–11. See also Watt's essay in Howard (ed.), *Restraints on War*, pp. 66–70.

15. Gooch, *Armies in Europe*, pp. 183–7.
16. Brian Bond, *British Military Policy Between the Two World Wars* (OUP, 1980). Michael Howard, *The Continental Commitment* (Temple Smith, 1972). Gooch, pp. 187–90.
17. Challener, *The French Theory of the Nation in Arms*, chapter 4 *passim*. de la Gorce, pp. 194–5.
18. Gooch, pp. 195–9.
19. Challener, pp. 151–3, 189–214.
20. Vagts, pp. 408–10, 426–39. Watt, pp. 116–17.
21. Howard, *War in European History*, pp. 133. Gooch, pp. 181–2.
22. Barry D. Powers, *Strategy Without Slide-rule* (Croom Helm, 1976).
23. B. H. Liddell Hart, *Paris or the Future of War* (Routledge and Kegan Paul, 1925), pp. 46–52, 59–61.
24. Powers, pp. 136–8.
25. I. F. Clarke, *Voices Prophesying War, 1763–1984* (OUP, 1966; Panther ed., 1970), pp. 162–75 and see his extremely useful *Checklist of Imaginary Wars*, ibid., pp. 227–49.
26. Howard, *War in European History*, pp. 128–30. Watt, p. 72. Bialer, pp. 113, 132–3, 159.
27. J. F. C. Fuller, *The Conduct of War, 1789–1961* (Eyre Methuen, 1972), pp. 242–6. For the details of 'Plan 1919' see Fuller's *Memoirs of an Unconventional Soldier* (Nicholson and Watson, 1936), pp. 322–41. For Fuller's career see A. J. Trythall, *'Boney' Fuller: the Intellectual General* (Cassell, 1977).
28. Challener, pp. 248–51.
29. Robert J. Young, 'Preparations for Defeat: French war doctrine in the inter-war period' in *Journal of European Studies*, 2 (1972), pp. 155–72. de la Gorce, pp. 266–79. For a biased but revealing contemporary critique of the defensive mentality in the late 1930s see Irving M. Gibson, 'Maginot and Liddell Hart: the Doctrine of Defense' in E. M. Earle (ed.), *Makers of Modern Strategy* (Princeton University Press, 1941; Atheneum, NY, 1966).
30. The importance of the economic element in Anglo-French war plans is well brought out by Robert J. Young's *In Command of France: French Foreign Policy and Military Planning, 1933–1940* (Harvard University Press, 1978). For the Royal Navy and maritime air power see Geoffrey Till, *Air Power and the Royal Navy, 1914–1945* (Jane's, 1979).
31. Vagts, p. 451. Watt, pp. 110–14.
32. Vagts, pp. 412–16. de la Gorce, pp. 209, 220, 249–51, 281–2.
33. Watt, pp. 51, 116–17.
34. Ibid., pp. 48–50. But in stressing that none of the general staffs wanted war (pp. 107–9) Watt fails to explain that whereas the German officers did not want war before they were ready, the British and French did not want war at all. On Hitler's personal influence on the broad direction of German foreign policy and rearmament from 1933 see Wilhelm Deist,

The Wehrmacht and German Rearmament (Macmillan, 1981), chapter 7 *passim*.

35. Thomas Jones, *A Diary with Letters, 1931–1950* (OUP, 1969), pp. 159–60. On the Italian air threat in the Mediterranean during the Abyssinian crisis see Arthur Marder, *From the Dardanelles to Oran* (OUP, 1974), pp. 64–104.
36. For complementary studies of the financial and economic aspects of British rearmament see G. C. Peden, *British Rearmament and the Treasury, 1932–1939* (Scottish Academic Press, 1979) and R. P. Shay, Jr, *British Rearmament in the Thirties* (Princeton University Press, 1977).
37. Michel Garder, *A History of the Soviet Army* (Pall Mall Press, 1966), pp. 73–95.
38. Watt, pp. 56–7. Garder, p. 96.
39. Watt, p. 57. Garder, pp. 96–101. For a less critical view of the effect of the military purges see Leonard Schapiro's chapter in B. H. Liddell Hart (ed.), *The Soviet Army* (Weidenfeld and Nicolson, 1956), especially pp. 70–2.
40. Deist, pp. 30–1, 48–51, 68–71, 84.
41. Ibid., pp. 91, 100.
42. R. J. Overy, 'Hitler's War and the German Economy: a Reinterpretation' in *Economic History Review*, vol. XXXV, no. 2 (May 1982), pp. 272–91.
43. Ibid., pp. 289–90.
44. Howard, *The Continental Commitment*, pp. 79–80, 128.
44. Marwick, *Britain in the Century of Total War*, pp. 251–5.
45. de la Gorce, pp. 274–5. Bond, *Liddell Hart*, chapter 4.

6

1. Peter Calvocoressi and Guy Wint, *Total War* (Allen Lane, the Penguin Press, 1972).
2. John Lukacs, *The Last European War, September 1939–December 1941* (Routledge and Kegan Paul, 1977), pp. 239–40.
3. Ibid. This is also a major theme in Watt, *Too Serious a Business*.
4. Quoted in Gordon Wright, *The Ordeal of Total War, 1939–1945* (Harper Torchbooks, NY, 1968), p. 235.
5. Calvocoressi, pp. 211–12.
6. Ibid.
7. Lukacs, p. 187, and for a map of flights and expulsions see Calvocoressi, p. 219.
8. Calvocoressi, pp. 213–14.
9. Overy, 'Hitler's War and the German Economy' in *Economic History Review*, pp. 283–4. See also Lukacs, pp. 192–3 and Marwick, *War and*

Social Change in the Twentieth Century, p. 109.

10. Overy, pp. 285–9.
11. Wright, pp. 61–3. A. S. Milward, *War, Economy and Society 1939–1945* (Allen Lane, Penguin Books, 1977), pp. 57–8.
12. Calvocoressi, pp. 426–7. Wright, pp. 47–52.
13. Wright, p. 52. Marwick, p. 158. Roberts, *Europe 1880–1945*, pp. 527–8.
14. Wright, pp. 57–61. Marwick, pp. 123–32.
15. Marwick, pp. 168–71. Roberts, p. 531.
16. Milward, p. 13.
17. Quoted by Wright, p. 123.
18. Ibid., pp. 107–8.
19. Milward, pp. 136, 141–50. Calvocoressi, pp. 255–7, 260. He calculates that in 1944 there were 7 million foreign workers in the Reich. Western and Italian workers were responsible for 25–30 per cent of the German war effort.
20. Milward, pp. 148–53.
21. Wright, pp. 63–5. Calvocoressi, pp. 500–1.
22. Quoted by Marwick, p. 113.
23. Wright, pp. 124–6.
24. Joll, *Europe Since 1870*, pp. 397–8.
25. Wright, pp. 137–9.
26. Calvocoressi, pp. 220–6. Joll, pp. 398–400.
27. Lukacs, pp. 448–51. For a powerful statement of this thesis see Sebastian Haffner, *The Meaning of Hitler* (Weidenfeld and Nicolson, 1979).
28. For example, Walter Laqueur, *The Terrible Secret* (Weidenfeld and Nicolson, 1980) and Martin Gilbert, *Auschwitz and the Allies* (Heinemann, 1981).
29. Group Captain Cheshire, VC, was interviewed in Rex Bloomstein's documentary 'Auschwitz and the Allies' shown on BBC Television on 16 September 1982.
30. Werner Rings, *Life with the Enemy: Collaboration and Resistance in Hitler's Europe, 1939–1945* (Weidenfeld and Nicolson, 1982), pp. 278–9.
31. Joll, pp. 394–7.
32. Calvocoressi, pp. 263–7, 271. He points out that strikes were a dangerous weapon. Strikers risked loss of jobs, deportation for forced labour and even, in the case of Dutch strike leaders, execution.
33. Rings, pp. 265–70, 280. Note however Calvocoressi's more favourable conclusion (p. 279) 'the combination of Resistance and Allied Governments was a considerable factor in winning the war . . . The Resistance could have become a separate war, but it did not.'
34. Lukacs, pp. 375, 378–80.
35. Calvocoressi, pp. 503–7. Wright, pp. 67–72. For an excellent comparison of British and German war propaganda see Michael Balfour, *Propaganda in War, 1939–1945* (Routledge and Kegan Paul, 1979).
36. M. Balfour, 'The Origin of the Formula "Unconditional Surrender" in

World War II' in *Armed Forces and Society*, vol. 5, no. 2 (February 1979), pp. 281–301.

37. Wright, pp. 72–3. See also Balfour, *Propaganda in War*, and Ian McLaine, *Ministry of Morale* (Allen and Unwin, 1979).

38. Wright, pp. 74–7.

39. Milward, p. 303, calculates that German forces, including the V-weapons, dropped 74,172 tons of bombs on Britain whereas the Allies dropped a total of 1,350,000 tons of bombs on Germany, excluding Austria. Cf. Tom Harrisson, *Living Through the Blitz* (Collins, 1976), pp. 331–3.

40. Roberts, p. 527. Milward, pp. 315–17. Calvocoressi, pp. 493–508.

41. Milward, pp. 304–5, 313–14.

42. Ibid., p. 328.

43. Harold C. Deutsch, *The Conspiracy Against Hitler in the Twilight War* (OUP, 1968).

44. Balfour, 'The Origin of the Formula.' Calvocoressi, pp. 399–401, 545. For an interesting discussion about British attitudes to the German anti-Nazi groups see C. Sykes, 'The German Resistance in Perspective' in *Encounter* (December 1968) and subsequent rejoinders and correspondence in the June, July, August, September and October issues (1969).

45. Calvocoressi, p. 552.

46. Calvocoressi, pp. 552–3. Marwick, pp. 138–9. Wright, pp. 263–4.

47. Wright, pp. 250–1, 263–4. Lukacs, p. 188.

48. See W. Laqueur, *The Terrible Secret*, pp. 1–2, for the shock caused by the British discovery of Belsen on 15 April 1945. See also Bond, *Liddell Hart* (Cassell, 1977), pp. 155–6 for a humane journalist's scepticism about the Nazi death trains in 1943.

49. Wright, p. 251 points out that we know little about the long-term psychological effects of exposure to intense and prolonged bombing. A British study of mental cases in 1948 showed only 3 per cent of the sample to be clearly connected with air-raid experience, but there may have been hidden damage which went undetected. See also the Postscript in Tom Harrisson, *Living Through the Blitz*. It has become a popular, but extremely dubious assertion, that bombing actually strengthened civilian morale in the Second World War.

50. Calvocoressi, pp. 553–4.

51. Ibid. See also M. Charlton, 'The Spectre of Yalta' in *Encounter* (June 1983).

52. Wright, pp. 244–5, 266–7. Calvocoressi, pp. 386–8, 428–34. Roberts, pp. 541–8. Marwick, p. 165.

53. A. J. P. Taylor, *The Second World War: an Illustrated History* (Hamish Hamilton, 1975), p. 234.

54. Roberts, p. 540.

55. Calvocoressi, p. 546.

56. Calvocoressi, p. 568.

7

1. Alastair Buchan, *War in Modern Society* (C. A. Watts, 1966), pp. 41–2. Though dated in some respects, this is still an admirably clear general introduction to the subject.

2. Ibid., p. 39. B. H. Liddell Hart, *The Defence of the West* (Cassell, 1950), pp. 81, 85, 88.

3. David Reynolds, *The Creation of the Anglo-American Alliance 1937–1941* (Europa Publications, 1981), p. 204.

4. Joll, *Europe Since 1870*, pp. 426–8.

5. Ibid., pp. 430–5, 451.

6. Ibid., pp. 436–7, 441, 454–5.

7. Ibid., pp. 458–9. Reynolds, p. 285. Wilfrid Knapp, *A History of War and Peace 1939–1965* (OUP, 1967), p. 291.

8. Alastair Buchan, 'Between Sword and Shield' in *Encounter* (July 1959), pp. 28–34.

9. M. R. D. Foot, *Men in Uniform* (Weidenfeld and Nicolson, 1961), p. 7. Leonard Beaton, *The Struggle for Peace* (Allen and Unwin, paperback ed., 1966), chapter VI.

10. Knapp, pp. 270–2. Liddell Hart, *Deterrent or Defence* (Stevens, 1960), pp. 133–42. Beaton, pp. 35–40.

11. Joll, pp. 462–3. Knapp, pp. 292–3, 308–9.

12. Buchan, p. 63. Beaton, pp. 57–8.

13. Buchan, pp. 159–160. Liddell Hart, pp. 39–41.

14. Buchan, pp. 46–7. Beaton, pp. 39–40.

15. Beaton, p. 42. Buchan, pp. 89–90. Howard, *War in European History*, p. 139.

16. Knapp, pp. 335–6, 362–7. John Keegan (ed.), *World Armies* (Macmillan, 1979), pp. 296, 299.

17. Michael Howard, *Studies in War and Peace* (Temple Smith, 1970), pp. 251–9. Keegan, p. 165.

18. Buchan, p. 191.

19. Raymond Aron, 'The Evolution of Modern Strategic Thought', *ISS Adelphi Paper*, no. 54 (February 1969), pp. 1–17. Buchan, pp. 48, 148–51, 160–1. Bernard and Fawn M. Brodie, *From Crossbow to H-Bomb* (Indiana University Press, paperback ed., 1973), pp. 279–80.

20. B. H. Liddell Hart (ed.), *The Soviet Army* (Weidenfeld and Nicolson, 1956), pp. 397–419. Foot, pp. 54–6. For a concise account of the Soviet army in 1979 see Richard Holmes's entry in Keegan's *World Armies*, pp. 729–46.

21. See J. M. Mackintosh's chapter 'The Satellite Armies' in Liddell Hart's *The Soviet Army*, pp. 439–51.

22. P.-M. de la Gorce, *The French Army*, chapters 15 and 19. Foot, pp. 35–42. Keegan, pp. 220, 223.
23. J. C. M. Baynes, *The Soldier in Modern Society* (Eyre Methuen, 1972), pp. 27–31. Foot, pp. 132–6. Marwick, *Britain in the Century of Total War*, p. 411.
24. Baynes, pp. 30–4. Sir John Hackett, *The Profession of Arms* (The Times Publishing Co., 1962), p. 57.
25. Foot, pp. 108–16. Keegan, pp. 247–50.
26. Foot, pp. 60–71. Keegan, pp. 675, 680–1.
27. Foot, pp. 71–6. Keegan, pp. 666, 672.
28. Foot, pp. 30, 97.
29. Marwick, pp. 412–13. Baynes, pp. 56–76.
30. The author did not particularly enjoy the months he served as a gunner and officer cadet but life as a subaltern in Germany was more interesting. Clearly much depended on the individual's expectations – and on luck. For the varied experiences of twenty-four national servicemen which collectively convey something of what it was like, see B. S. Johnson (ed.), *All Bull* (Quartet Books, 1973).
31. Marwick, pp. 413–14.
32. Howard, *War in European History*, p. 143.

GLOSSARY

Armageddon	the site of the great battle on the Day of Judgement, hence war on a grand scale
arme blanche	cavalry armed with lance or sabre
armée de métier	a professional and usually long-service army
blitzkrieg	literally lightning war, more specifically short, decisive campaigns waged by armoured forces with close air support
Bundeswehr	armed forces of the Federal Republic of Germany
CID	Committee of Imperial Defence
couverture	a defensive screen for frontiers or large military formations comprising both mobile units and fortifications
Drang nach Osten (see also *Lebensraum*)	literally drive to the east, an important ingredient in German nationalist and Nazi doctrine
Einsatzgruppen	in general, operation groups, specifically Nazi extermination squads in the Second World War
francs-tireurs	irregular light infantry or undisciplined partisans
Freikorps (or Free Corps)	armed volunteer bands largely composed of demobilized soldiers and mostly on the extreme right politically
Garde Mobile (or *Garde Nationale Mobile*)	French military reserve force loosely resembling the Prussian *landwehr* (q.v.) but largely composed of men who had esacaped regular training
guerre à outrance	all out, unlimited war

guerre de course	a naval strategy based on commerce destruction, as distinct from seeking command of the sea by fleet battle (see *Jeune École*)
Jeune École	French naval group in 1880s which advocated a commerce war against Britain
Junker	East Prussian landowning nobility, more generally the aristocratic military elite that dominated the Prussian/German army
landwehr	German reserve forces, or militia
Lebensraum	living space, Nazi policy of expansion, mainly to the east
muette (la grande muette)	figurative reference to the French army's strict neutrality and non-involvement in domestic politics (literally, the silent female)
poilu	French private soldier
Reichstag	Prussian/German national assembly or parliament
Reichswehr	German armed forces under the Weimar Republic, officially restyled the *Wehrmacht* by the Nazis in May 1935
SS	*Schutzstaffeln* – black-uniformd Nazi paramilitary elite
Untermensch	Subhuman. Nazi term for the peoples of eastern Europe, particularly the Slavs

SELECT BIBLIOGRAPHY

(Author's note: titles published before 1984 are quoted or referred to in the text; titles published since 1984 are included as examples of the recent surge of scholarly interest in the theme of 'War and Society'.)

Addison, Paul & Calder, Angus (eds) *Time to Kill: the Soldier's Experience of War in the West 1939–1945*. (1997)
Audoin-Rouzeau, Stéphane *Men at War, 1914–1918*.

Balfour, Michael *Propaganda in War, 1939–1945*. (1979)
Barnett, Correlli *Britain and Her Army, 1509–1970*. (1970)
—— *The Audit of War*. (1986)
Bartov, Omer *Hitler's Army: Soldiers, Nazis and War in the Third Reich*. (1991)
Baynes, J.C.M. *The Soldier in Modern Society*. (1972)
Becker, Jean-Jacques *The Great War and the French People*. (1985)
Beckett, Ian & Simpson, Keith (eds) *A Nation in Arms: A Social Study of the British Army in the First World War*. (1985)
Berghahn, V.R. *Militarism: the History of an Internation Debate*. (1982)
—— *Germany and the Approach of War in 1914*. (1973)
Bessel, Richard *Germany after the First World War*. (1993)
Best, Geoffrey *Humanity in Warfare*. (1980)
Best, Geoffrey & Wheatcroft, Andrew (eds) *War, Economy and the Military Mind*. (1976)
Bialer, Uri *The Shadow of the Bomber*. (1980)
Bond, Brian *The Pursuit of Victory: from Napoleon to Saddam Hussein*. (Paperback edition 1998)
—— *British Military Policy between the Two World Wars*. (1980)
Brodie, Bernard & Fawn, M. *From Crossbow to H-Bomb*. (1973)
Buchan, Alastair *War in Modern Society*. (1966)
Bull, Hedley (ed) *The Challenge of the Third Reich*. (1986)

Calder, Angus *The Myth of the Blitz*. (1991)
Calvocoressi, Peter, Wint, Guy & Pritchard, John *Total War*. (1989)
Cecil, Hugh & Liddle, Peter (eds) *Facing Armageddon: the First World War Experienced*. (1996)
Challener, R.D. *The French Theory of the Nation in Arms*. (1955)

Clarke, I.F. *Voices Prophesying War 1763–1984.* (Paperback edition, 1970)
Colin, Jean *The Transformations of War.* (1912)
Craig, Gordon A. *The Politics of the Prussian Army.* (1964)
Creveld, Martin Van. *Supplying War: Logistics from Wallenstein to Patton.* (1977)
—— *On Future War.* (1991)
Deist, Wilhelm *The Wehrmacht and German Rearmement.* (1981)
—— (ed) *The German Military in the Age of Total War.* (1985)
Eksteins, Modris *Rites of Spring: The Great War and the Birth of the Modern Age.* (1989)

Ferro, Marc *The Great War 1914–1918.* (1973)
Florinsky, M.T. *The End of the Russian Empire.* (Paperback edition, 1961)
Foot, M.R.D. *Men in Uniform.* (1961)
—— *Resistance: European Resistance to Nazism, 1940–45.* (1976)
—— (ed) *War and Society.* (1973)
Förster, Stig & Nägler, Jörg (eds) *On the Road to Total War: The American Civil War and the German Wars of Unification.* (1997)
Fuller, J.F.C. *The Conduct of War, 1789–1961.* (1972)
Fussell, Paul *The Great War and Modern Memory.* (1975)
Girardet, R. *La société militaire dans la France contemporaine, 1815–1939.* (1953)
Glover, Michael *The Velvet Glove: the Decline and Fall of Moderation in War.* (1982)
Goltz, Colmar von der *The Nation in Arms.* (1903)
Gooch, John *Armies in Europe.* (1980)
—— *Army, State and Society in Italy, 1870–1915.* (1989)
Gorce, P.M. de la *The French Army.* (1963)

Hackett, Sir John *The Profession of Arms.* (1962)
Harrisson, Tom *Living Through the Blitz.* (1976)
Herwig, Holger H. *"Luxury" Fleet: the Imperial German Navy 1888–1918.* (1980)
—— *The First World War. Germany and Austria-Hungary 1914–1918.* (1997)
Horne, Alistair *The French Army and Politics, 1870–1970.* (1984)
Howard, Michael *The Franco-Prussian War.* (Paperback edition 1967)
——, *Studies in War and Peace.* (1970)
——, *War in European History.* (1976)
——, *The Causes of Wars.* (1983)
—— (ed) *The Theory and Practice of War.* (1965)
——, *Restraints on War.* (1979)
Hynes, Samuel *A War Imagined: the First World War and English Culture.* (1990)

Joll, James *Europe since 1870.* (1976)

Keegan, John *The Face of Battle.* (1976)
Kennedy, Paul M. *The Rise of the Anglo-German Antagonism, 1860–1914.* (1980)
—— *The Rise and Fall of British Naval Mastery.* (1976)
—— (ed) *The War Plans of the Great Powers, 1880–1914.* (1979)

Kitchen, Martin *The German Officer Corps, 1890–1914*. (1968)
—— *Europe between the Wars*. (Paperback edition, 1988)
Kocka, Jürgen *Facing Total War: German Society 1914–1918*. (1984)

Leed, Eric J. *No Man's Land: Combat and Identity in World War I*. (1979)
Liddell Hart, B.H. *Paris or the Future of War*. (1925)
—— *The Revolution in Warfare*. (1946)
—— *The Defence of the West*. (1950)
—— *Deterrent or Defence*. (1960)
Lukacs, John *The Last European War 1939–1941*. (1977)

Martin, Laurence W. *The Two-Edged Sword: Armed Force in the Modern World*. (1982)
Marwick, Arthur *War and Social Change in the 20th Century*. (1974)
—— *The Deluge: British Society and the First World War*. (1967)
—— *Britain in the Century of Total War*. (1970)
McNeill, William H. *The Pursuit of Power*. (1983)
Milward, Alan S. *War, Economy and Society 1939–1945*. (1977)
Montheilet, Joseph *Les institutions militaire de la France 1814–1924*. (1932)
Mosse, George L. *Fallen Soldiers: Reshaping the Memory of the World Wars*. (1990)
Müller, K-J *Das Heer und Hitler. Armee und National sozialistiches Regime, 1933–1940*. (1969)
—— *Army, Politics and Society in Germany, 1933–1945*. (1987)

Nickerson, Hoffman *The Armed Horde, 1793–1939*. (1940)

O'Neill, Robert J. *The German Army and the Nazi Party. 1933–1939*. (Paperback edition 1968)

Pearton, Maurice *The Knowledgeable State: Diplomacy, War and Technology since 1830*. (1982)
Pedroncini, Guy *Les Mutineries de 1917*. (1967)
Porch, Douglas *The March to the Marne: the French Army 1877–1914*. (1981)

Ralston, David B. *The Army of the Republic*. (1967)
Rings, Werner *Life with the Enemy: Collaboration in Hitler's Europe, 1939–1945*. (1982)
Ritter, Gerhard *The Sword and the Scepter*. 4 vols (1969–1973)
Roberts, J.M. *Europe 1880–1945*. (Paperback edition 1962)
Ropp, Theodore *War in the Modern World*. (Paperback edition 1962)
Royle, Trevor *The Best Years of Their Lives: the National Service Experience, 1945–1963*. (Paperback edition 1988)

Simkins, Peter *Kitchener's Army*. (1988)
Spiers, E.M. *The Army and Society 1815–1914*. (1980)

SELECT BIBLIOGRAPHY

Stevenson, David *Armaments and the Coming of War: Europe 1904–1914.* (1996)
Stone, Norman *The Eastern Front, 1914–1917.* (1975)

Taylor, A.J.P. *The Struggle for Mastery in Europe.* (1957)
—— *The Second World War.* (1975)

Vagts, Alfred *Militarism* (Revised edition 1959)

Waite, R.G.L. *Vanguard of Nazism: the Free Corps Movement in Postwar Germany, 1918–1923.* (1969)
Watt, D.C. *Too Serious a Business: European Armed Forces and the Approach to the Second World War.* (1975)
Weinberg Gerhard L. *A World at Arms: A Global History of World War II.* (1994)
Whittam, John *The Politics of the Italian Army.* (1986)
Wright, Gordon *The Ordeal of Total War.* (1968)

Zeman, Z.A.B. *The Break-up of the Habsburg Empire 1914–1918.* (1961)

INDEX